Effective Universal Instruction

The Guilford Practical Intervention in the Schools Series

Kenneth W. Merrell, *Founding Editor*
Sandra M. Chafouleas, *Series Editor*

www.guilford.com/practical

This series presents the most reader-friendly resources available in key areas of evidence-based practice in school settings. Practitioners will find trustworthy guides on effective behavioral, mental health, and academic interventions, and assessment and measurement approaches. Covering all aspects of planning, implementing, and evaluating high-quality services for students, books in the series are carefully crafted for everyday utility. Features include ready-to-use reproducibles, appealing visual elements, and an oversized format. Recent titles have Web pages where purchasers can download and print the reproducible materials.

Recent Volumes

Promoting Student Happiness: Positive Psychology Interventions in Schools
Shannon M. Suldo

Effective Math Interventions: A Guide to Improving Whole-Number Knowledge
Robin S. Codding, Robert J. Volpe, and Brian C. Poncy

Emotional and Behavioral Problems of Young Children, Second Edition:
Effective Interventions in the Preschool and Kindergarten Years
Melissa L. Holland, Jessica Malmberg, and Gretchen Gimpel Peacock

Group Interventions in Schools: A Guide for Practitioners
Jennifer P. Keperling, Wendy M. Reinke, Dana Marchese, and Nicholas Ialongo

Transforming Schools: A Problem-Solving Approach to School Change
Rachel Cohen Losoff and Kelly Broxterman

Evidence-Based Strategies for Effective Classroom Management
David M. Hulac and Amy M. Briesch

School-Based Observation: A Practical Guide to Assessing Student Behavior
Amy M. Briesch, Robert J. Volpe, and Randy G. Floyd

Helping Students Overcome Social Anxiety: Skills for Academic and Social Success (SASS)
Carrie Masia Warner, Daniela Colognori, and Chelsea Lynch

Executive Skills in Children and Adolescents, Third Edition:
A Practical Guide to Assessment and Intervention
Peg Dawson and Richard Guare

Effective Universal Instruction: An Action-Oriented Approach to Improving Tier 1
Kimberly Gibbons, Sarah Brown, and Bradley C. Niebling

Supporting Successful Interventions in Schools:
Tools to Plan, Evaluate, and Sustain Effective Implementation
Lisa M. Hagermoser Sanetti and Melissa A. Collier-Meek

High-Impact Assessment Reports for Children and Adolescents:
A Consumer-Responsive Approach
Robert Lichtenstein and Bruce M. Ecker

Conducting School-Based Functional Behavioral Assessments,
Third Edition: A Practitioner's Guide
Mark W. Steege, James L. Pratt, Garry Wickerd, Richard Guare, and T. Steuart Watson

Effective
Universal Instruction

An Action-Oriented Approach
to Improving Tier 1

KIMBERLY GIBBONS
SARAH BROWN
BRADLEY C. NIEBLING

THE GUILFORD PRESS
New York   London

Copyright © 2019 The Guilford Press
A Division of Guilford Publications, Inc.
370 Seventh Avenue, Suite 1200, New York, NY 10001
www.guilford.com

Printed in the United States of America

This book is printed on acid-free paper.

Last digit is print number: 9   8   7   6   5   4

Library of Congress Cataloging-in-Publication Data is available from the publisher.

ISBN 978-1-4625-3683-2 (paperback)

About the Authors

Kimberly Gibbons, PhD, is Director of the Center for Applied Research and Educational Improvement at the University of Minnesota. Prior to that, she was Executive Director of the St. Croix River Education District in Minnesota. During this tenure, she was named Outstanding Administrator of the Year by the Minnesota Administrators of Special Education (MASE); she is also a past president of MASE. Dr. Gibbons provides national consultation and has numerous publications on multi-tiered systems of support (MTSS) and data-based decision making.

Sarah Brown, PhD, is Senior Director of Learning and Development at FastBridge Learning in Minnesota. Her work focuses on implementing MTSS at multiple levels of the education system and improving systems to support high achievement for every student. Previously, Dr. Brown has had several administrative roles, including serving as Bureau Chief at the Iowa Department of Education, where she led statewide implementation of MTSS, and as a Unique Learners' Manager at the St. Croix River Education District in Minnesota. She also worked at the Center for Applied Research and Educational Improvement at the University of Minnesota and at Heartland Area Education Agency 11 in Johnston, Iowa.

Bradley C. Niebling, PhD, is Bureau Chief for Learner Strategies and Supports at the Iowa Department of Education, where he leads statewide implementation of MTSS, supports Iowa's statewide implementation of the Iowa Core State Standards, and works with schools to improve Tier 1 practices within MTSS. Prior to that, Dr. Niebling worked at the university, school, and intermediate service agency levels as a school psychologist, trainer, and researcher. He has published multiple journal articles and book chapters on standards-based practices, curriculum alignment, and response to intervention/MTSS.

Acknowledgments

We dedicate this book to all educators who work tirelessly to improve the instruction they provide to students through collaboration with their colleagues. This book is a synthesis of all our experiences working with teachers and administrators to evaluate and improve instruction and intervention. We would like to thank our respective families for their endless patience and support throughout the writing process: Aaron, Eli, Zach, and Isabella Gibbons; Andy Heggenstaller; and Suzy, Madison, and Nora Niebling.

Contents

CHAPTER 1

Introduction

Sweeping changes have occurred in the last 15 years in the area of accountability and educational reform. Educators in the 21st century have been charged with ensuring high levels of learning for all students (DuFour, 2004), and progress toward this goal is now measured and publicly reported in the form of statewide accountability tests. Countless debates have occurred and numerous "reform initiatives" have been studied to try to discover the best way to improve our public education system. In an attempt to respond to the charge of improving outcomes for all learners, our nation's schools have been subjected to a constant stream of new programs, initiatives, and frameworks to solve the problem, with little success. Results from the 2017 National Assessment of Educational Progress (NAEP; National Center for Education Statistics, 2017) indicate a continued need to accelerate student growth in both reading and math. In the area of reading, 35% of fourth graders and 35% of eighth graders were "proficient" or "advanced" in reading. Results from the 2017 NAEP in the area of math indicated that 40% of fourth graders and 33% of eighth graders were "proficient" or "advanced" in math. Additionally, achievement gaps continue to persist between racial and ethnic groups.

According to Kastberg, Chan, and Murray (2016), results from the 2015 Program for International Student Assessment (PISA) indicate that the average scores of U.S. 15-year-olds in reading literacy were lower than the averages in 14 educational systems, higher than in 43, and not measurably different than in 12 educational systems and the OECD average. In math literacy, the U.S. average was lower than more than half of the other education systems (36 of 69) as well as the OECD average, higher than 28 education systems, and not measurably different than 5.

Finally, significant gaps in academic performance exist between the general school population and subgroups of students, such as those with disabilities, members of minority groups, and children living in poverty.

1

The response-to-intervention (RTI) or multi-tiered systems of supports (MTSS) framework has quickly emerged as a methodology for improving outcomes for all students through high-quality instruction tailored to student needs within a data-based decision-making model. In fact, a recent national survey of K–12 administrators indicated that 61% of respondents are either in full implementation or in the process of districtwide implementation of an RTI/MTSS framework, up from 24% in 2007 (Spectrum K–12 School Solutions, 2010). Although it is promising that so many school districts around the country are beginning to implement the RTI/MTSS framework, we have observed that many districts implementing this framework immediately try to intervene and provide supplemental services and supports to all students who are not meeting grade-level expectations (e.g., Tier 2 and Tier 3 services). While we agree it is a natural tendency to focus on helping students who are at risk, we believe that a critical first step is to evaluate the effectiveness of the universal tier (e.g., Tier 1, core instruction). Most school districts in this country do not have the resources to intervene their way out of ineffective universal instruction. The universal tier is the first intervention for all students and is our largest opportunity to have an impact on student achievement. We hope that this book will bring the attention back to quality universal instruction to prevent large numbers of students from falling off track and needing additional services and supports.

DEFINITION OF THE UNIVERSAL TIER

Universal instruction is what "all" students receive in the form of academic and social–emotional instruction and supports. Universal instruction focuses on the implementation of the district's core curriculum and is aligned with state academic content standards. It is differentiated to ensure that this instruction meets the needs of students. The amount of time dedicated to content-area learning and the focus of instruction are based on the needs of the students in a particular school. Some schools require more time than others in particular core curriculum areas, based on student demographics (readiness, language, economic factors) and student performance levels, to ensure that all students reach and/or exceed state proficiency levels. Schools spend significant amounts of time and money and enlist a significant number of personnel to make sure that universal instruction is well designed and based on empirical research documenting what works.

Teaching staff must receive sufficient and ongoing professional learning to deliver the universal instructional program in the way it was designed. The expectation is that if the universal tier is implemented with a high degree of integrity by highly trained teachers, then most of the students receiving this instruction will show outcomes upon assessment that indicate a level of proficiency that meets minimal benchmarks for performance in the skill area. The universal tier is more than a single textbook. It is all the materials and instruction used to provide the main classroom instruction in a particular content area—or, simply put, whatever it takes to get most students meeting grade-level standards!

EVOLUTION OF THE UNIVERSAL TIER

To understand what the universal tier is and its role in MTSS, it is important to dig into the history of factors that influence our current definition of universal tier. In addition, to continue improving the universal tier over time, it is also important to understand the factors that are likely to influence MTSS in the future. Such factors are likely to include key findings from research, influential policies, and our collective experiences as we work to meet the needs of all students by providing a common set of learning experiences.

Where We Have Been

An extensive review of the history of public education in the United States is beyond the scope of this book. However, developments in the last 30–40 years do provide a helpful perspective on what has preceded the current-day realities of education. In particular, there were several social, political, and educational forces in the 1970s and 1980s that, in many ways, started separately but have served as the precursor for a convergence of efforts into what we know today as the universal tier in MTSS. These efforts included individual student problem solving, standards-based reform, as well as several federal policies.

Individual Student Problem Solving

Individual student problem solving in education evolved from the late 1970s through the early 2000s. In many ways, it evolved because the approach of identifying students who required special education services by disability category, and trying to match treatments based on those categories, was not producing many positive outcomes for students with disabilities (e.g., Reschly & Tilly, 1999). Individual student problem solving, by contrast, was focused on matching treatments to student needs by answering four questions: (1) What is the problem?; (2) Why is the problem happening?; (3) What should be done about it?; and (4) Did the intervention work? (e.g., Bergan, 1977; Bergan & Kratochwill, 1990; Tilly, 2002). This is considered a functional approach to identifying student needs, as opposed to a categorical approach that is grounded in information gathered about students and their needs that occur naturally within their school experience.

Although some of these early efforts focused on special education identification, what emerged was a more collaborative approach to identifying student needs, with groups of educators and parents working in teams (Pluymert, 2014). This work took place before making decisions about students regarding their special education eligibility. Although the individual student problem solving approach was grounded in solid research regarding matching interventions to student needs, it fell short as a viable approach to meeting the needs of all students in schools. Trying to solve student learning and behavioral difficulties one student at a time was inefficient and very resource intensive. Although individual student problem solving remains an important part of school practice today, it is typically considered a part of a larger, more systems-based approach to using data to meet student needs—that is, MTSS.

Standards-Based Reform

Briefly, *standards-based reform* is a movement that rests on the assumption that setting high academic standards, then developing accountability for schools based on students' attainment of those academic standards, will drive changes in teachers' practice. Standards-based reform also assumes that all students can learn if they are held to a common or universal set of high academic standards (Porter & Smithson, 2001).

In general, this movement developed in response to U.S. students' low performance on standardized tests of achievement, compared to students in other countries. For example, the 1983 report *A Nation at Risk*, from the National Commission on Excellence in Education, described this low student performance. Based on this finding, one of the primary claims of this report was that educational goals for all students needed to be identified. In addition, the Second International Mathematics Study and Third International Mathematics and Science Study revealed differences in the content, depth, and breadth of instruction and the relationship of this instruction to student achievement (e.g., McKnight et al., 1987) across different countries, including the United States.

Findings from studies such as these gave rise to the phrase *mile-wide, inch-deep curriculum*. In other words, the instruction that students generally received in the United States covered a lot of different topics, but did not cover many of them well. This factor was cited as a primary contributor to the poor academic performance of students in the United States, when compared to students in other countries. These studies also highlighted the lack of clearly defined standards in the United States, when compared to other developed countries.

Important Policies

The efforts around standards-based reform and individual student problem solving, as well as the growing sentiment on social, political, and educational fronts, all culminated in the reauthorization of two important federal laws. The cornerstone policy for standards-based reform is known as the 1965 Elementary and Secondary Education Act (ESEA). Although this act has been reauthorized several times since 1965, the reauthorization that has received perhaps the most public attention was the reauthorization in 2001, known as the No Child Left Behind Act (NCLB). NCLB placed an unprecedented emphasis on the results of tests used in accountability systems, as well as on the importance that strong alignment exist between academic content standards and large-scale accountability measures. The spirit and intent of NCLB, as well as the growing support of problem solving and RTI as an alternative to the discrepancy approach to determining students' eligibility for special education services, was reinforced in the reauthorization of the Individuals with Disabilities Education Act (IDEA) in 2004. Under IDEA 2004, students with disabilities are required to participate in accountability assessments, and schools and districts are held accountable to ensure that increasing numbers of these students are proficient. In addition, RTI was codified as an alternative to the discrepancy model as a means by which schools could determine whether or not a student was eligible for special education services.

Where We Are Going

Developments in the last 15 years have brought the importance of a strong universal tier within MTSS into stronger focus. These efforts have included a more systems-based preventive approach to problem solving, the Common Core State Standards (CCSS), and the reauthorization of NCLB.

Systems-Based Intervention as a Preventive Approach to Problem Solving

We have learned through the implementation of individual student problem-solving efforts that although the approach can be effective for individual students, most school systems do not have the resources to meet the needs of all students using only this approach—especially when it comes to making universal tier improvements. In recent years, we have shifted the tactic to include individual student problem solving within a whole-system approach to problem solving known as *MTSS*. This shift arose both from the experience of educators implementing these practices in schools, as well as from public health models of disease prevention that differentiate primary, secondary, and tertiary levels of intervention, which increase in cost and intensity depending on the patient's response to treatment (e.g., Fletcher & Vaughn, 2009; Vaughn, Wanzek, & Fletcher, 2007).

Standards-Based Reform: The CCSS

The CCSS movement evolved in response to the inconsistency of state standards across the nation, along with large numbers of students exiting high school unprepared for college and/or employment. It was not uncommon for students to be rated "proficient" in one state and "below basic" in another state. Questionable student outcomes, as well as concerns about the rigor of content to which students were exposed, prompted the National Governors Association (NGA) and the Council of Chief State School Officers (CCSSO) to draft clear, consistent, and more rigorous standards known as the CCSS. Though optional for states to adopt, the CCSS were nonetheless partially adopted and implemented in 45 states. This widespread implementation may have been influenced largely by the U.S. Department of Education, which required states to adopt "college and career readiness standards" similar to the CCSS in order to be eligible for federal dollars as part of the Race to the Top grants, as well as to obtain a waiver on NCLB requirements.

Like many educational efforts that are implements on such a large scale, the CCSS has drawn its fair share of both support and criticism, often based on incomplete or inaccurate information. For example, some critics of the CCSS have claimed that the Standards are curricula. However, they are not curricula, and despite a great deal of rhetoric, they do not dictate how teachers teach content. Although CCSS implementation has been controversial and "rocky," it has resulted in an increased interest in core, or universal, instruction, and many teachers are enthusiastic about the challenge of implementing the Standards in their classrooms. This interest and enthusiasm are often the result of both increased access to information and ongoing interaction with the Standards while collaborating with others around how to support and implement them. Although we agree that genuine debate about the CCSS, in the interest of ascertaining what is best for students, is critically important, it is a debate full of landmines and should be done with thoughtfulness and caution. For every poll that shows declining support for the CCSS, there is another poll showing support for the CCSS holding steady or even increasing.

The purpose of this book is not to take a side in this debate, but rather to inform and clarify two key areas: (1) the multiple perspectives in that debate, and (2) to put those perspectives in the context of the universal tier in MTSS. At the end of the day, academic content standards have been, and continue to be, a part of the educational system in the United States. As such, it is important that we, as educators, are informed about those standards and know how to use them effectively. With that said, some of the most common criticisms of the CCSS are that (1) they were not validated as research-based before being implemented, (2) teachers are not well-enough prepared to implement them, (3) textbooks and other curriculum materials published prior to the implementation of CCSS are not well aligned with them, (4) they are a federal overreach and an intrusion on student privacy, and (5) they minimize teachers as professionals.

ISSUE 1: RESEARCH BASE OF THE CCSS

- *Criticism: The CCSS were not validated by research before they were implemented.* The primary perspective of this criticism is that states were quick to adopt the CCSS and require schools to implement them before they had been tested in real-life classrooms, with real-life teachers and students, to see what impact the Standards would have on student learning. Without testing the Standards in smaller pilot projects, it was inappropriate for states to require schools to implement them. There is little debate about whether or not the Standards themselves were tested before adoption or implementation; they were not.

- *Support: The CCSS were developed based on research-based content and rely on aligned systems.* Supporters of the CCSS point to the fact that the Standards are internationally benchmarked and developed using information from research on what is important for students to know and be able to do in order to be college and career ready by the time they graduate. Furthermore, the impact of standards on student learning is the result of many factors, not just their content. Of central importance is that teachers provide adequate opportunities for students to learn what is in the Standards and that content needs to be rigorous (e.g., Gamoran, Porter, Smithson, & White, 1997). This holds true for students from the full range of socioeconomic levels and for students who have a wide range of prior achievement. Furthermore, assessments used to measure student learning, as part of a comprehensive and balanced assessment system, should be aligned with the CCSS. This alignment requirement can be viewed as necessary to be able to determine the impact the Standards have on student learning.

ISSUE 2: SPEED OF IMPLEMENTATION EXPECTATIONS

- *Criticism: Expectations to implement the Standards were too fast for states to be adequately prepared.* When the CCSS were first adopted by states, and schools were expected to start implementing the Standards, a great deal of concern was expressed by teachers, administrators, and other educators that not enough time was provided for teachers to prepare to implement them. In some cases, schools were given only 1 or 2 years to "fully implement" the Standards. States did not have enough time to develop and provide the professional learning programs and support to schools that were needed to implement the Standards effectively.

- *Support: The speed and nature of implementation expectations are flexible.* Supporters of the CCSS often point out that issues related to the speed of implementation expectations are not dictated by the CCSS per se. States have flexibility in how they increase the supports and professional learning needed by teachers to increase their preparedness, while taking an approach of improving implementation of the CCSS over time. State preparedness has increased faster than anticipated due to the fact that resources can be shared across the country, since most states have adopted the Standards (or a form of them).

ISSUE 3: ALIGNMENT OF TEXTBOOKS AND OTHER CURRICULUM MATERIALS

- *Criticism: There are very few textbooks and curriculum materials aligned with the CCSS.* Related to the speed of implementation expectations, critics of the CCSS often claim that the options schools have for textbooks and other curriculum materials aligned with the CCSS are very limited. In addition, there has been growing distrust of the textbook industry because of the claims that some publishers make that their materials are "aligned" with the CCSS. However, upon inspection, educators and researchers often find that the claims on the shiny gold "Aligned with the Common Core" sticker on the front cover of the materials is misleading, at best. Coupled with many educators' feeling of uncertainty about how well the materials they find online, get from colleagues, or develop themselves align with the CCSS, critics often claim that it is unreasonable to expect teachers to implement the CCSS.

- *Support: Alignment of textbooks and curriculum materials is improving since the development of the CCSS.* Supporters of the CCSS will often point out that a variety of resources and tools have been developed and made freely available online to help educators and publishers of curriculum materials review and develop materials more tightly aligned with the CCSS. For example, Achieve, the CCSSO, and Student Achievement Partners have developed a resource called the Toolkit for Evaluating Alignment of Instructional and Assessment Materials (Achieve, Inc., Council of Chief State School Officers, & Student Achievement Partners, 2014). The purpose of the toolkit is to catalyze the impact that the CCSS can have on student achievement by increasing the prevalence of CCSS-aligned, high-quality instructional and assessment materials.

• Furthermore, researchers and educational organizations have started formally reviewing textbooks and other curriculum materials for CCSS alignment and making those reviews freely available online, such as Achieve the Core, Ed Reports, and the Open Education Resources Commons (OER Commons). Supporters claim that the CCSS have made it possible for unprecedented cross-state collaborations, leveraging the collective wisdom and influence of the education community to rapidly increase access to high-quality, standards-aligned instructional materials and to reduce costs to districts.

ISSUE 4: ROLE OF THE FEDERAL GOVERNMENT

• *Criticism: The CCSS are a product of federal overreach.* One of the most-cited criticisms of the CCSS is that the federal government has a significant and negative hand in the development and implementation of the Standards. In addition to accusations of backroom deals with influential groups that shaped the content and rapid implementation expectations of the CCSS, critics point to two main actions that involved the federal government. First was the U.S. Department of Education's requirement that states adopt college- and career-readiness standards in order to obtain a waiver for NCLB requirements that coincided with the rolling out of the CCSS. For critics, this requirement was viewed as the federal government's attempt to coerce states into adopting the CCSS. Second, the U.S. Department of Education also provided funding for two state-led assessment consortia, the Smarter Balanced Assessment Consortium (SBAC), and the Partnership for Assessment of Readiness for College and Careers (PARCC) to develop assessments aligned with the CCSS. For critics, this was viewed as providing financial benefits to both states and testing companies to engage in more unnecessary testing.

• *Support: The CCSS are a state-led effort.* Supporters of the CCSS will often point out that the federal government neither led nor paid for the development of the CCSS. The development of the CCSS was led by the NGA and the CCSSO. It was launched in 2009 by state leaders, including governors and state commissioners of education from 48 states, two territories, and the District of Columbia. In addition, NCLB waivers did not require adoption of the CCSS. States could adopt a different set of college- and career-readiness standards, including developing their own. States were also free to develop or select their own large-scale accountability assessments. Since 2010, many states have decided to adapt the CCSS, or have adopted different standards and assessments.

ISSUE 5: ASSESSMENT OF STUDENT LEARNING

• *Criticism: The CCSS will cause an increase in inappropriate testing.* The era of NCLB was one of increasing angst and backlash from educators regarding the use of testing. In particular, the use of large-scale, standardized summative assessments to make high-stakes decisions about areas such as school funding, whether or not teachers and principals kept their jobs, and the public's perception of schools contributed to an increase in the stress educators experienced. Inside these concerns is perhaps one more directly related to the teacher–student experience: namely, that these assessments are not sensitive to student learning from week to week, month to month, and don't provide timely, instructionally relevant information. Critics have viewed the federal funding of SBAC and PARCC as an attempt to further standardize education across the country by using tools that are punitive and not instructionally relevant.

● *Support: The CCSS can help drive more appropriate assessment practices.* Supporters of the CCSS will often point out that the Standards do not come with testing requirements or even tests. They detail important knowledge for students to acquire and be able to use. As college- and career-readiness standards, the CCSS contain a wide range of higher-order thinking skills that are difficult to assess with large-scale, standardized summative assessments. Recognizing this, as well as the compelling research behind formative assessment practices (e.g., Black & Harrison, 2006), both SBAC and PARCC are also developing resources to support comprehensive, balanced assessment systems (i.e., interim, formative, and diagnostic tools) in addition to summative assessments. These are tools that support teachers to make day-to-day instructional decisions.

ISSUE 6: RESPECT FOR THE PROFESSIONALISM OF TEACHERS

● *Criticism: Standards minimize teachers as professionals.* Perhaps at the center of all of these criticisms is a sense that teachers are not getting the respect they deserve as professionals. The resistance from critics when states were mandated to develop their own standards that were required to be implemented in the era of NCLB escalated when most of the United States adopted or adapted the CCSS. Critics argue that not only were teachers not represented in the development or adoption of the CCSS, but that even having standards as requirements was a negative intrusion into the decision making of classroom teachers who know what is best for their students. Additionally, many critics blame the CCSS for the other issues raised above, because each of these issues magnified and accelerated the impact of those issues.

● *Support: Standards help teachers maximize their time and skills in working with students.* Supporters of the CCSS will often point out that the Standards were developed with the input of a wide range of teachers and other education stakeholders. An extensive review of the development process is described at *www.corestandards.org.* Furthermore, many supporters of the CCSS claim that the Standards were developed to support teachers in their efforts to meet the needs of all students, not to restrict teachers or to convey a lack of respect. As professional learning and instructional resources have become more available, teachers are beginning to feel more comfortable with the CCSS. Teachers spend countless hours trying to meet the needs of their students, being asked to do more and more with less and less. Supporters of the CCSS claim that be defining at least part of what students are supposed to know and be able to do, that can help free teachers to spend more time understanding what their students need to be successful in learning those standards.

Important Policies: Every Student Succeeds Act

The combination of NCLB and IDEA brought an unprecedented level of pressure and external accountability to schools in the United States. As the years have passed since 2001, backlash against NCLB has increased as well. A great deal of criticism was directed toward the U.S. Department of Education for several reasons, including what many perceived to be an overreliance on test scores and unrealistic expectations that all students be proficient in reading and mathematics. At the same time, with the increased attention on test scores, many in the public as well as the research community were critical of states that set the bar for student proficiency on their tests too low, and of schools that continued to demonstrate stagnant student achievement.

NCLB was reauthorized in 2015, and is now known as the Every Student Succeeds Act (ESSA; 2015). Currently, much remains to be defined and understood about the practical implications of ESSA when compared to NCLB. However, one of the points that is currently known is that even though the adequate yearly progress method of holding schools accountable is no longer in place, what is in place is the continued use of large-scale, standardized tests required for grades 3–8 and one grade in high school. These tests still need to be aligned with high-quality standards—which currently means college- and career-readiness standards like the CCSS. Moving forward, state departments of education have been given increased responsibility to define accountability systems for their states to replace those in the NCLB. How this effort will impact the implementation of effective universal tier practices within MTSS remains to be seen. With that said, this is an excellent opportunity for educators to get involved in the opportunities offered by states to shape what ultimately becomes the accountability systems for ESSA in your states.

THE UNIVERSAL TIER AND MTSS: QUALITY COMPONENTS

When defining high-quality universal instruction, the challenge is to develop instruction that is articulated and taught in the way it is intended to be taught. We also expect universal instruction to be viable, with content sequenced and paced appropriately in the time available for instruction. In addition, universal instruction needs to be rigorous and challenging to all students. And finally, we want universal instruction to be relevant and make the connection between what is being learned and students' everyday lives. To overcome these challenges and ensure high-quality instruction, several components must be in place.

The Center on Response to Intervention (*www.rti4success.org*) has developed a rubric for assessing the implementation of an MTSS framework. The multilevel instruction section of the rubric focuses on universal instruction, and five key areas are included as indicators of quality universal instruction: (1) research-based curriculum and materials, (2) articulation of teaching and learning processes, (3) differentiated instruction, (4) standards-based, and (5) exceeding benchmark levels. First, we expect that all universal curriculum materials and instructional strategies are research-based for all students to the extent possible. Second, we expect that teaching and learning objectives are well articulated from one grade to another and within grade levels so that students have highly similar experiences, regardless of their assigned teacher. Third, we expect that teachers can describe how they differentiate instruction for students on, below, or above grade level, using classroom-level data to identify and address the needs of students. Fourth, we expect that universal reading and math curricula are aligned with the CCSS or other state standards. Finally, we expect that schools provide enrichment opportunities for students exceeding benchmark levels and that these opportunities are implemented consistently at all grade levels. We know that in order to meet all of these expectations, teachers need relevant and timely data to inform their instruction, and schools need to be organized in a way that provides ample collaboration time for teacher teams to use these data to inform their instructional practices.

BARRIERS TO ADDRESSING UNIVERSAL TIER INEFFECTIVENESS

Making lasting impact on the universal tier is not something that can be done with a few small changes implemented by a handful of dedicated crusaders. Because of that, and other reasons, improving the universal tier is often avoided or even ignored. Common barriers to addressing the universal tier are described next.

Assuming That MTSS Are about Intervention

Many schools go into MTSS endeavors expecting to start by identifying the students who need interventions and exploring the interventions that will change outcomes in their buildings for these at-risk students. This is, in fact, how many of us were trained to implement RTI decades ago, and it appears to be a logical place to start. However, we found that the practice of first identifying students with additional needs rarely resulted in *all* students performing successfully for multiple reasons. First, we relied on the existing infrastructure to provide interventions. Rarely were new resources added or existing resources used in a different manner, which resulted in the system "maxing out." Teachers were doing all they could with the resources available, as they continue to do today. Second, interventions were often created one student at a time, which resulted in low-intensity, ineffective practices being put in place. Furthermore, the master schedule often was never modified. For instance, a student in fourth grade may be identified as a student who struggles with math. An intervention is identified, but, due to staff availability and the schedule, the student receives the intervention for only 15 minutes a day, 4 days a week. Assuming that this intervention is matched to the student's need, the lack of intensity is likely to result in very slow learning progress. Instead, we assert that initial MTSS work must address the foundation of universal instruction. The universal tier is the first intervention for all students and is our opportunity to have the largest impact on student achievement by creating a sustainable and strong learning foundation upon which to build edifying supports for those who need them.

Assuming We Have Done It Already

We also encounter school teams that shun universal tier improvements because they believe this work has been occurring for years in their district. This work on the universal level is ongoing, so it is understandable that schools would want to shift focus and try new interventions to support struggling students. However, the lack of success at improving universal tier services does not absolve us from continuing this important work. It should, in fact, give us greater urgency to get it right!

Challenging Beliefs about Learners' Abilities to Achieve Academic Success

Many educators sometimes believe that outside, unalterable factors are strong enough to keep a child from learning, despite our best efforts. In these cases, excuses are made for not providing the most intensive interventions, delivered with relentless fidelity by the best teachers. In these cases we often ask teachers to think about which parents they want to tell that the system has given up on their child. It is important to empower teachers by reviewing the research on factors related to student achievement. Chapter 6 discusses several high-impact research-based instructional strategies that are related to curriculum, teaching, and the school environment.

Most educators believe (and research supports) the importance of holding high expectations for students. We know that students often rise to the expectations set for them. At the same time, our expectations may be directly related to what we have seen happen in the past. So, if we have always seen about 70% of students meeting expectations, we will not be surprised when only 70% meet current expectations. Subsequently, we will not necessarily feel a sense of urgency to change something about the system in order to improve achievement. Additionally, if we have seen students who struggle in kindergarten continue to struggle through their school career, we will start to have lower expectations for those students who have academic and/or social–emotional challenges early on. In reality, the goal of system improvement is to allow each and every child to succeed. Overcoming complacency with low achievement is a barrier that will need to be actively addressed throughout the process of system improvement. As achievement rises, though, this complacency will diminish, becoming less of a concern.

It is also interesting to examine our expectations about interventions. Additional resources (time, instruction, etc.) are provided, in theory, in order to raise achievement and close the achievement gap. However, often a team predicts that just the opposite will occur. They will hypothesize that an intervention will not have the intended impact and the child will need more intensive intervention, prior to implementation of an initial intervention! This pattern should be addressed immediately, every time it is conveyed. If members of the team believe an intervention will not be successful, it should be intensified immediately.

The Swinging Pendulum of Initiatives

Education is notorious for the syndrome of the swinging pendulum of initiatives. Think about it: What is the main professional learning focus for the current year? What was it last year? The year before? Chances are your answer is not the same for each year. If we believe that something is worth our time, and our time is precious, our focus should remain relentless on the implementation of that work, regardless of a new school year and a new fad.

The Culture of Closed Classroom Doors

Until recently, our education system was notorious for its culture of isolation. Each classroom teacher was assigned a group of students, and it was his or her responsibility to ensure success. Collaboration with other staff did not happen regularly (aside from professional learning days). With the more recent focus on professional learning communities (PLCs), the responsibility for success of grade-level students is shifting to all teachers in that grade level. We also see additional instructional resources being allocated to the universal tier (e.g., instructional coaches, paraprofessional support, specialized services). School culture should ensure that teachers feel safe discussing their instructional challenges with each other. Teachers should also feel comfortable with grouping children differently, which may result in children shifting classrooms, or even grade levels, for particular lessons. Furthermore, teachers should feel comfortable accepting additional support into their classrooms. In those cases, we also need to ensure that *everyone* who teaches each child feels accountable for that child's success. It is not enough to collaborate. We have to take responsibility for our outcomes and share our results—celebrations and challenges alike.

System versus Teacher Issues

When poor student outcomes occur in education, the system is quick to blame the teacher. The result is that individual teachers feel afraid and then unwilling to share their instructional challenges. In reality, when teachers are not successful, it is most often a system-level problem. Teacher success is dependent on many variables, including the materials to which they have access, the training they receive, the additional support and collaboration that are available to them, and countless other variables. When teachers are not successful, it is the job of the *system* to identify barriers and address them.

Lack of Knowledge about the Current State of the Universal Tier

Educators have a long history of trouble-shooting problems with individual students, and they often come ready to solve those problems with a comprehensive knowledge of the student's skill sets. System-level needs are much more challenging to address for multiple reasons. First, we find that principals often are not aware of the universal instructional practices being used in their schools. They know that training has occurred and materials have been purchased, but they are unable to answer the question, for example, "What does second-grade reading look like in your school?" Even more surprising, perhaps, is that they know how many minutes are scheduled for literacy instruction but rarely know how the time is being used. We find, over and over, that the schedule does not necessarily match practice for multiple, systemic reasons. At times, it is because classes such as art and physical education interfere. Other times, teachers have modified the master schedule to meet other classroom needs. And sometimes, other student services, such as speech therapy, interrupt universal instruction. Adequate knowledge of instructional practices in a school is essential if a principal is to lead the effort to improve the effectiveness of the universal tier.

Lack of Collaborative Teams

Collaboration is essential if school improvement efforts are to succeed. Teams allow staff to share ideas and discuss problems. They also allow for improved consistency of implementation when teams discuss new practices, model effective instructional practices for each other, examine student data, and problem-solve implementation problems. However, even though collaborative teams are important, an MTSS adoption survey (Spectrum K–12 Solutions, 2010) indicates that only 25% of districts implementing MTSS have collaborative leadership teams in place! Without these teams, extensive systems change is unlikely to occur.

THE CHALLENGE

After reading through the introduction to this book, with discussions of stagnant student achievement and lists of systemic barriers to successful implementation of universal tier changes, it is tempting to throw up our hands and say, "Too much!" This is an understandable reaction, as it is hard enough to navigate the day-to-day challenges of teaching students without needing to figure out how to make potentially significant changes to universal instruction. However, we have embarked on the journey of writing this book to share with you our experiences in tackling this change process.

We have found that making systemic changes to the universal tier is a big challenge. But, we have also seen amazing professionals undertaking extraordinary challenges to make meaningful changes to universal instruction that effect a difference in the lives of their students. All of us have worked with multiple school districts and have witnessed impressive outcomes for all students when universal instruction is the "target." So, we pose to you that it is, in fact, possible to engage in the ongoing process of improving universal instruction. After all, educators are in the business of facilitating continual improvement to enhance outcomes. The key to success in making effective changes to universal instruction is starting with a positive perspective, thinking systemically, and working collaboratively. We highlight these key factors throughout this book as we describe our approach to improving universal instruction.

Our challenge and your challenge, then, is this: to use a positive, systemic, collaborative approach to improving universal instruction. To accomplish this goal, we outline four actions for teams: (1) Dig deeply into universal tier work; (2) allocate time and resources to this system-level work; (3) identify barriers and develop plans to address them; and (4) continue conversations by monitoring, evaluating, and modifying action plans as implementation unfolds.

Digging into Universal Tier Work

What exactly do we mean by "digging into universal tier work"? After all, teachers are working hard every day to support the learning of their students; constantly trying to figure out what those students need; and adjusting what they, as teachers, are doing to help them. Many teachers believe they are already digging in! When we talk about digging into universal tier work, we mean that the whole school is working collaboratively to reflect on the work happening at all levels as a way to ensure effective instruction. Truly digging into universal tier work is a long-term commitment to improvement; it is not an initiative, a purchase, or a formation of professional learning teams. Digging into universal tier work requires regular, systemic work that involves everyone in the process, and that is considered part of regular practice and not something else to add on top of what is already done day in and day out. The barriers to success can be many and varied and require ongoing attention and effort. We address some ways to commit to the work of improving the universal tier in Chapters 4 and 5.

Allocating Time and Resources

Allocating time and resources to improving universal instruction may seem daunting and overwhelming to educators. After all, we haven't even discussed all of the important work that is needed to support targeted and intensive interventions, with progress monitoring, for learners who are struggling and need additional support. Although this is understandable, it is nonetheless critical that districts and schools find a way to push past this barrier. Districts and schools that ensure that analyzing universal instruction is a top priority by embedding it in their school cultures remove the barrier of feeling overwhelmed. One step toward making universal instruction a top priority is to declare it publicly and to document the decision. Many districts include improving universal instruction in their strategic plans. At the risk of minimizing this important step (which is certainly not our intention), the next step is necessary to ensure that the intention is met: namely, to allocate time and resources to engage in the work.

Taking this step can also seem overwhelming. After all, time and resources are typically in short supply. That is why it's important that digging into the universal tier becomes embedded in the culture, and not viewed as an add-on to existing work. Another way to put it is this: You may be at a place where you need to think differently about allocating the resources that you already have in order to truly prioritize digging into universal tier work. This is a very common conversation that is had, and it can be a difficult one. It is important to understand and believe that this conversation is needed, not because people have been making bad choices or have not already dedicated time and resources to working on the universal tier. But in our experience with schools implementing an MTSS framework, discussions about universal tier typically focus exclusively on curriculum materials and collecting universal screening data. After a few years, these discussions shift to the next new "initiative." The result is that there has not been enough time to facilitate conversations about deep, meaningful improvements to the universal tier, to implement strategies for improvements, and to evaluate the impact of these changes.

The challenge, then, is figuring out how to allocate adequate time and resources to ensure that the work of improving the universal tier is regular, ongoing, and deeply embedded in the fabric of the district and school. Every school system is different in terms of available resources and the needs that must be addressed. There is, therefore, no specific amount of time or resources a school system needs to allocate to improve the universal tier. In Chapters 4 and 5, we describe some specific ways to determine how much time and which types of resources are needed specific to the local context. Briefly, it is necessary to examine overall levels of achievement using information such as universal screening data, policy requirements, and degree of consensus and skills to engage in the work. These considerations can help with decision making regarding budgets, improvement and professional learning plans, and the master schedule that should all help drive what happens, day in and day out, in districts and schools.

Identifying Barriers and Developing Plans to Address Them

Earlier in this chapter, we identified several common barriers to reflecting on and working to improve the universal tier. We revisit these barriers throughout the book. Barriers need to be identified and addressed at this global level, just to get the conversations and work started. Once the work has begun, you will examine barriers at an even deeper level by using the practices and strategies that we describe in this book.

At times, it may feel like the process is getting personal and focuses too much on the negative and not enough on the positive. Let us be perfectly clear: Digging into universal tier work is about building on the strength of what you and your colleagues are already doing, and providing you with the resources and support you need to do it in a more efficient and effective manner. This is an important point because it can influence how everyone collectively thinks about trying to improve the universal tier. It is common to hear educators talk about all of the factors that influence student learning that are outside of their control (e.g., socioeconomic status, home factors, medical diagnoses). In this book, we focus on factors that are under the direct control of educators—curriculum, instruction, environment, and schoolwide organization. We emphasize all the factors we *can* control that have an influence on student outcomes.

The challenge, then, is for districts and schools to examine their systems with an assumption that the solutions lie within the local context. So, this is not about blaming those who work in the school or viewing the problem as located within students or their caretakers. Instead, we ask districts and schools a basic but challenging question: "What are the barriers to successful implementation of the universal tier?" Thinking about the work of improving the universal tier is foundational to everything else that needs to be done. The assumption is that there are *elements in the system* preventing teachers, administrators, and other school personnel from successfully implementing some necessary aspects of the universal tier. Once the barriers are accurately identified and successfully removed, the educators working in that system will have a clearer path to successfully implementing universal tier practices.

For example, a school may be losing instructional time due to noninstructional events like morning announcements and assemblies. In this example, the barriers to implementing a schedule that maximizes instructional time are noninstructional activities that may be positive but are often overlooked as factors that can interfere with instruction. Removing these barriers may be as simple as having a committee review the schedule and provide alternatives to how announcements and assemblies are handled. In Chapters 5–8, we go into more detail about ways in which districts and schools can identify and remove barriers to successful universal tier implementation, and to monitor the impact of those changes over time.

Continuing the Conversations

As we have said, improving the universal tier is not about purchasing materials, nor should it be viewed as a new "initiative." Improving the universal tier is about collaborative, ongoing work that gets embedded in the fabric of the district and school. Even as barriers to implementation are successfully identified and removed, it is important to continuously evaluate improvements to the universal tier. As new students come through, as school personnel come and go, as new requirements and exciting new initiatives come to the forefront over time, it is easy to lose track of what has already been successfully changed and which efforts were not as effective at positively impacting change.

The challenge, then, is to ensure that the positive changes are sustained and that less effective practices and strategies are not repeated. To successfully face this challenge, it is critical that the culture of collaboration continue to be nurtured, and that the positive changes that have been made are documented, regularly revisited, and ultimately sustained over time. Strategies to keep the conversations going include incorporating them into local handbooks, other policy documents, and the schedule and to show staff how those conversations are acted upon and lead to positive change.

ORGANIZATION OF THIS BOOK

Throughout this book, we suggest using an action planning process that incorporates answering the following five questions:

1. Is universal instruction effective?
2. If the universal tier is not sufficient, what needs must be addressed?
3. How will the needs identified in universal instruction be addressed?
4. How will the effectiveness and efficiency of universal instruction improvements be monitored over time?
5. Have improvements to universal instruction been effective?

Chapters 2 and 3 provide prerequisite information on learning targets and universal assessments. Then we dive into the five questions just listed. Chapter 4 provides information on how teams can use assessment data to determine if a school's universal instruction is effective. Chapter 5 provides a framework for determining why universal instruction may not be effective. Chapter 6 describes how to address the needs identified to improve universal instruction. Chapter 7 discusses how teams can monitor the effectiveness and efficiency of universal instruction and changes in the universal tier over time. Finally, Chapter 8 provides a framework for evaluating improvements to universal instruction. We conclude with a chapter on "continuing the journey" and tips for sustainability. The challenges are many, and the work is daunting, but we know it is possible to achieve. The universal tier impacts each and every child who walks into the school and therefore is worth the time and attention needed to improve it. Throughout this book, we offer strategies and supports to engage in universal tier improvement, as well as encouragement to continue this journey!

Discussion questions are included at the end of each chapter to support district, building, and grade-level teams as they read this book. As each chapter is read, the questions are designed to prompt reflection and to be applied to the specific setting of each school.

DISCUSSION QUESTIONS

1. How is the universal tier defined in your building or district?

2. What process does your building or district use to ensure that universal curriculum and instructional materials are research-based?

3. What else, in addition to curriculum and instructional materials, is used to support student learning in the universal tier?

4. What assumptions do educators in your building or district hold about the MTSS framework? If the majority of educators believe that the framework is about providing supplemental and intensive interventions to at-risk students, how will you go about addressing this implementation barrier?

5. How are educators in your building or district challenged to hold, and held accountable for, high expectations for all students? How does the system support a focus on "alterable variables" or factors that can be changed within the instructional day?

6. How familiar are educators in your building or district with the CCSS? What supports are in place to assist teachers to implement the Standards?

7. How has your building or district established a collaborative culture for discourse and decision making?

CHAPTER 2

Learning Targets

In this chapter, we discuss the importance of having clearly defined learning targets as the foundation of an effective universal tier. As we examine the background, importance, and practices related to identifying clearly defined learning targets, it will be important to remember that we are setting the stage for what we teach and assess as part of the universal tier. We acknowledge and discuss in detail throughout this book the importance of the materials and practices that help schools implement effective curriculum, instruction, and assessment. These materials and practices are at the very center of what teachers use daily as part of the universal tier. Learning targets, on the other hand, may or may not be what teachers think about actively in their ongoing role of supporting student learning—and that is completely understandable. Our goal is to describe what learning targets are; why they are important for an effective universal tier; and to provide practical ideas about how learning targets can inform your work in curriculum, instruction, and assessment.

DEFINITION OF LEARNING TARGETS

At the center of all the complexities of education is a relatively simple idea: We want students to grow in their learning and in their overall well-being. Statements to this effect are found in school vision and mission statements; countless professional learning materials and resources; theme statements for the conferences; books (like this one!); and even in many of the laws, rules, and regulations that govern our collective work. Indeed, there is little debate about what school should be about, and that is learning. Ensuring that students grow in their learning and overall well-being, we believe, is a non-negotiable aspect of a successful universal tier. The discussion gets sticky, however, when we step beyond the easy-to-agree-with purpose of school. What should students learn? Who should decide? Should curriculum materials dictate what students are supposed to learn? How do we know what students have learned as a result of school? We certainly cannot make those decisions for schools, but we can describe some ideas that can help them do so.

In the spirit of trying to keep this aspect of the process as simple and straightforward as possible, we propose that schools define what they want their students to know and be able to do in the form of learning targets. A web search for *learning targets* produces a variety of definitions and descriptions. Learning targets are discussed in the context of areas such as formative assessment, lesson plans, and academic content standards. For the purposes of this book, we define *learning targets* as statements defined by a district or school that describe what students are supposed to know and be able to do. Many districts word learning targets as "I can" statements. For example, Mrs. Jones is a fourth-grade teacher who is using the CCSS English language arts (ELA) standards. She is working with her students on CCSS Language Standard CCSS.ELA-LITERACY.L.4.5: "Demonstrate understanding of figurative language, word relationships, and nuances in word meanings." Specifically, Mrs. Jones is working on a specific part of the standard with her students, Standard CCSS.ELA-LITERACY.L.4.5.A: "Explain the meaning of simple similes and metaphors (e.g., *as pretty as a picture*) in context." She develops the following student-centered learning target: "I can explain the meaning of simple similes and metaphors in what I read."

If a district is currently using a similar definition of learning targets, then we recommend continuing to use it. If brand new to the idea of learning targets, our definition can serve as a place to start. In either case, we do need to be up front about one aspect of defining the concept of learning targets about which we feel quite strongly. That is, *learning targets need to be grounded in the academic content standards required by the state in which you work*. We dig more deeply into this concept later in this chapter.

With that said, the important point is that in MTSS implementation efforts, learning targets are a focal point of the universal tier—which, in turn, ensures that MTSS implementation efforts are standards-based. There are three main questions to address when working with learning targets in an MTSS system: (1) Who should develop learning targets?; (2) How should learning targets be developed?; and (3) How should learning targets be used to implement an effective universal tier?

WHO SHOULD DEVELOP LEARNING TARGETS?

In our exploration of learning targets, we include a feature that indicates that they should be *defined* by a district or school. What we do *not* claim, however, is that a district or school should *develop* the learning targets. This is an important distinction. A district or school may choose to develop their own learning targets, select learning targets that have been developed by someone else, or they may choose to use a combination of both approaches. We do not want to get in the middle of debates about whether or not it is more effective for learning targets to be developed by those who will be using them. In our experience and in our review of the research, we have not found any compelling evidence to suggest that one approach is better than the other. What is important is that there is consensus in a district or school about how learning targets will be defined and a common understanding about how they will be used in MTSS implementation efforts.

Establishing and maintaining consensus around learning targets is essential for the efforts to be successful. There are several issues related to learning targets that need to be taken into consideration when working to establish and maintain consensus: (1) how the learning targets are defined, (2) how the learning targets are used, and (3) each person's roles and responsibilities with the learning targets. If administrators and teachers are not largely on the same page regarding these issues, it will be incredibly difficult for all of the work that draws on those learning targets (curriculum, instruction, and assessment) to be successful. That is why it is important for district and building leaders to determine not only their level of consensus on these issues, but to engage with staff members to learn what they need in order to continue to go on the journey of using learning targets to improve the universal tier.

At the outset, simply asking staff whether or not they are willing to work collaboratively on defining and using learning targets can help determine the extent to which consensus exists in a building. Developing a survey is another way to gather the information. With either approach, it is important that staff have at least a surface-level understanding of what they are being asked to do with learning targets before asking them whether or not they agree to use them. Another consideration is whether or not learning targets are going to be required by the district or school. If so, then staff needs to know the reason they are being required. If learning targets are not required, your initial conversations may be slightly different, more focused on making the case for why using learning targets can be a good thing for both staff and students.

Regardless of whether or not learning targets are required, staff should play an active role in defining them. Ultimately, teachers and students will be the ones engaged with the learning targets on a daily basis. Making it clear at the outset that teachers will have a role in defining the learning targets can help establish and maintain consensus about, and commitment to use, those learning targets. Actively including teachers in the definition of learning targets will also provide more frequent opportunities to check in with teachers in an authentic way, to see how they are feeling about the process and supporting them when questions and concerns arise.

HOW SHOULD LEARNING TARGETS BE DEFINED?

There are many outstanding resources available on how to develop learning targets, such as Heritage's (2010) framework for developing learning goals and success criteria, and the Understanding by Design or Backward Design process (Wiggins & McTighe, 2005). Our goal is not to re-create the work of others in this area. Instead, we lay out some basic issues on how learning targets should be defined. As a reminder, learning targets need to be standards-based. With that as a foundation, we pay particular attention in this chapter to district and school considerations, the different roles needed in the process, the role of academic content standards (i.e., the standards-based part), what high-quality learning targets look like, and how the process of defining learning targets can be used to promote a healthy universal tier.

District and School Considerations

Since we have established that learning targets should be defined by the district or school, the next step is to determine how a district or school can go about defining those learning targets. As we mentioned previously, there are two basic approaches a district or school can take in defining learning targets: developing learning targets themselves, or selecting learning targets developed by others. In determining which method to use, a district or school should consider factors such as existing time and financial resources to engage in the process, knowledge and skills present in their system that are needed to develop high-quality learning targets, and how all of that fits into the list of everything else that needs to be done. If any of these things is in short supply, it is likely advantageous for a district or school to select a set of learning targets developed by someone else. With that said, there should still be broad staff involvement using either approach to ensure strong consensus in implementing the targets.

Roles Needed in Defining Learning Targets

Simply having broad staff involvement will not necessarily lead to a high degree of consensus if you do not build on staff members' strengths and establish clear roles based on those strengths. There are several roles necessary to successfully define learning targets. Those roles include content expertise grounded in the required academic content standards (e.g., the CCSS), assessment expertise, process facilitation, and administrative authority. Staff members with *content expertise* have deep awareness of the knowledge and skills that need to be learned by students; such expertise is needed to ensure that the learning targets are accurate. A related role, that of *assessment expertise*, is particularly helpful in ensuring that the learning targets that are developed can be assessed using a variety of formative and summative methods. Ultimately, this assessment is necessary because students, teachers, parents, and other education stakeholders need to be informed about student learning progress in relation to the learning targets.

A sometimes overlooked role in the development of learning targets is that of *process facilitator*, which requires someone with the knowledge and skills needed to ensure that the details of the process are followed with fidelity. This can be a challenging role, as often those participating in the process of defining learning targets want to provide direct input into the process itself. However, in order for the process to be successful, one or more people need to focus on making sure that the process is followed so it can be completed well, without overly influencing the specific decisions being made. Otherwise, you run the risk of diminishing the involvement of others and reducing the ongoing consensus that is needed for the work.

Finally, someone with *administrative authority* is needed to ensure that the resources needed to complete the work are allocated in a timely fashion. Resources include time, personnel, money, and materials. Without active administrator participation in the process of developing learning targets, you run the risk of those engaged in the "nuts and bolts" of the process not having what they need to complete their work. Furthermore, having someone with final decision-making authority is needed to ensure that the work will have administrative backing to provide it vision as well as support to navigate the bumpy patches in the road that always occur when implementing something new.

The Role of Academic Content Standards in Defining Learning Targets

Academic content standards serve as the overarching set of what students are supposed to know and be able to do as a result of engaging in learning at school. In the areas of ELA and mathematics, most states have adopted and added to the CCSS (*www.corestandards. org*). As was previously mentioned, the CCSS movement evolved due to the inconsistency of state standards across the nation, along with large numbers of students exiting high school unprepared for college and/or employment. Despite the widespread adoption of the CCSS, a number of misconceptions about the Standards remain.

- *The CCSS are not curriculum.* A curriculum includes a wide range of instructional materials (e.g., textbooks, audio/video files), teacher directions, and content articulation (e.g., curriculum maps, scope and sequence charts). The CCSS do not include any of these resources and materials, though examples of materials such as books that have sufficiently complex text are provided in the appendices to the Standards.

- *The CCSS do not prescribe or require how teachers teach content.* The role of academic content standards is to define *what* students need to learn, not *how* teachers are supposed to teach. The CCSS do not contain a list of required instructional practices. However, in looking at the CCSS, teachers should collaboratively reflect on the extent to which the instructional practices they currently use help students engage in learning the desired knowledge identified in the CCSS. If not, changes to practice are necessary, but still not dictated by nor described in the CCSS.

- *The CCSS are not specific enough to serve as the learning targets for a district or school.* Although the CCSS may or may not be more specific than previous editions of the academic content standards you have used, you will still need to decide whether or not you want to use the CCSS as your learning targets, or if you need to have learning targets that are more specific or that address smaller chunks of each standard. In fact, a single standard might have more than one learning target associated with it, or one learning target may cut across multiple standards. For example, the overarching Kindergarten CCSS Foundational Skills—Phonics and Work Recognition Standard CCSS.ELA-LITERACY.RF.K.3 may have three "I can" statements as learning targets derived from the substandards: (1) "I can distinguish between similarly spelled words by identifying the sounds of the letters that are different"; (2) "I can associate the long and short sounds with common spellings for the five vowels"; and (3) "I can say the most common sound for each consonant."

- *The CCSS are not a test.* A test is a form of assessment that is used to gather information about student learning. The CCSS is a list of what students are supposed to know and be able to do. In this era of standards-based practice, tests should be aligned with academic content standards like the CCSS. But that does not make the CCSS themselves a test; they just provide the list of what should be tested.

- *The CCSS were not developed by the federal government.* As we previously mentioned, the NGA, in partnership with the CCSSO, worked with content experts and educators from around the country to develop the CCSS. What is often confusing is that the federal government *incentivized* states to adopt college- and career-readiness standards to be eligible to apply for Race to the Top funds, and also provided grant money to state-led assessment consortia to develop tests aligned with the CCSS. Although debate remains about whether or not it was appropriate for the federal government to do these two things, what is not debatable is who developed the standards and who funded it—and it was not the federal government.

Despite these wide-ranging misconceptions and some states wavering in their support of the CCSS, these Standards remain an unprecedented opportunity for improving education in the United States. For all of the opposition, there continues to be widespread support of the CCSS. Those states that continue to adopt CCSS as their academic content standards provide amazing opportunities to create efficient standardization of overarching learning expectations, while still allowing a wide range of latitude for decision making at the district and school levels. Indeed, the CCSS are incredibly well suited to be used in the defining of learning targets for the following reasons.

- *The CCSS are rigorous.* The preponderance of evidence from research reviews and evaluation studies suggests that the CCSS are a rigorous set of learning expectations (Conley et al., 2011; Porter, McMaken, Hwang, & Yang, 2011). In this context, *rigorous* means that the standards are cognitively demanding, providing students with opportunities to be challenged to apply learning to real-world, complex, and open-ended situations. The standards call on students to use their prior knowledge, to develop in-depth understanding, and to communicate their learning.

- *The CCSS are internationally benchmarked.* One of the primary points of reference for the movement toward standards-based education in the United States is evidence from international studies of academic achievement, which place the performance of our education system well below the highest-achieving countries. One of the factors that are typically identified as distinguishing education in those countries from education in the United States is the rigor of the learning expectations for students in other countries. By internationally benchmarking the CCSS, the Standards are similar to the learning expectations from countries that have high levels of student achievement.

- *The CCSS are grounded in research on college and career readiness.* Another area of motivation for the development and adoption of the CCSS, in addition to evidence from international research, was that too many students in the United States were graduating from high school unprepared for college or careers (American College Testing Program, 2008; Hart, 2005). With input from researchers, postsecondary learning institutes, and members from the business and workforce community, the CCSS were developed to ensure that students who learned what is detailed in the Standards would be much more likely to be ready for college and/or career upon graduation from high school.

• *Widespread CCSS adoption has potential for increased efficiency in defining learning targets.* Before the development of the CCSS, there were limited options for districts and schools to easily access work on learning targets done by others that would be relevant and applicable in their contexts. Any standards-based work with learning targets was only possible within states or by vendors at a cost to districts and schools. However, with the CCSS, a growing body of work on learning targets is being done across the country that can be accessed by districts and schools without significant expense. Whether a district or school chooses to adopt learning targets developed by others, or to use that work to develop learning targets locally, the work can be done more efficiently with a wider range of options available to help guide the work.

• *Widespread adoption of CCSS has the potential to increase efficiency in using learning targets for curriculum and assessment purposes.* A great deal of the work on learning targets being done nationally is in the context of developing curriculum materials as well as formative and summative assessment tools. For example, several state departments of education and professional organizations have "unpacked" the CCSS into themes such as enduring understandings and learning targets. Doing a basic web search for these topics will yield many quality resources and tools that can help you either select or develop learning targets grounded in the CCSS. Several additional tools that are discussed in different chapter of this book—such as instructional units from organizations such as Student Achievement Partners (*http://achievethecore.org*) and the Digital Library, developed by the Smarter Balanced Assessment Consortium (*www.smarterbalanced.org*)—have curriculum and assessment resources that can be used to develop learning targets. Districts and schools can extract the learning targets from these resources to use locally.

The key point in discussing these misconceptions and opportunities related to the CCSS and learning targets is to emphasize that, if your state has adopted the CCSS, it is important to ground universal tier practices in these standards. This work should start with defining learning targets, whether you simply take learning targets developed by others or develop your own. If your state has not adopted the CCSS, your practice should still be grounded in the academic content standards of your state. Doing so will ensure that you are not only in compliance with federal and state requirements, but also that your efforts to define learning targets will have a degree of coherence and quality—which is more likely to have a practical, day-to-day influence on your practice.

High-Quality Learning Targets

Having established the importance of learning targets, as well as the role of academic content standards in identifying learning targets, it seems appropriate at this point to describe what high-quality learning targets look like. After all, investing all of this time and energy learning about learning targets and planning to pursue the use of learning targets, they should be good, right? What follows are several features of high-quality learning targets. They are organized into two main categories: characteristics of individual learning targets and characteristics of a set of learning targets.

A few points are worth mentioning before describing these characteristics of high-quality learning targets. First, it is critical for schools to elicit stakeholder input. In determining what students should know and be able to do, it is important for a district or school to ensure that there is consensus among key stakeholders around what that knowledge and those skills should comprise. As such, those stakeholder groups (e.g., teachers, administrators, parents) should have opportunities to provide input on the learning targets. Such input can take many forms, including participation in focus groups and surveys, providing written feedback, or being part of decision-making committees. Second, each of the characteristics of individual learning targets applies to the full collection of learning targets. Third, the best evidence we have available suggests that the CCSS generally display all of the features listed for high-quality learning targets. With that said, on to the characteristics!

Characteristics of Individual Learning Targets

There are several features to look for in defining learning targets. These features apply to each learning target defined, as well as to the full set of learning targets taken as a whole. The more of these features that are in place, the stronger the set of learning targets.

RESEARCH BASED

One of the initial characteristics to take into consideration is the extent to which the knowledge and skills embodied in the learning targets is based on research. In the case of early literacy, a resource such as the National Reading Panel and National Institute of Child Health and Human Development (2000) is an excellent source to help you accomplish this goal. Of recent interest has been the idea of academic content standards like the CCSS (which can be used as learning targets) defining the knowledge and skills students need to be college and career ready. This idea, too, is derived from research on what students know when they graduate from high school and how likely they are to succeed academically when they get to college (American College Testing Program, 2008).

INTERNATIONALLY BENCHMARKED

Another source of determining the quality of content in learning targets is to define targets that have been internationally benchmarked (e.g., Jerald, 2008). Being *internationally benchmarked* means that the knowledge and skills in the learning targets can also be found in the learning targets (e.g., academic content standards and national curricula) of other countries that have high student achievement. Using internationally benchmarked learning targets ensures that you will be focusing on knowledge and skills that have a high likelihood of identifying learning that is truly important for later success.

RIGOR

One of the characteristics that should result from using research-based, internationally benchmarked learning targets is that they are rigorous. *Rigor* is a concept that is often discussed but rarely defined in a consistent way. One method of defining *rigor* is using a framework of cognitive complexity such as Bloom's Revised Cognitive Taxonomy (Anderson & Krathwohl, 2001) or Webb's Depth of Knowledge framework (Webb, 2005). *Cognitive complexity* means that the learning targets are cognitively demanding, providing students with opportunities to be challenged to apply learning to real-world, complex, and open-ended situations. The learning targets call on students to use their prior knowledge, develop in-depth understanding, and communicate their learning.

MEASURABLE

The language used in learning targets should allow them to be easily measurable. It is difficult to know how effective instruction focused on a learning target has been if it is difficult to assess the knowledge and skills in that learning target. For example, "Students should understand syllables" is much vaguer and harder to measure than "Students should decode multisyllabic words." The second statement is more concrete and direct in terms of what students are supposed to do. Learning targets should lend themselves to easy measurement.

MINIMAL JARGON

If learning targets are going to be used effectively by a school, then those who are going to be using them should both understand them and be able to explain them easily. Learning targets should be examined for confusing and overly technical language to reduce the use of jargon as much as possible. Sometimes schools will reword learning targets for parents and also for students so that they are easier to understand and to use by those individuals. In the end, if learning targets are going to be used, they need to be relatively easy to understand.

Characteristics of a Set of Learning Targets

In addition to those characteristics that individual learning targets should have, there are some additional considerations that schools should take into account when considering a full set of learning targets such as the CCSS. Evaluating a full set of learning targets comprehensively is important if schools are to have confidence that those targets are designed to work together in harmony to support student learning.

VERTICAL ARTICULATION

There should be a comprehensive set of learning targets for each grade level in a school building. That way, there is a purposefully designed flow of learning from one grade level to the next. This flow is known as *vertical articulation*. High-quality learning targets are vertically articulated from grade to grade in such a way that there is little overlap in desired knowledge and skills from one grade to the next. At the same time, there should be no missing pockets or gaps in knowledge and skills from one grade level to the next. In order words, there should be natural connecting points between the learning targets as they proceed from grade level to grade level.

SCOPE AND SEQUENCE

While it is important that there be strong vertical articulation of learning targets from one grade level to the next, it is also important that the knowledge and skills are organized in a logical fashion within a grade level across an entire school year. Organizing learning targets within a school year helps schools keep student learning at a reasonable pace and provides clarity for decision making regarding instruction and assessment. Going through a process of organizing the learning targets within a grade level in terms of their a scope and sequence can also help schools determine how much can be reasonably accomplished in one school year.

COMPREHENSIVE

One of the challenges schools face is trying to "fit everything in." One of the points we have learned from international studies is that highly successful countries focus on fewer topics and dig into those topics more deeply than we typically do in the United States. What we mean by *comprehensive* learning targets is that the they are designed to cover a wide enough range of knowledge and skills deemed important by both research and stakeholders, while allowing enough time to dig into them deeply. In other words, the learning targets are characterized both by *breadth* and *depth*.

COHERENT

One of the standing challenges in developing a comprehensive, research-based set of learning targets is to make sure that the set is coherent. A *coherent* set of learning targets is one in which the targets work together with one another to form an interconnected web of learning for students. This is best accomplished when professionals with both content expertise and skill in articulating learning targets work together in a planful manner. Coherence of learning targets helps schools deliver more meaningful learning experiences and helps students make connections among their different learning experiences.

THE ROLE OF LEARNING TARGETS IN PROMOTING A HEALTHY UNIVERSAL TIER

We have gone to great lengths to describe what learning targets are and how they should be defined by a school. We have discussed the role of the CCSS in defining learning targets (they should either be the learning targets, or the learning targets should align with them).

What we have not done yet is address the role of learning targets in MTSS, and in particular for universal instruction. Explaining the role of learning targets in universal instruction is quite straightforward. Universal instruction is what all students in a school should receive daily. Learning targets define what all students should know and be able to do as a result of universal instruction. Learning targets, therefore, actually serve as one of the first bricks in the foundation of universal instruction. They are the main point of reference for all of the decisions made by a school related to curriculum, instruction, and assessment. Learning targets promote a healthy universal tier when they embody the high-quality characteristics we have described.

HOW SHOULD LEARNING TARGETS BE USED?

It is important that schools do not invest a great deal of time and energy defining learning targets, only for them to land on a shelf, never to be seen again. Schools do not have extra time and energy to waste. At the same time, learning targets cannot be an "add-on" to everything else that schools need to do. Instead, learning targets need to be that main point of reference for engaging in the work of universal instruction. Specifically, there are four main roles that learning targets should play in universal instruction: They should drive curricular decisions, drive instructional decisions, drive assessment decisions, and engage students in their learning.

To Drive Curriculum

There are a variety of important factors that schools need to consider when selecting and using curriculum materials, such as budget, professional learning needs, and teacher input. Critically important in these decisions is the extent to which the curriculum materials support teachers in their efforts to teach the learning targets. This is a consideration that, candidly, is often either overlooked by schools, or schools take the word of vendors that their materials align with standards such as the CCSS. Initial research on the alignment of curriculum materials with academic content standards like the CCSS suggested that there was *very little alignment* to be found (e.g., Polikoff, 2015). Although a group called EdReports.org has found recent improvement in alignment between curriculum materials and the CCSS (*www.edreports.org*), overall there continues to be a great deal of missing alignment. This is not a minor point. Curriculum materials, no matter how well designed they are, should not drive the decisions about what students should learn. They should be tools that are used to engage students in learning that is focused on what the school has defined as important for students to learn.

By the same token, if schools decide to develop their own curricular materials, it is important that their process is driven by what is defined in the learning targets that have been collectively and collaboratively defined by the school. Schools should be mindful with this approach, as it can be very resource intensive and requires a high level of training to do well. The curricular processes described in books such as *Understanding by Design* (Wiggins & McTighe, 2005), *Aligning and Balancing the Standards-Based Curriculum* (Squires,

2004), and *Total Instructional Alignment* (Carter, 2009) allow schools to use learning targets to drive the design and development of curriculum, but do require training, coaching, and support. Teachers need to have a deep understanding of the learning targets and how instructional materials should be designed to follow the scope and sequence within a grade level and the vertical articulation across grade levels. That is not to say it is impossible. This is just a friendly "heads up" regarding what it will take for schools to develop their own curricular materials.

Regardless of whether a school chooses to adopt/purchase curriculum materials, design their own, or some combination of the two, learning targets need to drive the discussions and decisions being made through the process. Some strategies that can help schools use learning targets to drive curricular decisions include the following:

- Engage staff in a process of studying the learning targets to deepen their understanding of them. This could take a variety of forms. The learning could focus on the structure of the learning targets, identifying key vocabulary used, or having collaborative conversations among teachers and other instructional staff on what each target means. The type of conversations can help staff develop a common understanding about what the learning targets mean. These conversations can be further enhanced by examining student work products using the learning targets.

- Review evaluations of curriculum materials for alignment with the CCSS. Organizations such as EdReports.org and AchievetheCore.org are taking different but promising approaches to reviewing curricular materials for alignment with the CCSS. Reviewing these evaluations can be instructive for schools as they work to establish their learning targets as drivers of the curriculum process.

To Drive Instruction

In many ways, instruction should be an extension of the curricular materials. That is, curricular materials should provide a great deal of structure, ideas, and resources for the delivery of instruction. If learning targets were used to drive curricular decisions, and if the curricular materials are implemented with fidelity, it should follow that the instruction being delivered is focused on the learning targets. The reality is that this is very difficult to do. Schools are full of both predictable disruptions to schedules and learning (e.g., assemblies) and unpredictable disruptions (e.g., when several teachers are out sick with the flu), and they are also full are students with learning needs that may vary from day to day.

And, like the research on curricular materials, there is very little evidence to suggest that instruction is closely aligned with learning targets. Although there has been a modest increase in alignment between what is taught with academic content standards and assessments in the era of NCLB (Polikoff, 2012), this change in practice has not led to the wide-sweeping changes in instruction that the architects of that policy envisioned. We therefore cannot assume that just because learning targets exist, and just because our curricular materials may align with those learning targets (which the available evidence indicates is unlikely), that instruction will align with those learning targets.

As such, it is important that learning targets continue to be kept in the forefront of a school's work with instruction, actively using it to drive the instructional process. Planning to use the learning targets to inform daily instructional decisions can be incredibly helpful in assuring that the learning targets actually drive daily instructional decisions. Some strategies that can help schools use learning targets to drive instructional decisions include the following:

• Include the learning targets for lessons at the top of lesson plans. By having the learning targets front and center at the top of the lesson, they serve as a point of reference for teachers and it can help to keep them fresh in their minds. This is especially helpful with all of the decisions and distractions teachers face daily.

• Post the learning targets for the day publicly in the classroom. This extends beyond simply posting all of the learning targets for a grade level in the classroom, and having them hang there all year. Although that is a fine practice, what we are talking about is highlighting and making present in an obvious, visible way the learning targets for *each day*. This can be helpful in letting students know what specifically they will be learning that day.

• Focus professional learning conversations among teachers on specific learning targets. Instead of having professional learning focus only on specific teaching techniques, couple those conversations with the learning targets that can be effectively taught with those techniques. This can serve as another reminder of what students should know and be able to do as a result of those instructional techniques.

To Drive Assessment

Assessment is covered in great detail throughout this book. As such, we don't spend a great deal of time discussing it here. The key concept to discuss at this juncture is that what gets assessed should be driven by what students are supposed to know and be able to do—which should be defined in a school's learning targets. Assessments that are aligned with learning targets provide many benefits, including helping us to develop different types of assessments for different purposes (e.g., universal screening formative assessment, diagnostic assessment, progress monitoring, and summative assessment) that help identify the extent to which students are learning what is described in the learning targets.

At the risk of sounding like a broken record, there is not a great deal of evidence from research to suggest that the assessments used by schools are closely aligned with learning targets. Before the CCSS, most evidence suggested that assessments either were not closely aligned with learning targets, or that there was not much evidence to even see if those assessments were aligned with learning targets or not (Porter, 2002). However, there is renewed optimism that this research gap might be lessening with the work being done by the two state-led assessment consortia, the SBAC (*www.smarterbalanced.org*) and the PARCC (*www.parcconline.org*).

With that said, there is a great deal of assessment work done daily in schools that these assessment consortia cannot feasibly address. It is therefore the responsibility of schools to ensure that the assessment practices they use address the learning targets they have defined. Some strategies that can help schools use learning targets to drive assessment decisions include the following.

• Use the learning targets when developing local assessments. Whenever rubrics, checklists, quizzes, or tests are developed by teachers, it can be helpful to have the learning targets present and reviewed as the assessments are being developed. This can increase the likelihood that those assessments are actually addressing those learning targets.

• Ask for evidence from assessment vendors of alignment between their assessments and the learning targets. Although this may not win a school many favors with assessment vendors, schools have an obligation to ensure they are using high-quality assessments. Schools can ask vendors to describe which learning targets are assessed, how they are assessed, and how they determined that those assessments were aligned with the learning targets.

To Engage Students

Using learning targets to drive curricular, instructional, and assessment decisions is a helpful way for schools to ensure that they have a system that is coordinated and highly like to provide students with opportunities to succeed with the learning targets. With that said, having a coordinated system is a necessary but not sufficient condition for that success to occur. Students need to be actively engaged in their own learning to increase their likelihood of success with the learning targets (DiPerna, Volpe, & Elliott, 2002).

It is beyond the scope of this chapter to discuss student engagement in great detail. Instead, we briefly describe how learning targets can be used to engage students in their own learning. Using learning targets to facilitate student engagement has the benefit of grounding their engagement in what they are supposed to be learning. This focuses learning on big ideas and skills, instead of on activities and exercises. Some strategies that can help schools use learning targets to engage students in their own learning include:

• Reframe the learning targets in a more student-friendly format. Learning targets are typically written for adults, specifically teachers and curriculum leaders. Schools can help students better understand what they are learning about by rewriting the learning targets in student-friendly language that is developmentally appropriate. One format is called "I can" statements. For example, the third-grade Common Core Foundational Skills standard CCSS.ELA-LITERACY.RF.3.3.C—"Decode multisyllabic words"—can be rewritten in more student-friendly language such as "I can read words with more than one syllable."

• Explain how the exercises and activities help students increase their learning of the targets. The act of explaining why students are being asked to do what they are doing can address that eternal question of students: "Why do I need to know this?" Learning targets, especially those that have been reframed using more student-friendly language, can provide helpful answers to that question.

- Have students reflect on their learning in the context of the learning targets. Instead of just telling students a score or grade they obtained on a quiz or test, for example, having students reflect on how their learning is progressing on the targets can help them better connect to what they are learning and why they are learning it. This is one of the central tenants of formative assessment practices that research has shown to yield positive results for student learning (Black & William, 1998).

THE ROLE OF COLLABORATIVE TEAMS

A theme you will find running throughout this book is the role of collaboration in ensuring that a school has a healthy universal tier. Collaborative teams allow staff to share ideas and discuss problems. When it comes to learning targets, collaborative teams provide opportunities for school personnel to work through challenges together to successfully define and use learning targets to drive their decisions. Using clearly defined, high-quality learning targets to improve the universal tier is about collaborative, ongoing work that gets embedded in the fabric of the district and school. That collaborative work includes defining/developing learning targets, engaging in professional learning around the learning targets, bringing student work and lessons to collaborative teams for improvement and feedback, and providing feedback to the school system for improvements to the learning targets.

Define/Develop Learning Targets

The majority of this chapter has focused on what learning targets are, what role they play, and who should define them. We have discussed the importance of both administrators and teachers being involved, and that the roles of content expert, assessment expert, process facilitator, and administrative authority be present. We have talked about how these personnel in the specified roles, along with input from other stakeholder groups, are necessary in the process of defining learning targets. It is at this juncture—the forming of collaborative teams—where all of these pieces need to come together.

In the current policy context of education in the United States, academic content standards are likely to continue to be present in our work for a long time to come. We would argue that the most straightforward approach to defining learning targets for a school is to use the CCSS (or the academic content standards adopted by your state, if not the CCSS) as the learning targets. After all, schools are required to implement their state's academic content standards. The CCSS can be viewed objectively as meeting most to all of the characteristics of high-quality learning targets. However, in order to own the learning targets, schools need to have collaborative conversations about how they want to define their learning targets.

In the end, a school's collaborative teams may decide that it makes the best sense to use the CCSS as the learning targets. Or, they may decide that developing learning targets that are framed differently but still aligned with the CCSS is the best route to take in order to own and implement them. In the end, the learning targets are more likely to be used if the defining of them occurs collaboratively at the school level. Having structured collaborative teams that have been given this charge is an excellent approach to defining learning targets at the school level.

Engage in Professional Learning around Learning Targets

Once the school's collaborative teams have defined the learning targets, the next step is to ensure that staff has a deep, common understanding of the learning targets and how to use them. This learning should have begun during the defining process. With that said, the processes of developing deep, common understanding of the learning targets and how to use them is an ongoing process that really never ends. As such, having an established set of collaborative teams and routines for those teams can help facilitate this ongoing learning. Some helpful strategies for using collaborative teams to engage in this ongoing learning include the following.

- Schedule specific times for collaborative teams to engage in professional learning around the learning targets. As we have previously mentioned, using practices like studying the architecture of the learning targets or unpacking the learning targets can be helpful first steps in learning more about them. Just spending time discussing the learning targets in collaborative teams provides all staff with opportunities to discuss them and to build common understanding around them.

- Have teachers take turns facilitating the professional learning. Providing teachers with both opportunities and expectations to lead professional learning for the collaborative teams can create ownership and accountability to engage in the professional learning. And, teachers are much more likely to buy into what they are hearing from their teaching peers than from administrators or external experts or consultants.

- Develop a learning syllabus for the collaborative teams for a school year. Creating a syllabus, or a scope and sequence, of professional learning topics for an entire school year provides a vision for the learning. This is much more likely to be effective if teachers have an opportunity to help build that syllabus.

Bring Student Work and Lessons to the Team for Improvement and Feedback

Although professional learning on learning targets can provide important, foundational knowledge for school staff, by itself it is not enough to translate the learning targets into action with students. To take the next step, collaborative school teams need to discuss their practice and how learning targets are and could be used. This step requires teachers to bring their lesson plans, units, and other materials they use to teach their students to their collaborative teams for improvement conversations. It also requires teachers to bring examples of student work to reflect on how student assignments were built around learning targets and how students performed relative to those learning targets. In order for this practice to be successful, several things need to be in place, including the following.

• Administrators and teacher leaders need to create a safe, welcoming environment. Teaching is a highly personal experience, and it can often be challenging for teachers to expose themselves to feedback from peers. They run the risk of exposing their perceived or actual shortcomings as teachers in these types of conversations. Administrators and teacher leaders can help create a safe environment by publically setting expectations for purpose and behavior during collaborative team meetings, holding people accountable to those expectations, and modeling that behavior for everyone else.

• Establish routines for the process of bringing lessons and student work to the collaborative team for feedback. Simply laying out the steps that teachers will take to bring their work to the team for feedback, and what will happen before, during, and after the collaborative team meeting, can help create clarity and consistency in the process for all involved. This clarity and consistency can help reduce anxiety about the process, as well as save time and energy to focus on the feedback instead of the process. This approach can also help facilitate consistency across collaborative teams, creating a culture of using learning targets to grow professionally.

• Teacher leaders can model what it looks like to bring their work to the collaborative team for collective reflection and improvement. This modeling has the benefit of not only showing colleagues what the processes can look like in terms of routines and procedures, but also how to respond to feedback. Having clarity on these components can help put other teachers at ease. And, it has the added bonus of someone going first—a step that even adult professionals often fear taking.

Provide Feedback to the System for Improvements to Learning Targets

We have stated our view that collaborative teams should be used by schools to define learning targets. As you will see in the way we have organized this book, we are big believers in engaging in a process of continuous improvement to ensure that schools have a healthy universal tier. The practice of continuous improvement absolutely applies to learning targets as well. If there are aspects of the learning targets that are not working as well as they should, there needs to be a way for those problems to be resolved. For example, if there is persistent confusion regarding learning targets related to vocabulary development, collaborative teams need to be able to systematically go back through the process to understand where challenges may have arisen and then to try and resolve those challenges. Perhaps not enough time was spent on professional learning related to the learning target structure. Following are two strategies a school can use to provide teachers with opportunities to provide feedback on the learning targets:

• The expectation for gathering feedback should be set at the beginning of the learning target definition process. By doing this, the school is letting everyone know, up front, that everything about the process is open to improvement, and that everyone is responsible for making sure that improvements are made so learning targets can be successfully implemented over time. This also provides collaborative teams with the opportunity to help develop the feedback process, thereby increasing understanding, buy-in, and accountability for improving learning targets over time.

   • The approach to improving learning targets should be tied directly back to how they were defined in the first place. If there are problems with the learning targets themselves, or with how they were defined or supported, the school needs to be able to retrace its steps to identify what went wrong and what needs to be changed. Otherwise, feedback sessions can lack focus or turn into an airing of grievances, as opposed to collaborative problem solving.

CONCLUSION

We started this chapter by examining the importance of having clearly defined learning targets—statements of what students should know and be able to do—as the foundation of an effective universal tier. By defining what students should know and be able to do in learning targets, schools set the stage for what teachers teach and assess as part of the universal tier. Learning targets should drive decisions related to curriculum, instruction, and assessment. We contend that the learning targets for a school should either be the CCSS or closely aligned with the CCSS. The details of how learning targets are defined and implemented in schools should be handled in collaborative teams. By using a collaborative team approach, schools can increase the investment by teachers and administrators alike in the learning targets as a central driving force for all subsequent decisions about student learning.

DISCUSSION QUESTIONS

1. Are learning targets used in your school or district? If so, how would you describe what they are and how you use them? If not, why not?

2. How are learning targets selected or developed in your school and district?

3. How aligned are the learning targets with those in the CCSS? How clearly is the process used to align them described?

4. How would you describe the quality of the learning targets in your school and district?

5. How do learning targets drive decisions about curriculum, instruction, and assessment?

6. How are learning targets used to engage students in their own learning?

7. What is the role of collaborative teams in using learning targets within MTSS?

CHAPTER 3

Universal Tier Assessments

It would not be uncommon to walk into any school building and be overwhelmed with the sheer volume of assessments administered to students. With the accountability movement in full swing, districts have realized that student assessment information is essential to improve instruction. However, not all assessments are equal; some assessments are better than others in terms of providing useful information to teachers. How is a professional educator supposed to make sense of the wealth of data now available? The answer lies in having an understanding of the different types of assessments along with the different purposes for which assessments are administered.

This chapter describes the purposes of assessment at the universal tier (Tier 1) and how these data may be used for decision making at four levels: (1) individual student, (2) classroom, (3) grade, and (4) building. We describe the differences between formative and summative assessments and discuss how formative assessment data should help drive instructional decisions. Finally, we describe the role of collaborative teams and the types of data they should review.

PURPOSES OF ASSESSMENT

School districts implementing an MTSS framework typically engage in assessment for four purposes: screening, diagnostic, progress monitoring, and outcome evaluation information. Screening assessments are given to all students and serve two purposes. First, they help educators identify which students are meeting, exceeding, or performing below grade-level expectations in the domain of interest (e.g., reading, math, social–emotional). Educators use screening data to determine which students may benefit from additional intervention and how to differentiate universal instruction. Second, screening assessments inform schools about the sufficiency of the universal tier. They point to grade levels that need additional focus for universal tier improvement.

At its simplest form, screening involves administering short-duration measures to all students multiple times per school year. Many districts implementing an MTSS framework screen students three times per year (e.g., fall, winter, and spring). When choosing screening tools, the intent is to identify reliable and valid measures that are simple, quick, and easy to administer. The goal is to obtain useful information in the shortest amount of time to minimize the amount of lost instructional time due to assessment. Screening assessments do not tell us everything we need to know about a student's strengths and weaknesses, but when reliable and valid screening measures are used, we can be confident that the screening data are related to the overall skill domain (e.g., reading, math). In addition, many school districts use screening measures that predict proficiency on statewide accountability measures. Rather than wait for the annual accountability measures, school staff can administer short measures that are highly correlated with proficiency on state tests. Students who are identified as at risk can receive intervention to change the trajectory of performance. As a result, screening data provide a quick way to make local comparisons among students and provide a way to check on the progress of all students so that no student "falls through the cracks."

Of equal importance, screening data may be used to evaluate the impact of universal instruction so that teacher collaborative teams can use data to improve that level of instruction. For example, suppose a building conducts screening on all students in the area of reading. When the data are reviewed, it is discovered that only 40% of students are on track at grade level. These data should prompt the question "What is happening (or not happening) in universal instruction that is resulting in so many students performing below target?" This question should be the start of a comprehensive process of analyzing universal instruction to identify instructional gaps and to develop a plan to fill the gaps and improve outcomes.

When selecting screening measures, we recommend that districts select tools that are supported by evidence as reliable, as having strong correlations between the tools and valued outcomes, and as predicting accurate risk status. Educators should be able to articulate the supporting evidence for tools that are used. Finally, screening data should always be used in concert with at least two other data sources (e.g., state assessments, diagnostic assessment data, progress monitoring data) to verify decisions about whether a student is, or is not, at risk. Remember, error is present in every screening tool. Relying only on one source of data to make decisions about students will increase the likelihood of making an inaccurate decision.

A second purpose of assessment is to collect diagnostic information. At the individual student level, diagnostic assessments are assessment measures given to help educators understand a student's skill level. Diagnostic measures may be given to help guide instructional grouping and to identify which skills are missing or weak that may need to be retaught or practiced. These measures also provide information to teachers about the level of support students need and their need for explicit instruction on targeted skills. When we know why students are experiencing difficulty in a specific skill area, we can use these data to help select appropriate interventions.

At this point, it may be helpful to distinguish between formal and informal diagnostic measures. Formal assessments have data that support the conclusions made from the test. We usually refer to these types of tests as *standardized measures.* In their development stages, these instruments have been pilot-tested on students and have accumulated statistics that support the conclusion, for example, that a particular student is reading below average for his age. The data are mathematically computed and summarized. Scores in the form of percentiles, stanines, or standard scores are commonly given from this type of assessment. Some examples of formal diagnostic tests include Key Math–3, Developmental Reading Assessment (DRA), and Gray Diagnostic Reading Tests.

Teachers often use informal assessments to determine whether students have mastered what has been taught. These assessments may be created by teachers or included as part of a published curriculum. Teachers naturally collect informal assessment on a daily basis for all students to help guide instruction and to assign grades. Scores of percent correct, number of items correct, and most rubric scores are provided by informal diagnostic assessment.

Diagnostic assessment is usually more time-consuming than screening assessment. Typically, these assessments are individually administered and can take between 20 and 60 minutes per student. As a result, we recommend that formal diagnostic assessments should not be administered to all students! Instead, conduct diagnostic assessment with students who are targeted for interventions or with students who are receiving intervention and are not making adequate progress. The danger with using formal individual diagnostic assessments with all students is the amount of instructional time lost with their administration. Teachers need to think strategically about which students need more diagnostic information to assist them in planning and delivering effective instruction.

At a system level, diagnostic assessment is used to identify the specific reasons the universal tier is not having the desired outcomes. If a grade-level team identified that only 35% of students are meeting grade-level proficiency targets, the team would want to start collecting information to determine *why* so many students are below target. More information on how to determine why universal instruction is not sufficient is provided in Chapter 5.

A third purpose of assessment is to monitor progress. Once teachers determine which students are at risk and what they need, progress monitoring measures are used to help determine whether instruction and interventions are successful for an individual student. Suppose you are about to undergo coronary bypass surgery. Does the surgeon assume that your heart is working just fine during and after surgery? After all, bypass surgery works well for most patients! Hospital staff does not assume that every surgical intervention will be successful. They collect data before, during, and after surgery so they can know at any point how the patient is responding and make changes in the course of treatment. In the field of education, research is extremely helpful at identifying interventions that have been shown to accelerate growth for groups of students, but we do not know ahead of time whether an intervention will be successful for an *individual* student. Progress monitoring data help teachers adjust their instruction when student progress is insufficient.

The Center on Response to Intervention at the American Institutes for Research recommends a number of criteria that should be met when selecting progress monitoring measures. Progress monitoring tools should have a sufficient number of alternate forms of equal and controlled difficulty to allow for progress monitoring of recommended interventions based on the student's intervention level. For example, many districts use progress monitoring tools that involve having students read aloud as the teacher counts the number of words read correctly per minute. When monitoring student progress using this tool, it would be important to have multiple reading passages of the same difficulty level. If a limited number of passages are used, students will become familiar with the content, and fluency will increase due to a practice effect. The progress monitoring tool should also include guidance on the minimum acceptable growth and provide benchmarks for minimum acceptable end-of-year performance. Finally, information should be provided on the reliability and validity of the performance-level score. Progress monitoring typically occurs at least monthly for students receiving supplemental intervention and at least weekly for students receiving intensive intervention.

Outcome assessments tell us whether we are seeing improvements at the system level. Data to inform system outcomes may be summative in nature and may include data from the screening or progress monitoring process (Burns & Gibbons, 2012). Many districts use outcome data to track the progress of groups of students over time and to evaluate implementation of the MTSS framework. To ensure sustainability of an MTSS framework, districts are encouraged to have an evaluation plan in place to monitor short- and long-term goals. Student data typically are reviewed for all students and subgroups of students to evaluate the effectiveness of MTSS. Outcome data are necessary in evaluating effectiveness of the intervention.

An activity that many districts have found useful is to conduct an inventory of the assessments used at each grade level and identify the intended purpose for each assessment. In our work with schools around the country, we have found many instances in which districts collect too many measures that are duplicative, or they find that they have gaps in decision making (e.g., due to lack of progress monitoring measures). Many districts have found it useful to complete an assessment inventory on which they list each assessment used by grade level, along with its purpose (e.g., screening, diagnostic, progress monitoring, or outcomes) and evidence of reliability and validity. The inventory helps them identify gaps and redundancies. A sample inventory is provided in Form 3.1.*

TYPES OF ASSESSMENTS

Summative Assessment

Another useful distinction to understand is the difference between summative and formative assessments. Both types of assessment are important to the instructional process

---

*All forms appear at the end of the chapters.

and lead to improved outcomes (Hattie, 2009; Salvia, Ysseldyke, & Bolt, 2013). Summative assessment is the process of collecting data *after* instruction has occurred to make judgments about student progress (Burns & Gibbons, 2012). For example, a teacher may administer a chapter or unit test to see how much students learned and to assign grades. Other examples include statewide accountability tests, end-of-course exams, and annually administered norm-referenced tests of achievement.

Formative Assessment

Alternatively, formative assessment is the process of collecting assessment before or during instruction with the intent of using the data to change or modify instruction. Formative assessments assist teachers by providing information on what students learned and where there are gaps in skills. Teachers may administer a pretest to their class to determine what students already know about the topic. Teachers may then use these data to differentiate instruction for students—providing more support to students with little prior knowledge and less support and more enrichment to students who have already mastered the content. Teachers may collect progress monitoring data on students who are receiving small-group interventions. Progress monitoring data are formative when teachers use the data to make changes in instruction when student progress is unsatisfactory. The essential attribute of formative assessment data is that the data are used to identify student needs and to plan instruction that will better meet those needs (Williams, 2006).

UNIVERSAL TIER ASSESSMENTS

Now that you have a good understanding of the purposes of educational assessments and the difference between summative and formative assessments, let's talk about assessments used in universal instruction and how they guide decision making. Assessments used for Tier 1 should provide answers to specific questions in order to guide decision making. Some of these questions include (but are not limited to) the following:

1. Are at least 80% of students meeting expectations at each grade level?
2. Are at least 95% of students who meet expectations in the fall still meeting expectations in the spring?
3. Are at least 80% of students in various subgroups meeting grade-level expectations?
4. Which students score below grade-level expectations?
5. What is the relationship between Tier 1 formative classroom assessments or benchmark assessments and performance on summative measures (e.g., statewide accountability tests, end-of-course exams)?

Screening data assist teams in answering these questions. The following section discusses the area of screening and provides examples of how screening data may be used at the individual, class, grade, and building level to aid in decision making.

SCREENING ASSESSMENTS

Another term for screening assessment is *benchmark assessment*. Both terms imply collecting information on all students and using the data to make decisions. Prior to conducting screening assessment, a number of logistical decisions need to be made. These decisions include which measures to administer, who will administer them, how to provide training on administration and scoring of measures, and the selection of an assessment window.

Identifying Screening Measures

One of the first decisions school leaders will be faced with in the area of assessment is that of determining which screening measures will be used at each benchmark period (e.g., fall, winter, and spring). A wide variety of screening tools already exist in basic academic skill areas and can be researched easily online; a review of each tool is outside the scope of this chapter. When identifying screening measures, careful consideration should be given to the classification accuracy, generalizability, reliability, validity, and efficiency of the measure. There are a variety of websites that assist districts in comparing various screening tools against these criteria. A commonly used website is the Center on Response to Intervention (www.rti4success.org) at American Institutes for Research.

Of particular interest is that many of the tools that have emerged as meeting the necessary criteria for screening are in the curriculum-based measurement (CBM)/general outcome measure (GOM) family. CBMs/GOMs are sets of standardized indicators that assess the proficiency of global outcomes associated with particular skill areas (Fuchs & Deno, 1991). A considerable amount of research has demonstrated the reliability of CBM/GOM data and the validity of the subsequent decisions made (Deno, Mirkin, & Chiang, 1982; Fuchs, Fuchs, & Maxwell, 1988; Shinn, Good, Knutson, Tilly, & Collins, 1992). In addition, research has shown a high statistical correlation between these types of measures and statewide accountability measures (Silberglitt et al., 2006). Because these measures are quick and easy to administer, reliable and valid, and sensitive to growth over time, they are commonly used for screening and progress monitoring purposes.

It should be noted that a variety of screening tools are commercially available for PreK through middle school. Unfortunately, there is not one single screening tool that works well for every grade level in secondary settings. As a result, secondary educators must use a variety of existing data to assist them in determining which students are at risk and in need of supplementary or intensive supports. It is commonly recommend that secondary settings use a combination of attendance data, performance data on standardized tests, course grades, credit attainment, and discipline data as part of the screening process (Burns & Gibbons, 2012). Students who fall off track in multiple areas should be targeted for additional support.

Selecting an Assessment Window

Once districts have selected appropriate screening measures, it is imperative that an assessment window be established. An *assessment window* is simply a standard time frame for collecting screening data. Using a standard time frame allows districts to make comparisons across buildings and grades within a school year and across school years for program evaluation purposes. Many school districts select a 3- to 4-week assessment window during the fall, winter, and spring benchmark assessment period. Typically, screening is not conducted during the first two weeks of the school year to allow students to acclimate to a new setting and to recoup the skills lost over the summer vacation.

Identifying the Screening Process

After screening measures and an assessment window have been selected, the next steps are to identify who will administer the screening measures and the training procedures needed for administration and scoring. Two options exist for determining who will administer screening measures. Districts may decide to have an assessment team administer individual screening measures (e.g., CBM measures of reading [CBM-R]), or they may decide to have classroom teachers administer the measures. Districts that utilize an assessment team typically include paraprofessionals, specialist teachers, school psychologists, and community volunteers. An obvious advantage to having an assessment team is less disruption to the classroom environment and lost instructional time. With a team of 10 testers, it should take around 15 minutes to screen a classroom of 25 students (e.g., 5 minutes per child). In comparison, it would take a classroom teacher over 2 hours to screen the class, requiring students to work independently during this time period. The advantage to having each teacher conduct screening is that teachers have more ownership over the data and more understanding of the assessment. It is essential that any staff person who administers screening measures be adequately trained on standardized administration and scoring of the measures. We recommend a comprehensive initial training, and then brief refreshers following each screening period. We have also found it useful to conduct random reliability checks to ensure the fidelity of administration and scoring procedures.

After screening data are collected, school staff must determine how the data will be reviewed to aid in decision making. Remember, it is pointless to collect screening data if a process has not been established to review them and use them for instructional decision making. Most of the commercially available screening tools have systems to manage the data and provide useful data reports. In the next section, we discuss the role of collaborative Tier 1 teams in reviewing screening data.

THE ROLE OF COLLABORATIVE TEAMS

Successful implementation of an MTSS framework depends on a strong collaborative team infrastructure within each building (Burns & Gibbons, 2012). Many districts implementing an MTSS framework have district-, building-, grade-level, and problem-solving teams. This section focuses on how building- and grade-level teams can use screening data to assist in decision making and evaluate universal instruction. We provide examples of how teams may use screening data at the individual, class, grade, and building level to aid in decision making.

Building Leadership Teams

Building leadership teams (BLTs) guide the implementation of MTSS within a building. They perform several activities, including assisting with collecting assessment data for buildingwide needs, identifying professional learning needs, and facilitating consensus and commitment. The primary role of this team is to evaluate schoolwide screening data (academic and social–emotional) to identify themes *within the building* and to identify the appropriate tools, training, and support to facilitate continual improvement. For example, the BLT may examine their screening data in the area of reading and find low percentages of students proficient across the grade levels. This information could prompt discussion at the building level about curriculum, instructional time allocated, and the need for increased professional learning and coaching around effective reading instruction. The BLT could develop an action plan, set goals, and monitor implementation of professional learning and coaching by examining screening data. The screening data provide insight as to how effective school improvement plans have been at increasing the growth of all students. A sample agenda for building-level teams is provided in Form 3.2.

Grade-Level Teams

As stated earlier, once schools have a system in place for collecting screening data on all students, there must be a process established so that teachers actually use the data to make instructional decisions. One way to accomplish this task is to form grade-level teams consisting of teachers and support staff who meet regularly to review the achievement of all students in the grade level. These teams should focus on reviewing screening data to set grade-level goals. The focus of these teams is to evaluate gradewide data. They should collaborate on the important task of creating universal instruction that meets the needs of most students by identifying ways in which to differentiate instruction. Finally, they need to identify the students who need additional academic support, plan standard interventions, and engage in regular reviews of progress monitoring data.

Many districts around the country have formed PLCs (DuFour, 2004). The grade-level team process is similar to the PLC, as long as the focus is on finding out what students need to learn, how educators know when students have learned the intended skills, and what to do when students do not meet expectations. This format is in contrast to a PLC structure wherein teams select a topic they want to learn more about and engage in self-directed professional learning. This PLC format does not guarantee a laser-like focus on student achievement data and on strategies for continual improvement.

Recent research in the area of effective data teams suggests that for grade-level data teams to see results, they must (1) establish measurable goals for instructional improvement based on data, (2) measure and report progress toward the instructional goals using data, and (3) establish a common planning time for collaboration. The most successful grade-level teams meet weekly and have regular meeting times, active facilitation, protocols for decision making, and leadership by example. We also suggest that each team member commit to assume a role; come prepared to the meeting; be punctual; engage fully in the process; and participate honestly, respectfully, and constructively. All team members should be engaged participants, as demonstrated by committing, listening, questioning, and contributing. Each grade-level team should consider assigning roles for facilitator, note taker, timekeeper, focus monitor, and data specialist to facilitate positive outcomes. Roles and tasks are summarized in Table 3.1 and reflection cards for each role are provided in Form 3.3. A Data Action Teams Integrity Checklist is provided in Form 3.4.

The agenda for grade-level teams should focus on student achievement data and the action plan. A sample protocol for agenda topics by month is provided in Form 3.5. Having a structured agenda maximizes the probability that time will be used in the most effective manner with a focus on results. On a monthly basis, the grade-level team facilitator should meet with the principal to discuss achievement gaps, successes, and challenges in implementing the action plan, team interactions and performance, progress monitoring and assessment schedule, professional learning needs, and resources.

TABLE 3.1. Roles and Tasks of Collaborative Team Members

Role	Task
Facilitator	• Sets agenda • Sets norms • Listens well • Asks the right questions • Reinforces member roles • Facilitates team's reflection on process and progress
Note taker	• Records minutes • Distributes to facilitator, colleagues, administrators
Timekeeper	• Follows time frames allocated on agenda • Informs group of time frames during dialogue
Focus monitor	• Reminds members of tasks and purpose • Refocuses dialogue on processes and agenda items • Keeps the focus on things that can be changed in the instruction, environment, curriculum, and organizational structure
Data specialist	• Gathers all data from team members • Creates tables, charts, and graphs • Shares results with team members
Engaged participant	• Commits • Listens • Questions • Contributes

Individual teachers will be required to reflect on the screening data for their class and determine whether large numbers of students are below the benchmark target. If so, teachers may decide to implement classwide interventions. For example, upon a review of fall screening data, Mrs. Johnson concludes that 55% of her students are below the benchmark target in the area of reading as measured by CBM-R. Further examination of the data reveals that of the 55% below target, 90% of these students have a fluency problem. Although they are reading with 95% or greater accuracy, their fluency is below target. Mrs. Johnson decides to implement a classwide intervention for 15 minutes per day, using the Read Naturally (Ihnot, 2002) intervention.

Problem-Solving Teams

The last type of team that may interact with schoolwide screening data is the building problem-solving team. Many names for such teams exist, including but not limited to *student assistance teams, teacher assistance teams, building assistance teams,* and *intervention teams.* Regardless of what the team is called, the primary function of problem-solving teams is to collaborate to design intensive interventions for students who have not made progress with more standard Tier 2 interventions. It is critical that these teams be viewed as general education rather than a special education teams. Whereas a more traditional framework relied on teachers to make referrals to a problem-solving team, we suggest that problem-solving teams examine the schoolwide screening data at each benchmark period and determine students who are scoring at or below the 10th percentile. Cross-team collaboration should occur to identify those individual students who are in need of a more individualized and intensive intervention. These could be students for whom supplemental interventions (Tier 2) have been unsuccessful or students who are severely discrepant from grade-level expectations and need a more individualized and intensive intervention. It is recommended that the problem-solving teams utilize a problem-solving decision-making model to identify and analyze problems, develop intervention plans, implement those plans, and evaluate the intervention outcomes. A sample problem solving team checklist is provided in Form 3.6.

CONCLUSION

Assessments serve the four purposes of providing screening, diagnostic, progress monitoring, and outcome data. Districts should look for assessments that meet more than one purpose to help pare down the number of assessments given per grade level. At the end of the day, it is screening data that form the foundation for evaluating the effectiveness of universal instruction and for evaluating whether attempts to improve universal instruction have been effective. Systems-level staff who are lacking valid and reliable screening measures, administered at multiple points per school year, will struggle in their attempts to evaluate the effectiveness of universal instruction and to determine whether improvements have been successful. Collaborative teams are essential for reviewing data, setting goals, and developing and monitoring plans.

DISCUSSION QUESTIONS

1. What assessments are available to you at each grade level? Thinking about the four purposes of assessment described in this chapter, are there any gaps or redundancies in your current assessments?

2. How are screening assessments used in your building? Are these data used to evaluate universal instruction?

3. How are diagnostic assessments used for some students to target specific needs?

4. How are grade-level teams accessing and using progress monitoring data?

5. What types of collaborative teams exist in your building? Which team reviews schoolwide data? Which team reviews grade-level data? Which team helps design intensive interventions for students who have not responded to supplemental interventions?

6. How are team agendas developed? Are there standard team routines and protocols? How are team decisions documented?

FORM 3.1

Assessment Inventory by Purpose of Assessment

Grade	Measure	Screening	Diagnostic	Progress Monitoring	Outcomes

(continued)

SCREENING

Valid: Validity refers to the degree to which evidence and theory support the interpretations of test scores entailed by proposed uses of tests. Correlations between the instruments and valued outcomes are strong.

Reliable: Performance is stable and consistent. Reliability coefficients should be .8 for screening and .9 for important individual decisions.

Accurate: Predictions of risk status are accurate.

Grade	Measure	Reliable	Accurate	Simple and Quick to Administer	Easily Understood

(continued)

PROGRESS MONITORING

Selected progress monitoring tools meet all of the following criteria:

Simple and quick to administer; easy to understand; reliable and valid; sufficient number of alternate forms of equal and controlled difficulty to allow for progress monitoring at recommended intervals; specify minimum acceptable growth; sensitive to change over small amounts of time; and provide benchmarks for minimum acceptable end-of-year performance.

Grade	Measure	Reliable	Valid	Alternate Forms of Equal Difficulty	Simple and Quick to Administer	Easily Understood	Sensitive to Change	Specify Minimum Acceptable Growth	Benchmarks for End of Year Performance

Building Leadership Agendas by Month

AUGUST

☐ Assign team roles

- Facilitator: _____

- Note taker: _____

- Timekeeper: _____

- Focus monitor: _____

- Data specialist: _____

☐ Review spring screening and statewide accountability test data across grade levels

☐ Flag grade levels that have fewer than 80% of students proficient and follow up with these grade levels for specific plans

☐ Identify whether at least 95% of students who met expectations in the fall met expectations in the spring at each grade level

☐ Review data on subgroups of students

☐ Discuss how information will be shared with building staff

SEPTEMBER

☐ Review fall benchmark screening data

☐ Identify the percentage of students who meet fall proficiency targets and record this information

☐ Identify the percentage of students are who are at some risk (Tier 2) and high risk (Tier 3), and record this information

☐ Review grade-level team-meeting notes

☐ Identify any "proficiency themes" that are emerging in the building or common themes from grade-level team notes

☐ Set an end-of-year building goal

☐ Develop building plan to address themes

☐ Discuss the training and supports required to address needs

☐ Discuss how fidelity of implementation data will be collected

☐ Discuss issues around programming for students with the highest skill levels

☐ Discuss how information will be shared with building staff

(continued)

OCTOBER

- ☐ Review building goal
- ☐ Review grade-level team-meeting notes
- ☐ Identify any building needs or themes across grade levels
- ☐ Confirm that all students who scored below fall targets have progress monitoring graphs that use valid and reliable measures
- ☐ Discuss any progress monitoring support needs
- ☐ Discuss issues around programming for students with the highest skill levels
- ☐ Review fidelity data
- ☐ Discuss how information will be shared with building staff

NOVEMBER

- ☐ Review building goal
- ☐ Review grade-level team-meeting notes
- ☐ Identify any building needs or themes across grade levels
- ☐ Confirm that all students who scored below fall targets have progress monitoring graphs that use valid and reliable measures
- ☐ Discuss any progress monitoring support needs
- ☐ Discuss issues around programming for students with the highest skill levels
- ☐ Review fidelity data
- ☐ Discuss how information will be shared with building staff

DECEMBER

- ☐ Review building goal
- ☐ Review grade-level team meeting notes
- ☐ Identify any building needs or themes across grade levels
- ☐ Discuss any training and support needs
- ☐ Discuss issues around programming for students with the highest skill levels
- ☐ Review fidelity data
- ☐ Discuss how information will be shared with building staff

JANUARY

- ☐ Review winter benchmark screening data
- ☐ Review grade-level team-meeting notes and discuss the percentage of students who meet winter proficiency targets at each grade level

(continued)

- ☐ Identify any "proficiency themes" that are emerging in the building or common themes from grade-level team notes.
- ☐ Review end-of-year building goal
- ☐ Review building plan to address themes
- ☐ Discuss the training and supports required to address needs
- ☐ Discuss how fidelity of implementation data will be collected
- ☐ Discuss issues around programming for students with the highest skill levels
- ☐ Discuss how information will be shared with building staff

FEBRUARY

- ☐ Review building goal
- ☐ Review grade-level team-meeting notes
- ☐ Identify any building needs or themes across grade levels
- ☐ Discuss any training and support needs
- ☐ Discuss issues around programming for students with the highest skill levels
- ☐ Review fidelity data
- ☐ Discuss how information will be shared with building staff

MARCH

- ☐ Review team goal
- ☐ Review grade-level team-meeting notes
- ☐ Identify any building needs or themes across grade levels
- ☐ Discuss any training and support needs
- ☐ Discuss issues around programming for students with the highest skill levels
- ☐ Review fidelity data
- ☐ Discuss how information will be shared with building staff

APRIL

- ☐ Review team goal
- ☐ Review grade-level team-meeting notes
- ☐ Identify any building needs or themes across grade levels
- ☐ Discuss any training and support needs
- ☐ Discuss issues around programming for students with the highest skill levels
- ☐ Review fidelity data
- ☐ Discuss how information will be shared with building staff

(continued)

MAY

☐ Review spring benchmark screening data

☐ Review grade-level team-meeting notes and discuss the percentage of students who meet spring proficiency targets at each grade level

☐ Review grade-level team-meeting notes and discuss whether at least 95% of students who met expectations in the fall are still meeting expectations in the spring. Identify any building-level themes.

☐ Identify any "proficiency themes" that are emerging in the building or in the common themes from grade-level team notes.

☐ Review progress toward end-of-year building goal

☐ Review grade-level team-meeting notes regarding what each grade level wants to keep the same or change during next school year to address the full range of student needs

☐ Discuss the training and supports required to address needs

☐ Review fidelity of implementation data

☐ Discuss issues around programming for students with the highest skill levels

☐ Discuss how information will be shared with building staff

JUNE

☐ Review progress toward end-of-year building goal

☐ Review data on subgroups of students

☐ Evaluate effectiveness of supplemental and intensive interventions using data

☐ Review grade-level team-meeting notes regarding what each grade level wants to keep the same or change during next school year to address the full range of student needs

☐ Discuss the training and supports required to address needs

☐ Review fidelity of implementation data

☐ Revise the building plan for the following year based on data and needs

Reflection Cards for Grade-Level Team Members

FACILITATOR

Facilitates DAT meeting process:
- Set's agenda.
- Uses norms for effective meetings.
- Asks the "right" questions.
- Listens well.
- Reinforces member roles.
- Facilitates the team's reflection on process and progress.

How did I do? _____

_____

_____

NOTE TAKER

Documentation:
- Takes accurate minutes.
- Distributes to the DAT leader, colleagues, administrators, etc.

How did I do? _____

_____

_____

(continued)

TIMEKEEPER

Time is precious:
- Follows time frames allocated on the agenda.
- Informs the group of time frames during dialogue.

How did I do? _____

_____

_____

FOCUS MONITOR

Stay focused:
- Reminds team members of tasks and purpose.
- Refocuses dialogue on processes and agenda items.

How did I do? _____

_____

_____

(continued)

DATA SPECIALIST

Data informed:
- Gathers all data from team members.
- Creates tables, charts, and graphs.
- Shares results with team members.

How did I do? _____

_____

_____

ENGAGED PARTICIPANT

Be engaged:
- Commits.
- Listens.
- Questions.
- Contributes.

How did I do? _____

_____

_____

Data Action Team (DAT) Integrity Checklist

Date: _____ Completed by: _____ Data Action Team: _____

Step	Item (check ☑ if answer is "Yes")	Notes
Agenda and Minutes	☐ Agenda allocates time for each meeting component	
	☐ Agenda identifies standing and new business	
	☐ Agenda includes next meeting date or time to set a date	
	☐ Agenda identifies personnel to discuss each meeting component	
	☐ Minutes indicate prioritized needs	
	☐ Minutes include clear delineations of responsibilities among team members for assigned tasks	
	☐ Minutes include a clear description of meeting results	
	☐ Minutes include description of ongoing strategies implemented since last meeting	
	☐ Minutes include description of data being reviewed	
	☐ Team members adhere to meeting time as evidenced by all areas being reviewed in the meeting minutes	
Total/Score	# Yes/10 = % Agenda Implementation Integrity	

(continued)

Data Action Team (DAT) Integrity Checklist *(page 2 of 5)*

Step	Item (check ☑ if answer is "Yes")	Notes
Communication	☐ Minutes of DAT meeting are shared with leadership	
	☐ Minutes of DAT meeting are shared with appropriate staff	
	☐ Team has a means to communicate informally (Google Docs, email listserv, Hangouts)	
	☐ Implementation calendar detailing tasks to be completed throughout the year is accessible to all team members	
	☐ Building DAT shares data with district team (district team shares with state, state shares its findings back with districts)	
	☐ Team shares data with families/consumers	
	☐ Updates on action plans are communicated to all appropriate staff	
Total/Score	# Yes/7 = % Communication Implementation Integrity	
Data Organization	☐ Data are timely (extent to which data are reported on or before deadline using information from appropriate time period)	
	☐ Data are graphically depicted	
	☐ Team members have utilized guided data worksheets to aid in analysis	
	☐ Data to be discussed are made available to team prior to meeting	
	☐ Additional data needed based on actionable causes has been gathered	
Total/Score	# Yes/5 = % Data Org. Implementation Integrity	

(continued)

Data Action Team (DAT) Integrity Checklist *(page 3 of 5)*

Step	Item (check ☑ if answer is "Yes")	Notes
Action Plans	☐ Team has established action plan based on data analysis	
	☐ Action plan includes a detailed problem description	
	☐ Problem description answers all four "W" questions	
	☐ Action plan details actionable cause(s)	
	☐ Action plan includes goals relevant to actionable causes	
	☐ Data from formative assessments are being used to determine goals/outcomes (building level)	
	☐ Goal targets were determined according to baseline data	
	☐ Specified goals meet SMART requirements	
	☐ Goals are broken down into specific tasks	
	☐ Team members responsible for supporting each goal are identified	
	☐ Specific tasks are aligned with goals/outcomes	
	☐ Specific tasks/activities chosen to facilitate meeting-identified goals/outcomes are backed by evidence of effectiveness or research	
	☐ Team members are assigned to oversee tasks/activities goals to be implemented	
	☐ Team members can produce data that evidence implementation of tasks/activities to achieve goals	
	☐ Team members can produce data that evidence if tasks/activities are producing desired effects toward goal attainment	
Total/Score	**# Yes/15 = % Action Plan Implementation Integrity**	

(continued)

Data Action Team (DAT) Integrity Checklist *(page 4 of 5)*

Step	Item (check ☑ if answer is "Yes")	Notes
Infrastructure Leadership	☐ Professional learning is provided specific to the attainment of SMART goal(s)	
	☐ Specific professional learning occurs prior to initiating a new program or practice	
	☐ Feedback is given in a timely manner to all staff implementing tasks	
	☐ Evidence is provided that policy or procedures have been modified based on data gathered as a result of action plan implementation	
	☐ The school leader is present at each DAT meeting	
	☐ Walk-through or coaching observation data are provided as evidence of implementation of tasks	
	☐ Feedback is given in a timely manner (48 hours or less) to all staff responsible for implementation of tasks	
	☐ Evidence is given that a sustainability (or continuous improvement) plan exists to support future actions and improvements	
Total/Score	**# Yes/8 = % Infrastructure Implementation Integrity**	
Team Leadership	☐ Leader ensures that roles are assigned for members during meeting (facilitator, note taker, timekeeper, etc.)	
	☐ Leader ensures that team's operating norms for meetings are reviewed	

(continued)

Data Action Team (DAT) Integrity Checklist *(page 5 of 5)*

Step	Item (check ☑ if answer is "Yes")	Notes
Team Leadership (continued)	☐ Leader keeps team on task as directed by agenda	
	☐ Leader ensure that group ideas or decisions are prominently posted	
	☐ Leader encourages productive work relations (redirects to task, discourages side conversations, engages all team members)	
	☐ Leader ensures that tasks assigned to team members are reviewed at close of meeting	
	☐ Leader ensures that decisions made by team are reviewed at close of meeting	
	☐ Leader closes meeting with next meeting date reminder	
Total/Score	# Yes/8 = % Team Leadership Implementation Integrity	

Subset Measure	Percentage Score
Agenda and Minutes	
Communication	
Data Organization	
Action Plans	
Infrastructure Leadership	
Team Leadership	

Grade-Level Team Meeting Agendas by Month

AUGUST

☐ Assign team roles

- Facilitator: _____

- Note taker: _____

- Timekeeper: _____

- Focus monitor: _____

- Data specialist: _____

☐ Review spring screening and statewide accountability test data from previous grade level (if available). Identify students who will likely need additional support.

☐ Plan one to three standard intervention options that would address common concerns at this grade level

- Plans are evidence-based

- Plans are practical

- Curricular materials are available to implement plan or can be readily created

☐ Record these intervention plans as standard treatment protocols

- Discuss how your team will select students these interventions

- Discuss how these interventions will be delivered (time, space, people)

☐ Team assists all teachers in learning how to implement plans using peer modeling and coaching, grade-level chats regarding implementation, and/or assistance by content specialists.

☐ Team documents how fidelity of interventions will be assessed.

☐ Discuss what you plan to do this year to challenge your highest skilled students

☐ Share meeting notes and key decisions with the building leadership team

SEPTEMBER

☐ Review fall benchmark screening data

☐ Identify the percentage of students who meet fall proficiency targets, and record this information

☐ Identify the percentage of students are who are at some risk (Tier 2) and at high risk (Tier 3), and record this information

☐ Set an end-of-year team goal to work toward, noting the percentage of students you would like to see in each tier based on the assessment data

☐ Identify the initial list of students who should have their progress monitored more frequently than three times per year

(continued)

☐ If the percentage of students in Tier 1 is below 80%, discuss grade-level-wide opportunities to improve universal instruction

☐ Plan one to three standard intervention options that would address common concerns at this grade level or refine plans from August

- Plans are evidence-based

- Plans are practical

- Curricular materials are available to implement plan or can be readily created

☐ Record these plans as standard treatment protocols

- Discuss the basis for selecting students for these interventions

- Select students for participation in specific interventions

- Discuss logistics of intervention delivery (time, space, people)

☐ Team assists all teachers in learning how to implement plans using peer modeling and coaching, grade-level chats regarding implementation, and/or assistance by content specialists

☐ Team documents how fidelity of interventions will be assessed

☐ Discuss what you are doing to challenge your highest-skilled students

☐ Share meeting notes and key decisions with the building leadership team

OCTOBER

☐ Review team goal

☐ Confirm that all students who scored below fall targets have progress monitoring graphs using valid and reliable measures

☐ Review graphs for all students

- First pass through, look at graph and decide to keep current program or to make a change

- Second pass through, discuss the changes needed in the program. Share what you know about the student's instructional needs and ideas for making the current program work better for the student.

- Add or change participation in a standard intervention?

- Tweak an individual program within the regular classroom?

☐ Record decisions about program changes on district documentation form

☐ Decide if there are students who should be referred to the building-level problem-solving team

☐ Review fidelity data for interventions and adjust as needed

☐ Discuss what you are doing to challenge your highest skilled students

☐ Share meeting notes and key decisions with the building leadership team

(continued)

NOVEMBER

☐ Review team goal

☐ Confirm that all students who scored below fall targets have progress monitoring graphs using fluency measures

☐ Review graphs for all students

- First pass through, look at graph and decide to keep current program or to make a change

- Second pass through, discuss any changes needed in the program change. Share what you know about the student's instructional needs and ideas for making the current program work better for the student.

- Add or change participation in a standard intervention?

- Tweak an individual program within the regular classroom?

☐ Record decisions about program changes on district documentation form

☐ Decide if there are students who should be referred to the building-level problem-solving team

☐ Review fidelity data for interventions and adjust as needed

☐ Discuss what you are doing to challenge your highest skilled students

☐ Share meeting notes and key decisions with the building leadership team

DECEMBER

☐ Review team goal

☐ Confirm that all students who scored below fall targets have progress monitoring graphs using fluency measures

☐ Review graphs for all students

- On first pass through, look at graph and decide to keep current program or to make a change

- On second pass through, discuss any changes needed in the program. Share what you know about the student's instructional needs and ideas for making the current program work better for the student.

- Add or change participation in a standard intervention?

- Tweak an individual program within the regular classroom?

☐ Record decisions about program changes on district documentation form

☐ Decide if there are students who should be referred to the building-level problem-solving team

☐ Review fidelity data for interventions and adjust as needed

☐ Discuss what you are doing to challenge your highest skilled students

☐ Share meeting notes and key decisions with the building leadership team

(continued)

JANUARY

☐ Review winter benchmark data

☐ Identify the percentage of students who are falling in each tier based on the assessment data, and record this information

☐ Review progress toward your end-of-year team goal

☐ Update the list of students who should be monitored more frequently than three times per year using fluency measures based on winter data

☐ If the percentage of students in Tier 1 is below 80%, discuss grade-level-wide opportunities for making the universal program more robust for this cohort

☐ Review graphs for all students

- On first pass through, look at graph and decide to keep current program or to make a change

- On second pass through, discuss the changes the program needs. Share what you know about the student's instructional needs and ideas for making the current program work better for the student.

- Add or change participation in a standard intervention?

- Tweak an individual program within the regular classroom?

☐ Record decisions about program changes on district documentation form

☐ Decide if there are students who should be referred to the building-level problem-solving team

☐ Review fidelity data for interventions and adjust as needed

☐ Discuss what you are doing to challenge your highest skilled students

☐ Share meeting notes and key decisions with the building leadership team

FEBRUARY

☐ Review team goal

☐ Confirm that all students who scored below fall targets have progress monitoring graphs using fluency measures

☐ Review graphs for all students

- On first pass through, look at graph and decide to keep current program or to make a change

- On second pass through, discuss the changes the program needs. Share what you know about the student's instructional needs and ideas for making the current program work better for the student.

- Add or change participation in a standard intervention?

- Tweak an individual program within the regular classroom?

- Record decisions about program changes on district documentation form

☐ Decide if there are students who should be referred to the building-level problem-solving team

☐ Review fidelity data for interventions and adjust as needed

☐ Discuss what you are doing to challenge your highest skilled students

☐ Share meeting notes and key decisions with the building leadership team

(continued)

MARCH

☐ Review team goal

☐ Confirm that all students who scored below fall targets have progress monitoring graphs using fluency measures

☐ Review graphs for all students

- On first pass through, look at graph and decide to keep current program or to make a change

- On second pass through, discuss the changes the program needs. Share what you know about the student's instructional needs and ideas for making the current program work better for the student.

- Add or change participation in a standard intervention?

- Tweak an individual program within the regular classroom?

☐ Record decisions about program changes on district documentation form

☐ Decide if there are students who should be referred to the building-level problem-solving team

☐ Review fidelity data for interventions and adjust as needed

☐ Discuss what you are doing to challenge your highest skilled students

☐ Share meeting notes and key decisions with the building leadership team

APRIL

☐ Review team goal

☐ Confirm that all students who scored below fall targets have progress monitoring graphs using fluency measures

☐ Review graphs for all students

- On first pass through, look at graph and decide to keep current program or to make a change

- On second pass through, discuss the changes the program needs. Share what you know about the student's instructional needs and ideas for making the current program work better for the student.

- Add or change participation in a standard intervention?

- Tweak an individual program within the regular classroom?

☐ Record decisions about program changes on district documentation form

☐ Decide if there are students who should be referred to the building-level problem-solving team

☐ Review fidelity data for interventions and adjust as needed

☐ Discuss what you are doing to challenge your highest skilled students

☐ Share meeting notes and key decisions with the building leadership team

(continued)

MAY

☐ Review spring benchmark data as available

☐ Identify the percentage of students who are falling in each tier, based on the assessment data, and record this information.

☐ Review progress toward your end-of-year team goal

☐ Are at least 95% of students who met expectations in the fall still meeting expectations in the spring? If not, discuss possible reasons why and action items for change.

☐ Review graphs for all students

- On first pass through, look at graph and decide to keep current program or to make a change

- On second pass through, discuss the changes the program needs. Share what you know about the student's instructional needs and ideas for making the current program work better for the student.

- Add or change participation in a standard intervention?

- Tweak an individual program within the regular classroom?

☐ Record decisions about program changes on district documentation form

☐ Decide if there are students who should be referred to the building-level problem-solving team

☐ Review fidelity data for interventions and adjust as needed

☐ Plan and discuss what you want to keep the same or change during next school year to address the full range of student needs

☐ Identify training interests/needs related to new plans

☐ Share meeting notes and key decisions with the building leadership team

Problem-Solving Process Checklist

Problem-Solving Step	Completion Date
Problem Identification	
• An initial **discrepancy was defined** in observable measurable terms and was quantified. (List all concerns, prioritize one, and collect data to determine a discrepancy.)	
• Documented data from at least two sources converge to support the discrepancy statement (i.e., interview + observation, or test data + observation).	
• Student baseline data in the area of concern are collected using a measurement system with sufficient technical adequacy for ongoing frequent measurement, and include a minimum of three data points with standardized procedures for assessment. **Baseline data are graphed.**	
Problem Analysis	
• Data from a **variety of sources (RIOT[a]) and domains (ICEL[b])** were collected to consider multiple hypotheses for the cause of the identified discrepancy. These data are documented.	
• A **single hypothesis** for the cause of the discrepancy was selected. At least two pieces of data converged to support this hypothesis. At least one of these is quantitative.	
Plan Development	
• **A data-based goal** was established that describes the learner, conditions (time and materials for responding), expected performance, and a goal date. The goal is indicated on a graph.	
• The intervention selected meets the federal definition of a scientifically research-based intervention. The selected intervention directly addresses the identified problem and the hypothesis for the cause of the discrepancy.	
• **A written intervention plan** was clearly defined that explicitly described what will be done, where, when, how often, how long (per session), by whom, and with what resources.	
• A written description of the **progress monitoring plan** was completed and includes who will collect data, data collection methods, conditions for data collections, and schedule.	

(continued)

[a]RIOT, review, interview, observe, test.
[b]ICEL, instruction, curriculum, environment, learner.

Problem-Solving Step	Completion Date
• A **decision-making rule** was selected for use.	
• A plan **evaluation meeting was set** for no more than 8 weeks after the plan is established.	
Plan Implementation	
• A **direct observation of the intervention** was completed at least one time. Any discrepancies between the written plan and the intervention in action were noted and resolved. Observations continued until the intervention being delivered and the written intervention plan matched. Written documentation of each observation was made.	
• **Data were collected and graphed,** as stated in plan. The required number of data points was collected under the same intervention conditions after integrity was established.	
Plan Evaluation	
• The team documented agreement that the **plan was carried out as intended.**	
• The team determined and documented whether the **preintervention discrepancy decreased, increased, or stayed the same** during the plan implementation phase.	
• The team decided to **continue** the plan unmodified, **modify, fade, or terminate the plan.** The team documented this decision.	

CHAPTER 4

Determining the Effectiveness of Universal Instruction

This chapter examines the process teams use to explore the effectiveness of current universal instruction. Throughout this work, it is important to remember that this is an examination of the impact of current practice on students in the building today. What may have been very effective 10 years ago may not meet the rigorous outcomes of the Common Core. Many communities have also experienced significant population changes that may impact the effectiveness of previous practices. It is a common belief that universal instruction is always at the center of instructional considerations, and this chapter is about determining if the amount of resources currently directed toward universal tier improvement is sufficient. We provide processes and considerations for answering the question "Is the universal tier sufficient?"

HOW DO WE KNOW?

Simply put, universal instruction is effective when the vast majority of learners are successful without additional intervention. If forced to rely on intervention systems to bring large numbers of learners to proficiency, the goal of all learners being successful will never be achieved. We recommend setting a target of having 80% of students proficient without additional intervention supports. And remember, an effective universal tier will look different in various schools because each school has different students and different resources. If every school were the same, we could recommend purchasing a particular basal program that would result in an effective universal tier. Since every school is different, a basal program alone is typically not the solution. In addition to curricular materials, several factors—instructional strategies, the environment, and the structures of supports for teachers and student—all contribute to improving achievement. This chapter outlines the processes to follow to assess the effectiveness of the currently implemented universal tier.

Assessing the universal tier is a tricky endeavor for multiple reasons. First, effectiveness of the universal tier cannot be measured solely by evaluating current instructional practices. Schools must examine how learners are responding to those practices. A strategy that is successful in one school may not have the same impact in another. Secondly, in schools where learners walk in the door with more needs, universal instruction must be more robust and, frankly, intense right from the start to get to this target. Consensus issues are almost always encountered in these settings when discussing the effectiveness of universal instruction. It is hard not to associate the high failure rate of subgroups of students with factors over which the school has no control. However, there are many factors within the control of educators, including the instruction they provide, the curriculum that is being used, the classroom environment, and how the school building is organized. Every minute spent discussing variables outside the control of educators results in one less minute being spent on problem-solving how to make the universal tier more robust and effective.

DEFINITION OF UNIVERSAL TIER SCREENING

Universal tier screening is the process of using data on all students to determine the sufficiency of current universal tier instruction. This analysis allows for an evaluation of the sufficiency of current instruction to meet the needs of all the students in the building. The data analysis and resulting conversation are different from student screening because the focus is on the system, as opposed to the individual. However, it is also similar to student screening in that it clarifies only *if* the universal tier is sufficient. Universal tier screening does not identify *why* large numbers of students are below target or what to change to improve instruction.

METHODS AND TOOLS

Selecting a Tool

When selecting a tool to examine the effectiveness of the universal tier, schools apply the characteristics of screening. The same tools that are used in an MTSS system to screen for student concerns can also be used to determine the overall effectiveness of the instruction provided. As a result, we recommend using these tools to serve a dual purpose in buildings. There is little reason to use a different screening measure for the universal tier than is used for identifying individual student needs. This also provides an added benefit of saving instructional time, which is a goal of an efficient assessment system.

Methods

In order to determine the effectiveness of the universal tier, the following five questions can be considered after universal screening data are collected. These questions are important and unique, as well as wholly different from those asked about individual students. A checklist containing the questions can be found in Form 4.1. The questions are separated into basic and advanced. The basic questions are those that are answered first and represent universal tier screening at its simplest level. When the BLT has answered the basic questions in the affirmative, then the team will probe more deeply into universal tier sufficiency by considering the advanced questions. These questions are discussed in detail the following sections. Additionally, Table 4.1 summarizes the purpose of each question.

Basic Questions

Basic questions allow the BLT to consider the sufficiency of the universal tier. When data suggest the answer to either of these questions is "no," then the team will begin to dig more deeply into the needs within the universal tier. Remember, screening data only identify needs, not specific solutions. When screening information suggests that the answer to these questions is "yes," then the BLT will examine the advanced questions to determine priorities for universal tier improvements. The two basic questions are the following: (1) Are at least 80% of students meeting expectations at each grade level; and (2) Are at least 95% of students who met expectations in the fall still meeting expectations in the spring? These important questions are discussed further in this section.

- *Are at least 80% of students meeting expectations at each grade level?* Eighty-percent of students meeting expectations is typically identified as the target for a healthy universal tier. This target is chosen because the vast majority of schools do not have resources to effectively serve more than about 20% of students through intervention. MTSS is about utilizing resources effectively. With a finite number of resources and a goal of all students being successful, the foundation of the universal tier must be strong enough to support most students to allow for rigorous, intensive interventions to be provided for those learners who struggle. Schools should examine their universal screening data after each administration to answer this question. If fewer than 80% of students are meeting benchmarks at each grade level, then the BLT will work to identify changes that need to be made within the universal tier to achieve better results.

In the fall of each school year, this basic question is considered differently for kindergarten learners. Instead of asking if 80% of kindergartners meet expectations, as they had just begun school, we ask if our universal instruction is robust enough to meet their needs. When very high numbers of kindergartners start school with high needs (which happens in many places) it signifies that the universal tier instruction needs to be very intense to ensure that the students learn at a trajectory that allows them to meet expectations at the end of the year. Being able to consider that immediately as students enter kindergarten, by examining universal screening data, is invaluable to a BLT.

TABLE 4.1. Explaining Universal Tier Questions

Universal Tier Question	Rationale
Are at least 80% of students meeting expectations at each grade level?	• Allows for comparison between grade levels. • Grade levels with greater needs can be allocated more resources. • Provides information regarding prioritization of universal tier work.
Are at least 95% of students who met expectations in the fall still meeting expectations in the spring?	• Students who meet expectations in the fall are expected to meet expectations in the spring. • If large numbers of students who met expectations do not grow at a rate that allows them to continue to meet expectations in the spring, then it suggests that the universal tier is not sufficient.
Is our universal tier instruction robust enough for our kindergarten students?	• Kindergartners have not yet been exposed to our instruction, so expecting 80% to be meeting fall benchmarks is not reasonable in many schools. • When students come to school with higher needs, resources can be allocated to support greater learning.
Are at least 80% of students meeting expectations at each grade level without additional intervention?	• A sufficient universal tier is expected to meet the needs of most students without providing additional intervention. • Allows for utilization of resources in a more efficient and effective manner. Students who do need intervention can be provided with robust, intensive instruction to close achievement gaps.
Are there gaps in the percentage of subgroups of students meeting expectations?	• The universal tier should be strong enough that it meets the needs of most learners, regardless of background. • Allows for the identification of potential system bias against a particular group. • Racial subgroups, free-reduced lunch participation (FRP), and English learners (ELs) are typically included in these analyses.
Is the rate of students identified as having a learning disability at or below the state average?	• Most schools can expect that their building rate is similar to that of the state's average. • If the building identification rate is above the state average, it may suggest that some students are incorrectly identified as having disabilities but are, in fact, not receiving adequate universal tier instruction.

When these two questions elicit answers of "no," the degree of effectiveness of the universal tier will inform the team as to the severity of the universal tier problem. If large numbers of students are at risk of performing below proficiency, the team may recommend that immediate universal tier intervention be implemented; this is known as *classwide intervention*. This concept and its implementation are discussed further in Chapter 6. Briefly, classwide intervention is a way to provide immediate support to the universal tier when a large number of learners need additional support. Since the support is provided classwide, all students who need it have access. It is recommended that classwide intervention be implemented when fewer than 60% of learners meet expectations.

   • *Are at least 95% of students who met expectations in the fall still meeting expectations in the spring?* During a given school year, it is expected that a strong universal tier will adequately support those students who began the year meeting expectations. If Nonya began the year meeting benchmarks, adequate universal instruction should ensure that she progresses at rate to continue to meet benchmarks at the end of the year. If Kyle meets benchmarks in the fall but not in the spring, the universal tier has not been sufficient for him. This does not mean that Kyle lost skills over the course of the year. It signifies that he did not grow at a rate that would be sufficient for remaining on track. In other words, other students who met expectations at the end of the year experienced more growth. Schools should strive for at least 95% of students who begin the year meeting benchmarks to learn at a pace that keeps them on track by the end of the school year.

To answer this basic question, be aware that simply examining the percentage of students who meet expectations in the spring compared to the fall will not provide this information. Some students will rise to proficiency whereas others may fall from proficiency during the course of the year. Therefore, a visual display that shows how students moved between tiers over the course of the year is needed to answer this question. Table 4.2 provides an example of this visual display, and programs such as Excel or Numbers support this analysis. In the table, the last column displays movement from the fall to the spring. The team will notice that 14 students who began the year with a low level of risk ended the year at the "some risk" level. If only the first three columns were examined, the schools would likely assume that only three students dropped into a higher-risk category. This type of chart allows schools to consider questions related to student movement between tiers of

TABLE 4.2. Visual Display of Group Learning Trajectory across a School Year

Level of risk	Fall (No. of students)	Spring (No. of students)	Level of risk	Movement from fall to spring (No. of students)
Low risk	150	147	Low risk	136
			Some risk	14
			High risk	0
Some risk	43	46	Low risk	11
			Some risk	31
			High risk	1
High risk	5	5	Low risk	0
			Some risk	1
			High risk	4

support throughout the year. A sample grade-level team universal tier screening agenda is included in Forms 4.2–4.4 for fall, winter, and spring, respectively.

APPLICATION IN KINDERGARTEN

When considering the sufficiency of the universal tier in the fall at the kindergarten level, schools will use the same data in a slightly different manner. In kindergarten, students have not yet had exposure to universal instruction, so the team is not evaluating the sufficiency of the school's universal tier efforts. Rather, the team considers the level of support needed by students this year. For example, if fall universal screening data indicate that 45% of students are below expectations, the universal tier will need to be more robust than if screening data indicate only 15% of students are below expectations.

Advanced Questions

After answering the basic questions noted above, BLTs are encouraged to move to a set of more advanced questions. The purpose of these advanced questions is to further pinpoint specific needs for improvement within the universal tier. This effort allows for continued data-based decision making regarding the universal tier, even after basic proficiency levels are achieved. The three advanced questions are the following: (1) Are at least 80% of students meeting expectations at each grade level without additional intervention; (2) Are the rates of students meeting expectations similar between subgroups?; and (3) Is the rate of students identified as having a learning disability at or below the state average? These important questions are described further in this section.

- *Are at least 80% of students meeting expectations at each grade level without additional intervention?* The power of an MTSS system is in the ability to better allocate resources to effectively meet the needs of all students. Most of a school's resources (time and staff) are allocated toward the universal tier. That universal instruction—the foundation of education for students—needs to be successful for the vast majority of students in the building. When it is not successful, new intervention resources are not magically created. The same resources of time and staff are spread between a larger number of students, resulting in watered-down interventions. The three most often modified characteristics of interventions in these situations are (1) session frequency, (2) session duration, and (3) group size. To create more instructional groups, session frequency may be decreased from 5 days a week to 3 days a week. Also, session length could be reduced from 40 minutes to 20 minutes in order to double the number of groups that can be created. Lastly, group size could be increased from five or fewer students to 10 or more to accommodate all students who may need the intervention. These decisions are made with the best of intentions to serve all students who need interventions. The fact of the matter is, when a school has too many students who need to receive successful interventions, those students who need the most support often do not receive it.

If doubters remain about the importance of maintaining the integrity of these three variables (frequency, duration, and group size), we encourage you to obtain a student copy of any evidence-based intervention material used in your school. Go ahead, we will wait! Let's say that you decreased this intervention to 3 days a week from 5 days a week, and you cut the duration in half as well, resulting in 2 days to get through each lesson. You get through one and a half lessons a week instead of five. Examine the difference in student learning over a month's worth of time. In 4 weeks, the students would have finished Lesson 20 if a more intense intervention were implemented. In the less intense version, the same students have finished Lesson 6. Flip to Lesson 21 and Lesson 7. In one month's time, this is the difference in the skills of students in the two groups. Now multiply that out by 2 months, 3 months, and so forth, until you are convinced that these variables are essential. The only way we have the ability to intensify frequency, duration, and group size is by maximizing the impact of our universal tier! This approach minimizes the number of students who need access to evidence-based interventions with adequate resources and allows us to provide the amount of time and intensity that is needed to close the achievement gap.

Imagine a grade level with 100 students. The winter universal screening data are in, and 80% of students are meeting expectations. Teachers and the building-level team are excited that all their hard work to implement a strong universal tier has paid off. At the grade-level team meeting, they proceed to set intervention groups and find that many of the students who currently receive some of their low-intensity interventions are barely meeting benchmark targets. In fact, this accounts for another 10% of students in the grade. This group of teachers is nervous about ending these interventions, thinking that these interventions may be the reason these students are meeting benchmarks (albeit barely). Now, instead of 20 students who need intervention, they are back up to 30 students. In fact, each classroom has about seven or eight students who need interventions to be successful. In order to group and schedule all these interventions, the frequency and duration of the intervention sessions are decreased and the size of the groups are increased, resulting in less intensive interventions for participating students.

Are the rates of students meeting expectations similar between subgroups? Examining subgroups may seem counterintuitive. After all, there is no evidence that different interventions should be used for different subgroups. Remember, though, that this is about system improvement, not about identifying interventions for individual students. Subgroup analyses are important to identify potential bias within a system. The goal of an effective universal tier is to meet the needs of the vast majority of students, regardless of background. Each community, therefore, is responsible for ensuring that the universal tier is sufficient for the students it currently serves. Over time, as needs of incoming students change, the universal tier needs to adapt to those challenges. A system should be examined for potential bias when it is found that 80% of students are proficient, but a majority of those who are not proficient are students who are disadvantaged and/or of color.

• *Is the rate of students identified as having a learning disability at or below the state average?* Many students who are identified as having a learning disability have goals and services in the area of reading. By definition, these students are not yet proficient readers, and it is expected that a lower percentage of these students will meet expectations during universal screening periods. Because of this, examining the rate of students identified with learning disabilities may be a more accurate indicator of the sufficiency of the universal tier. When evaluating a student for a learning disability, schools are required to examine exclusionary factors, including if the student received appropriate instruction in reading (34 C.F.R. 300.306(b)). It can be postulated that in schools where higher than typical rates of students are identified as having a learning disability, some may be misdiagnosed and may have experienced a lack of appropriate instruction in reading. A strong universal tier will prevent this type of misdiagnosis, as well as save the system significant amounts of resources in serving students through special education who would not need these resources had they received strong universal instruction.

DECISIONS AND PRIORITIES

Determining the effectiveness of the universal tier is not a simple task. Upon taking a step back, thinking about these questions can help determine how to prioritize universal tier work. MTSS is powerful because it allows for the consideration of how all resources in the building are used to ensure student success. These universal tier screening questions can guide resource allocation within the universal tier. When answered yes, the screening data suggest that the appropriate resources are being provided to assure universal tier sufficiency. When answered no, the screening data suggest that additional resources (e.g., training, materials, and/or time) are needed to provide a more robust and effective universal tier. The screening data do not identify which resources need to be provided, but they do point BLTs in the direction of allocating these resources for further inquiry and improvement.

The screening data can also be used to identify priorities for improvement, such as grade level or content area. For example, if it if is discovered that fewer than 70% of students in the fall of second grade are meeting benchmark targets, first grade may be prioritized for improvement.

The size of the concern identified may also support prioritization of universal tier improvements. If it is discovered that only 60% of kindergartners meet benchmark targets when they begin in the fall, a classwide intervention may be prioritized as a universal tier improvement. As noted, classwide intervention is described in detail in Chapter 6; however, its name likely provides some context to its purpose. Classwide intervention is designed to allow for the quick improvement of the universal tier while the BLT is examining more specific improvements that may be needed. Throughout all decision making regarding the effectiveness of the universal tier, building-level and grade-level teams are crucial to success.

TEAMING OPPORTUNITIES

Examining data to determine effectiveness of the universal instruction offers multiple opportunities for collaborative teaming. Opportunities to examine data together, make decisions regarding needs, and proactively plan to deal with consensus concerns all require collaborative efforts to address systemically and effectively.

Examining Data

Building-level teams should look at grade-level data together in the fall and the spring to determine the strength and needs in the universal instruction. In the fall, data are used to determine how robust universal instruction needs to be in order to meet learner needs, and in the spring, data indicate the degree of success of the universal instruction throughout the year.

Resource Decisions

The building-level team will use spring data to determine grade-level resource allocation. For instance, if the BLT notes that one particular grade level has significantly more needs than another, collaborative time with a reading specialist, instructional coach, or other opportunities for learning may need to be prioritized for this grade level. Additionally, if additional supplemental instructional resources are available in the building, those may also need to be reallocated to provide the most needy grade levels with additional support. Data-based decision making extends to the system as well as the students. Gone are the days when every teacher gets exactly the same resources.

Consensus Planning

Universal instruction needs are the most difficult around which to obtain consensus. Staff (including principals and superintendents) can be quick to attribute lack of success in the universal tier to variables we have little control over, such as economic status, language barriers, and familial struggles. However, many schools have overcome these same hardships by embracing the need for strong universal instruction and a relentless pursuit of improvement in teaching practices (Carter, 1999).

Educators do not often consider their explanations for lack of achievement with the universal tier (namely because of population needs) a consensus barrier. Teachers truly believe that all children can learn; but, having experienced so many examples of children who struggle, they begin to expect that lack of achievement is inevitable. This is because the system has not been designed in a way to support all teachers and learners. When universal instruction is not effective, teachers are not to blame. The failure is a systemwide concern, and the system needs to change.

BLTs would be well-served to spend time considering consensus barriers and planning to address those in an ongoing, positive manner. For instance, in the situation described above, the leadership team may plan to do an activity in a staff meeting where a highly successful school with hardships similar to their own is examined briefly and discussed. Building consensus among all staff that universal instruction will be improved, and that resources will be put toward improving the universal instruction at a grade level or the entire building, should not be ignored. In fact, at times, the BLT may need to explain why more time is being spent on these improvements than in discussions and planning for small-group and individual interventions. Proactively planning for these conversations is critical in order to engage and encourage staff to continue in this challenging work.

CASE IN POINT

The following two examples depict the process of answering the question Is the universal tier sufficient? Exquisite Elementary is a school new to using an MTSS process, whereas Majestic Middle School has been implementing it for several years.

Exquisite Elementary School

The principal and BLT at Exquisite Elementary are eager to improve outcomes for their students. They have not been satisfied with the test scores of their third graders for a couple of years, but they are not sure what to do about it. After reading a book about MTSS and the universal tier as a team, they decide that they may need to shift their focus from trying new interventions to examining what they provide to everyone. They know they will need information on students before the end of their third-grade year and decide to implement universal screening in the area of reading for all students three times a year, starting in kindergarten. They use an online site to find a summary of the technical adequacy of several universal screening assessments and choose one for their school. After the fall screening data are collected, the BLT considers the data (see Figure 4.1). Based on the fall data, the team decides that it needs to explore a classwide intervention at the first-grade level and to improve universal tier implementation at other grade levels. At the kindergarten level, they can tell that the students starting school this year will need a strong universal tier. The BLT decides to share these data with the entire staff at their next staff meeting. They also decide that this year, they will focus on improving their universal tier supports.

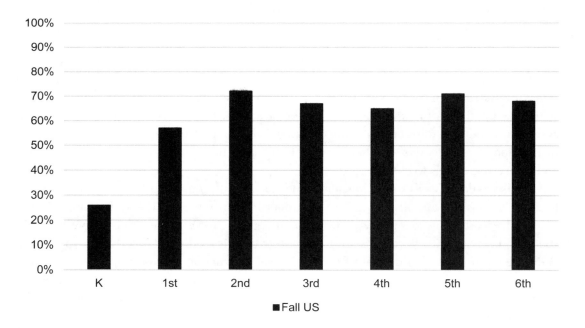

FIGURE 4.1. Fall universal screening results for all students at Exquisite Elementary School.

Majestic Middle School

Majestic Middle School has been using an MTSS framework for several years. The principal, BLT, and grade-level teams have experienced success through providing interventions that meet a variety of student needs. They have a large percentage of their students meeting proficiency on state tests and have few office referrals. However, their principal is concerned that the system of referrals and interventions they currently implement is extremely taxing on teachers. There are many more intervention groups than the principal thought they would have when they started their MTSS efforts, and more than a handful of students have been in interventions their entire middle school career. One spring, after reading a book about MTSS and the universal tier, the BLT members decide that maybe they should examine their universal screening data in a different way than they usually do. In addition to the grade-level and building-level reports that the team usually examines, the members use a new agenda to discuss the success of their universal tier. First, they look at the overall data—something they are used to doing as a team. Those data look very impressive (see Figure 4.2). They examine these data every spring and are always proud that their hard work is paying off. They have at least 80% of students meeting targets at every grade level.

This year, the team decides to also consider the question, "Are at least 95% of students who met expectations in the fall still meeting expectations in the spring?" The results are shocking to the team. They find that in sixth grade, only 85% of students who start the year on track end the year on track (see Table 4.3). In seventh and eighth grades the results are similar. The team members are surprised because they assumed the reason the percentage of students who were meeting expectations went from 82 to 84% during the school year was because 2% of students who were at risk were successful. They never thought that some of those students who began the year on track would not make enough growth to remain on track.

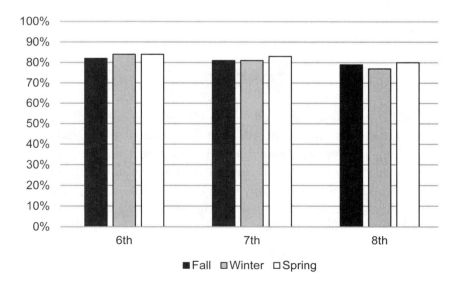

FIGURE 4.2. Universal screening data for all students at Majestic Middle School.

TABLE 4.3. Fall and Spring Universal Screening Data from Majestic Middle School

Level of risk	Fall (No. of students)	Spring (No. of students)	Level of risk	Movement from fall to spring (No. of students)
Low risk	283	290	Low risk	241
			Some risk	41
			High risk	1
Some risk	5	46	Low risk	48
			Some risk	4
			High risk	6
High risk	4	9	Low risk	1
			Some risk	1
			High risk	2

They wonder if this is a fluke and decide to consider the percentage of their students who are successful without intervention. Again, they are surprised to see that they have large percentages of students who are proficient only after intervention. Some of the team members want to celebrate these data. They now have evidence of something they have expected for a while. The interventions they provide are successful for their students. Their astute principal agrees that it is great news that their interventions are strong. However, she points out, unless the school team starts improving their universal tier, they will always be overwhelmed with their intervention needs. The team agrees that these are data the whole school staff should discuss; the team plans to share them at the next staff meeting. The team members realize that their focus for the next school year will be on improving the universal tier, and they are both nervous and excited to take on the challenge.

CONCLUSION

Universal tier screening allows for teams to determine if the universal tier is meeting the needs of students in the building today. Although the question is simple, the process allows for multiple teaming and consensus-building opportunities. Many buildings have become accustomed to having large numbers of students in interventions. Until teachers begin to see that the universal tier can successfully meet the needs of most students in their classroom, they are unlikely to believe it is possible. Although challenging work, identifying and coming to consensus that the universal tier needs additional attention has the potential to be the first step toward large and lasting impacts on student outcomes. Applying the same universal screening data used to identify specific students who need intervention, questions about the universal tier itself can be asked to determine needs and to set priorities for system-level improvements.

DISCUSSION QUESTIONS

1. What are ways we currently consider the effectiveness of our universal tier?

2. Do we currently have ways of answering the basic questions posed in this chapter?

3. What would we expect to see if we answered the basic questions?

4. If we found that our universal tier was not sufficient for the students in our building today, how could we ensure that resources were allocated to improving it?

5. Do we currently have ways of answering the advanced questions posed in this chapter?

6. What would we expect to see if we answered the advanced questions?

7. Do we have a common belief in our building that subgroups should perform similarly when provided a strong universal tier?

Is the Universal Tier Sufficient?: Checklist

FALL

Basic Questions

☐ Are at least 80% of students meeting expectations at each grade level?

☐ Is our universal tier instruction robust enough for our kindergarten students?

Advanced Questions

☐ Are at least 80% of students meeting expectations at each grade level without additional intervention?

☐ Are the rates of subgroups of students meeting expectations similar?

☐ Is the rate of students identified as having a learning disability at or below the state average?

WINTER

Basic Questions

☐ Are at least 80% of students meeting expectations at each grade level?

☐ Are at least 95% of students who met expectations in the fall still meeting expectations in the winter?

Advanced Questions

☐ Are at least 80% of students meeting expectations at each grade level without additional intervention?

☐ Are the rates of subgroups of students meeting expectations similar?

☐ Is the rate of students identified as having a learning disability at or below the state average?

SPRING

Basic Questions

☐ Are at least 80% of students meeting expectations at each grade level?

☐ Are at least 95% of students who met expectations in the fall still meeting expectations in the spring?

Advanced Questions

☐ Are at least 80% of students meeting expectations at each grade level without additional intervention?

☐ Are the rates of subgroups of students meeting expectations similar?

☐ Is the rate of students identified as having a learning disability at or below the state average?

Is the Universal Tier Sufficient?: Fall Team Agenda

Grade Level(s): _____ Assessment/Data Used: _____

BASIC QUESTIONS

☐ Are at least 80% of students meeting expectations at each grade level?

- If not, is a classwide intervention needed?
  - If yes, what classwide intervention will be used?

Name of the intervention	
Description of the intervention	
When will it be implemented?	
How often will it be implemented?	

☐ Is our universal tier instruction robust enough for our kindergarten students?

ADVANCED QUESTIONS (OPTIONAL)

☐ Are at least 80% of students meeting expectations at each grade level without additional intervention?

☐ Are the rates of subgroups of students meeting expectations similar?

☐ Is the rate of students identified as having a learning disability at or below the state average?

Is the Universal Tier Sufficient?: Winter Team Agenda

Grade Level(s): _____ Assessment/Data Used: _____

BASIC QUESTIONS

☐ Are at least 80% of students meeting expectations at each grade level?

  • If not, is a classwide intervention needed?

    ○ If yes, what classwide intervention will be used?

Name of the intervention	
Description of the intervention	
When will it be implemented?	
How often will it be implemented?	

☐ Are at least 95% of students who met expectations in the fall still meeting expectations in the winter?

ADVANCED QUESTIONS

☐ Are at least 80% of students meeting expectations at each grade level without additional intervention?

☐ Are the rates of subgroups of students meeting expectations similar?

☐ Is the rate of students identified as having a learning disability at or below the state average?

Is the Universal Tier Sufficient?: Spring Team Agenda

Grade Level(s): _____ Assessment/Data Used: _____

BASIC QUESTIONS

☐ Are at least 80% of students meeting expectations at each grade level?

- If not, are there any grade levels that need classwide intervention upon return in the fall?

Name of the intervention	
Description of the intervention	
When will it be implemented?	
How often will it be implemented?	

☐ Are at least 95% of students who met expectations in the fall still meeting expectations in the spring?

ADVANCED QUESTIONS

☐ Are at least 80% of students meeting expectations at each grade level without additional intervention?

☐ Are the rates of subgroups of students meeting expectations similar?

☐ Is the rate of students identified as having a learning disability at or below the state average?

CHAPTER 5

Identifying Barriers to Effective Universal Tier Implementation

In the previous chapters, we presented information on learning targets, universal assessments, and evaluating the effectiveness of universal instruction. In Chapter 4 we examined the ways in which process teams determine whether or not a school's universal tier is effective and efficient enough to meet the needs of at least 80% of students, without additional interventions and supports. If less than 80% of students are on track to be proficient, this chapter should be the next stop for a school. In this chapter, we describe a process schools can use to identify barriers to implementing an effective, research-based universal tier.

When schools examine their data and identify that their universal tier is not sufficient to meet the needs of the students enrolled at that time, they often jump straight to identifying potential solutions to pursue and implement. The reason we have included this chapter is because, in our experience, we have seen too many schools make this mistake. Jumping straight to solutions, without understanding *why* student learning is insufficient, is like trying to play darts in the dark. At best, schools may get lucky and hit the target and implement a new strategy that significantly increases student learning in a sustainable way. But it is highly unlikely. At worst, schools expend a great deal of time and energy trying to implement new practices that do not pay off in sustainable, improved student learning. This outcome is demoralizing to staff and not beneficial for students. It is critically important to understand why less than 80% of students are on track in order to select strategies that are matched to the needs of the school, teachers, and ultimately the students.

Throughout this book, we have suggested using an action planning process that includes answering the following five questions:

1. Is universal instruction effective?
2. If the universal tier is not sufficient, what needs must be addressed?"
3. How will the needs identified in universal instruction be addressed?

4. How will the effectiveness and efficiency of universal instruction be monitored over time?

5. Have improvements to universal instruction been effective?

Here, we focus on the second question: How will the needs identified in universal instruction be addressed? In this chapter, we discuss two main actions school teams can take collaboratively to answer this question: (1) Identify universal tier practices that are and are not sufficiently in place, and (2) identify systemic barriers to implementing universal tier practices. To support these actions, we also provide strategies for keeping this overall process manageable, some words of caution and common pitfalls, and the role of collaborative teams in answering the second question. Finally, a case study is included to illustrate addressing the second question. A checklist for keeping track of the entire process can be found in Form 5.1.

ACTION 5.1. THE STRUCTURE AND PROCESS FOR EXAMINING UNIVERSAL TIER PRACTICES

Considerations before Getting Started

For schools to accurately identify universal tier practices that are and are not in place, one of the first things they need to do is develop a clear definition of what the universal tier is. As we described in Chapter 1, our definition of universal tier is what "all" students receive in the form of academic and social–emotional instruction and student supports. In our experience, schools often define universal tier in terms of their textbooks. Although research-based textbooks that are tightly aligned with school-defined learning targets (which need to be aligned to state-required academic content standards like CCSS) can be an indispensable set of tools for teachers, they alone do not constitute a school's universal tier.

We describe the universal tier as being composed of an array of resources, tools, and practices. Basically, the universal tier is comprised of whatever it takes to get students to grade-level proficiency, and it may look different from school to school and even grade to grade. In short, the universal tier is comprised of the curriculum, instruction, assessment, and the collaborative work schools do to engage all students in learning the academic content standards. So, universal tier is "universal" within a school, but there is no one-size-fits-all package of universal tier practices that will work for every school.

Another important consideration for schools is to learn about a key concept in MTSS that is usually associated with interventions for struggling students: implementation fidelity. The concept of *implementation fidelity* has received an increased amount of attention in recent years in the area of interventions. Implementation fidelity is being scrutinized for several reasons, but the most important reason is that it is impossible to determine how effective an intervention is for a student if the intervention was not implemented with fidelity. In other words, if an intervention was not implemented consistently, as it was designed to be implemented or delivered with the intended dosage (e.g., time and frequency), then the student was not actually participating in that intervention.

Therefore, when teams examine student progress monitoring data, they also need to examine implementation fidelity data to make accurate decisions about what to do next. If a student is not making adequate learning progress but the intervention was being implemented with fidelity, then it is reasonable to assume that the intervention was not appropriately matched to student needs and changes to the intervention are needed. However, if a student is not making adequate learning progress and the intervention was not implemented with fidelity, the discussion should likely focus on why it wasn't implemented with fidelity so those challenges can be resolved and the intervention implemented as intended moving forward.

This concept can actually be applied to the universal tier as well, but to do so it is important to have a clear picture of what the universal tier is and how to examine implementation fidelity. Schools need to have observable, measurable practices and a set of processes and tools to use when collecting implementation fidelity data. Schools need a structure and process for examining universal tier practices, because if there are not enough students performing at a proficient level, it stands to reason that one of the reasons may be because the universal tier is not being implemented according to research and best practice. Given the challenges around allocating additional resources to improve universal tier instruction, we have dedicated a great deal of our time to supporting schools to do this work. We have focused on a collaborative approach that involves partnering with schools to improve their universal tiers. Our work has involved organizing the universal tier into key components, digging into key component practices, and trying to keep the process manageable.

Organizing the Universal Tier into Key Components

In the work of establishing key components of the universal tier, it is easy to drift into theory and away from the practical. In full disclosure, we actually find theories to be quite practical and useful. But, we also understand that in the day-to-day life of schools, theory is not always the first thing people think about. That is why we have tried to strike a balance between generating some practical strategies to organize the universal tier, but still using theory or frameworks to help us organize our thinking and our work. Having a theory or framework is helpful to keep the work grounded within a consistent vision, and prevents teams from jumping around from idea to idea.

In the end, the most useful strategy for breaking down the universal tier into smaller components is to use the definition of universal tier as a starting point and then divide it up into each part that is described in that definition. What follows is the summary description we are using for the universal tier in this book, this time with each different part italicized: "In short, the universal tier is comprised of the *curriculum, instruction, assessment,* and the *collaborative work* schools do to use *time* effectively to *engage all students* in learning a common set of skills and knowledge needed, as defined in the schools *learning targets.*"

The key areas of practice in this definition are curriculum, instruction, assessment, collaboration, time, student engagement, and learning targets. Stopping here and using these seven elements as our components would be perfectly reasonable. With these seven components, we have a broad set of considerations that are all still areas that a school can directly influence. However, there are some additional considerations related to these items that research suggests are likely to have an impact on the universal tier. First, *professional learning* and *coaching* are needed to change classroom practice (Fixsen, Naoom, Blase, Friedman, & Wallace, 2005; Joyce & Showers, 2002). Second, the *alignment* of curriculum, instruction, and assessment with learning targets, as well as with each other, can also have an impact on student learning and was discussed in Chapter 2 (Gamoran et al., 1997; Porter, 2002).

Adding these two elements (professional learning, alignment) give us nine components that we could examine to identify potential areas of universal tier improvements. In our experience, this list is too long to keep the work moving forward in a positive direction. It is just too many things to keep organized. We have found combining some of these elements can be helpful in that regard. In particular, the elements of alignment, student engagement, professional learning/coaching, time, and collaboration can largely be considered in the context of curriculum, instruction, assessment, and learning targets. This keeps the focus of the components on what happens in the classroom, while embedding these other concepts in those elements, as they can be excellent facilitators of a high-quality universal tier. Table 5.1 provides a quick summary of what we call the universal tier components–embedded elements (UTC-EE) framework.

Digging into Key Component Practices

The primary purpose of the UTC-EE framework is to provide an overarching organizational structure or framework for schools to use as the starting point in the process of digging into universal tier practices. To accomplish this goal, we have identified research-based and best practices for each key components, as well as a set of questions about those practices to answer collaboratively as a school.

Building Common Understanding of Research-Based and Best Practices

In our review of research and best practices, and drawing upon our experience working with schools to improve their universal tier, we have identified several practices that are important to explore. Each of these practices, when implemented, has the potential to facilitate positive student outcomes. That potential is expanded when these practices are used together. Table 5.2- provides a list of practices and resources that should be present in a

TABLE 5.1. The Universal Tier Components and Embedded Elements (UTC-EE Framework)

Universal tier components	Embedded elements
• Learning targets	• Alignment
• Curriculum	• Engagement of students
• Instruction	• Professional learning/coaching
• Assessment and data-based decision making	• Time
	• Collaboration

TABLE 5.2. Practices and Resources for a Healthy Universal Tier

List of practices	Embedded elements
Learning targets	
• Grounding in state-required academic content standards (e.g., CCSS)	• Alignment
• Background knowledge and information support for teachers	• Professional learning/coaching • Collaboration
• ScopeZ and sequence of skills articulated across school year	• Time
• Individually well-written (objective, measurable, minimal jargon, user-friendly)	
• Vertical articulation across grade levels with minimal gaps and redundancies	
• Comprehensive coverage of important knowledge and skills that are coherently designed	• Time
Curriculum	
• Learning targets reflected in materials	• Alignment
• Design of materials enhances student engagement	• Student engagement
• Background knowledge, information, and training support for teachers	• Professional learning/coaching • Collaboration
• Correspondence between materials' scope and sequence and the scope and sequence of learning target skills	• Alignment
• Extent of skill coverage not addressed in learning targets	• Alignment • Time
• Design of materials that is reflective of instructional shifts of the CCSS	• Alignment • Student engagement
• Use of research base of curriculum materials with high effect sizes	
Instruction	
• Learning targets reflected in instruction	• Alignment
• Amount of time allocated to instruction	• Alignment • Time
• Background knowledge, information, and training support for teachers	• Professional learning/coaching • Collaboration
• Effective use of time to maximize student engagement in learning	• Student engagement • Time
• Use of classwide interventions when large numbers of students display learning difficulties	• Student engagement

(continued)

TABLE 5.2. *(continued)*

List of practices	Embedded elements
Instruction (continued)	
• Use of research-based instructional strategies and routines with high effect sizes that support the instructional shifts of the CCSS	
• Use of data-based differentiation and flexible grouping	• Student engagement
• Fidelity of implementation of curricular materials	• Alignment
Assessment and data-based decision making	
• Learning targets reflected in assessments	• Alignment
• Background knowledge, information, and training support for teachers	• Professional learning/coaching
• Regular collection of universal screening data	
• Consistent use of universal screening data for making decisions	• Collaboration
• Use of formative assessment data to guide instruction and systemic changes	• Alignment • Student engagement • Collaboration • Time
• Opportunities for collaborative teaming focused on using student data	• Collaboration

healthy universal tier, organized by the key components, and includes the embedded elements as well. It is important for schools either to collaboratively reflect on a list like this one, or to generate their own list. If a school decides to add to this list or to generate its own, it is important to be mindful of research and best practices in these areas. You will also find that many of the practices listed in the table include one or more of the embedded elements from Table 5.1.

Questions about the Universal Tier to Answer Collaboratively

Gathering information about the universal tier is fundamentally about answering really important questions. These questions become the "what and how" for schools to dig into universal tier practices. Once schools have effective questions, they will be able to determine the best means of gathering the information needed to answer those questions. In developing questions for the practices associated with each key component, we have considered several factors: the extent to which the school or district has control over those practices, whether or not the practices exist along a continuum of more basic to more advanced practice, whether there is at least one question for each practice, and whether or not it would be possible to gather information to answer the question. The result of our work is a set of questions that, if answered, paint a fairly comprehensive picture of which universal tier practices are and are not in place. Those questions can be found in Tables 5.3–5.6. There were two specific factors we considered when developing these questions to help schools successful navigate the process of gathering complex information in a relatively simple manner: (1) focusing on a few things at a time, and (2) answering questions using a sequential approach.

Focusing on a Few Questions at a Time

One of the most common mistakes in this work is to try and capture as much information about as many areas as possible. Speaking as professionals that love a good rubric or inventory, we have been down that road before. Trying to collect too much data becomes overwhelming to schools and results in a lot of time, energy, and resources spent on trying to collect extraneous data. We would argue that too much data can make team decision-making inefficient and ineffective. Instead, schools should collaboratively select a small handful of questions to answer. This approach has several benefits. First, school personnel are given opportunities to provide input, up front, into how the process will go. Second, it establishes a set of priorities to pursue. Third, it allows schools to spend more time, energy, and resources digging more deeply into a small set of practices that facilitates effective decision making.

Answering Questions Using a Sequential Approach

We have already organized the questions by universal tier component. Schools can then take each of those questions within, and at times even across, universal tier components and organize them in a logical, sequential order. It helps to start with questions that are easier to answer. Relatedly, it may help to think about the questions in terms of prerequisites. That is, answer questions about practices that are prerequisite to the practices embodied in later questions. An example may be helpful here. Consider the questions in Table 5.5 related to the amount of time allocated to instruction and the effective use of time to maximize student engagement in learning. It is reasonable to view these questions as having a common theme of time (one of the embedded elements). It is also reasonable to view the practices embodied in these questions as potentially building on each other. Starting with the most basic question and going to the most complex question could look something like this:

1. How much time is allocated to the universal tier? Is it sufficient to engage all students in meaningful learning of the learning targets?
2. Is more time spent on prioritized learning targets?
3. What percentage of scheduled time is spent in instructional time versus transition or "management" tasks?
4. What percentage of instructional time is spent with students actively engaged in learning?

TABLE 5.3. Universal Tier Questions: Learning Targets

Universal tier practice	Questions
Grounding in state-required academic content standards (e.g., CCSS)	• To what extent is the content of the learning targets aligned with state-required academic content standards? • To what extent is the rigor of the learning targets aligned with the rigor called for in state-required academic content standards?
Background knowledge and information support for teachers	• What do teachers know and not know about the learning targets? • How frequently do teachers access coaching to deepen their understanding of the learning targets? • How frequently do teachers collaborate in teams to deepen their understanding of the learning targets?
Scope and sequence of skills articulated across the school year	• To what extent have the learning targets been organized for teaching from the beginning to the end of the school year? • To what extent is the organization of the learning targets logical so that prerequisite skills would be taught before more advanced skills? • To what extent does the organization of the learning targets enable meaningful learning to occur within 1 school year?
Well written (objective, measurable, minimal jargon, user-friendly)	• To what extent are learning targets written in terms that are observable, objective, and measurable? • To what extent are the learning targets written in clear, understandable language for multiple audiences?
Vertical articulation across grade levels with minimal gaps and redundancies	• To what extent are there clear connections between learning targets across multiple grade levels? • To what extent are their gaps between learning targets across multiple grade levels? • To what extent are there redundancies between learning targets across multiple grade levels?
Comprehensive coverage of important knowledge and skills that is coherently designed	• How comprehensive is the alignment of the learning targets with the state-required academic content standards? • How coherently do the learning targets work together to create an interconnected web of relationships among them? • To what extent is it possible to engage all students in meaningful learning for the full set of learning targets in 1 school year?

TABLE 5.4. Universal Tier Questions: Curriculum

Universal tier practice	Questions
Learning targets reflected in materials	• To what extent is the content of the curriculum materials aligned with learning targets? • To what extent is the rigor of the curriculum materials aligned with the rigor called for in the learning targets?
Design of materials enhances student engagement	• To what extent are the curriculum materials designed to maintain high levels of student engagement?
Background knowledge, information, and training support for teachers	• What do teachers know and not know about the content and design of the curriculum materials? • How frequently do teachers access coaching to deepen their understanding of how to implement the curriculum materials with fidelity? • How frequently do teachers collaborate in teams to work on implementation issues related to the curriculum materials?
Correspondence of materials' scope and sequence with scope and sequence of learning target skills	• How aligned is the organization of the curriculum materials with the scope and sequence of learning target skills?
Extent of skill coverage not addressed in learning targets	• To what extent do the curriculum materials minimize the amount of skill coverage not contained in the learning targets?
Design of materials that is reflective of instructional shifts of the CCSS	• To what extent do the curriculum materials reflect the instructional shifts of the CCSS?
Use of research base of curriculum materials with high effect sizes	• To what extent are the instructional materials designed based on research with high effect sizes? • To what extent have the curriculum materials been positively validated through empirical research?

By combining both of these approaches, schools should focus on the first question for each practice, for each of the universal tier components, and work to resolve any implementation issues they discover before moving on to the second questions. This has the benefit of quickly reducing the number of questions to answer, and therefore the number of different factors to consider.

Pulling It All Together

The structure and process for examining the current reality of universal tier practices is incredibly complex and potentially overwhelming. We have attempted to break this work down into smaller chunks, and to provide a method of engaging in this critical collab-

TABLE 5.5. Universal Tier Questions: Instruction

Universal tier practices	Questions
Learning targets reflected in instruction	• To what extent is the content of instruction aligned with learning targets? • To what extent is the rigor of instruction aligned with the rigor called for in the learning targets?
Amount of time allocated to instruction	• How much time is allocated to the universal tier? Is it sufficient to engage all students in meaningful learning of the learning targets? • Is more time spent on prioritized learning targets?
Background knowledge, information, and training support for teachers	• What do teachers know and not know about research-based instructional strategies and routines? • How frequently do teachers access coaching to increase their use of research-based instructional strategies and routines? • How frequently do teachers collaborate in teams to work on implementation issues related to research-based instructional strategies and routines?
Effective use of time to maximize student engagement in learning	• What percentage of scheduled time is spent in instructional time? • What percentage of instructional time is spent with students actively engaged in learning?
Use of classwide interventions when large numbers of students display learning difficulties	• To what extent do school personnel work to determine the need for classwide interventions? • To what extent are research-based classwide interventions implemented when needed? • To what extent are research-based classwide interventions implemented with fidelity? • To what extent are progress monitoring data regularly collected during classwide intervention?
Use of research-based instructional strategies with high effect sizes that support the instructional shifts of the CCSS	• To what extent are teachers using approaches to instruction that reflect the instructional shifts of the CCSS? • To what extent are research-based instructional strategies and routines regularly implemented?
Use of data-based differentiation and flexible grouping	• To what extent are differentiation strategies and flexible grouping used? • To what extent are differentiation and flexible grouping decisions made using student data?
Fidelity of implementation of curricular materials	• To what extent are research-based instructional strategies and routines implemented with fidelity? • To what extent are curricular materials implemented with fidelity?

TABLE 5.6. Universal Tier Questions: Assessment and Data-Based Decision Making

Universal tier practice	Questions
Learning targets reflected in assessments	• To what extent do universal screening measures reflect the broad constructs represented in learning targets? • To what extent are classroom summative assessments aligned with the content and rigor called for in learning targets? • To what extent are classroom formative assessments aligned with the content and rigor called for in learning targets?
Background knowledge, information, and training support for teachers	• What do teachers know and not know about development and use of classroom formative and summative assessments? • To what extent do teachers know how to engage in data-based decision making? • How frequently do teachers access coaching to develop and use classroom formative and summative assessments? • How frequently do teachers access coaching to engaging in data-based decision making? • How frequently do teachers collaborate in teams to work on development and implementation issues related to formative and summative classroom assessments? • How frequently do teachers collaborate in teams to engage in data-based decision making?
Regular collection of universal screening data	• Are universal screening measures sufficiently reliable and valid? • Are universal screening data collected at least three times per school year?
Consistent use of universal screening data for making decisions	• To what extent are universal screening data used to evaluate universal tier effectiveness? • To what extent are universal screening data used to determine which students need targeted or intensive supports?
Use of formative assessment data to guide instruction and systemic changes	• To what extent have learning goals and success criteria been developed for each learning target? • To what extent are learning data collected with and from students? • To what extent do students know about the learning goals and success criteria? • To what extent are students involved in reflecting on their learning with teachers, grounded in the learning goals and success criteria?
Opportunities for collaborative teaming focused on using student data	• How frequently do teachers meet in grade-level teams to review student data? • To what extent do teachers have access to student learning data? • To what extent are collaborative teaming sessions focused on student needs based on data?

orative work. Specifically, we organized the universal tier into key components and the essential elements that cut across multiple key components into the UTC-EE framework (Table 5.1). To use the UTC-EE framework to dig into universal tier practices, school leadership teams should work collaboratively with an instructional staff to answer a small set of sequentially organized questions aligned to the research-based and best practices within each key component/essential element (Tables 5.2–5.6). Schools can use the worksheets provided (Forms 5.1 and 5.2) to keep track of this work so successes can be celebrated and built upon, and areas that need improvement can be prioritized. Schools that accurately identify the current reality of universal tier practices only dig into a few things at a time, and work to make improvements in those areas first, before tackling additional, more complex practices.

ACTION 5.2. IDENTIFYING BARRIERS TO UNIVERSAL TIER PRACTICES

All of the work described up to this point has been intended to determine celebrations of success and identification of areas of practice that can be improved. The next step is to examine the reasons *why* some universal tier practices need improvement. Historically, this has been known as *diagnostics* or *problem analysis*. Problem analysis is the process of determining why a student, group of students, or even an entire school is having challenges. We prefer to think of this process as *identifying implementation barriers*. Implementation barriers are aspects of the school system that get in the way of universal tier practices that should be implemented (identified in Action 5.1) being successfully implemented. This might seem like semantics, but it quite intentional.

In our experience, most teachers acknowledge that they would like having help with their teaching practices, but do not have nearly enough assistance. Any entry into the world of improving the universal tier is likely to be a sensitive one, because often the environment for discussion is not likely to be considered a safe one in which teachers would be asked to share their challenges and frustrations related to their practice. It is for these reasons that we genuinely view the problem analysis process as one of identifying barriers to implementation. This can help avoid finger pointing and personalizing the work, and instead focus on what can be done about the system to remove that problematic factors and to provide a clear path of support for teachers. To keep this work not only front and center, but the reason for it as well, we call this the *barrier identification and prioritization to support implementation by teachers* (BIP-SIT) approach.

The Process of Identifying Barriers

Schools can follow three steps to successfully identify implementation barriers: (1) prioritize missing practices for barrier identification, (2) learn about common implementation barriers, and (3) gather information to identify barriers.

Prioritize Missing Practices for Barrier Identification

In most cases, schools are only going to be able to work on two or three different implementation issues in any given school year. Any more and the efforts get watered down and it becomes very difficult to make meaningful process. It is therefore necessary to prioritize the list of implementation issues to address. This list can be taken from the list of universal tier practices identified as needing improvement in the Summary of Universal Tier Practices Worksheet (Form 5.3). Factors that may be helpful to consider when prioritizing implementation areas include factors such as whether or not the issue can be addressed relatively quickly, how directly it is related to student learning, staff consensus on the importance of the issue, and the level of impact staff believe would occur if the issue were resolved. Schools may decide on additional considerations during the prioritization conversation. In the end, schools should prioritize one to three implementation areas for which to identify barriers.

Learn about Common Implementation Barriers

In Chapter 1, we described eight common barriers to addressing universal tier ineffectiveness that we often encounter: (1) assuming that MTSS are about intervention, (2) assuming we have done it already, (3) challenging beliefs about learners' abilities to achieve academic success, (4) the swinging pendulum of initiatives, (5) culture of closed classroom doors, (6) system versus teacher issues, (7) lack of knowledge about the current state of the universal tier, and (8) lack of collaborative teams. These are concepts that most educators are familiar with, and often identify things that present them with challenges in their work. Unfortunately, rarely are these barriers connected to specific implementation challenges and used to drive solutions to those implementation challenges. Instead, they simply become reasons why change can't happen. However, we have found that when staff and administrators briefly discuss this list together—with the understanding that the next step will be to identify which barriers are actually causing implementation problems for teachers—it can be an empowering process.

Gather Information to Identify Barriers

With a prioritized list of implementation issues to tackle, schools start gathering information about barriers in their system (see Form 5.4). This is yet another opportunity for schools to engage in collaborative work to identify those areas that are interfering with implementation efforts. When identifying barriers, it may be helpful to start with the list of common barriers in Table 5.7. By starting with a simple list and brainstorming additions to it, teams may proceed to a process that consists of the following steps:

1. At a staff meeting or PLC session, make the list of implementation concerns available and review it with staff.
2. Post the implementation concerns in an easily viewed format, such as on chart paper or hook up a computer to a projector and use a word-processing or slide presentation application to list the implementation concerns.

TABLE 5.7. Common Implementation Barriers

- Low levels of consensus among staff to implement the practice
- Lack of adequate professional learning and coaching support for teachers
- Lack of access to the necessary tools to implement the practice
- Lack of initial success with students when trying to implement the practice
- Too many competing priorities in the school
- Insufficient resource allocation

3. For each implementation concern, have staff individually, and then in pairs, document their ideas about what has made implementing the missing practices challenging. Those ideas are then shared and noted next to each implementation concern. This list of brainstormed challenges serves as the first pass at identifying potential barriers.

4. For each implementation challenge, have a discussion about all of the potential barriers and come to consensus about the barriers that staff think should be prioritized to validate. If several potential barriers were brainstormed, the list may need to be narrowed down to two or three barriers on which to focus.

5. Validate the barriers. All that term means in this context is that the school should collect some information on the proposed barrier to see if it is really a barrier. RIOT procedures (described in the next section) can be used again to collect information, this time to determine if the brainstormed list of potential barriers is accurate. For example, follow up with other teachers to see if they also believe the brainstormed barriers are accurate. This task may extend beyond a single meeting.

Create an Organizer for the Information That Will Be Collected

One of the common challenges for schools as they work to improve the universal tier is to keep track of all the information that is collected about implementation and potential barriers. We recommend that schools use a framework known as RIOT—which stands for *review, interview, observe, test*—to organize collected information regarding implementation and potential barriers. Table 5.8 provides examples of the types of information that can be collected with RIOT procedures.

One of the benefits to using RIOT procedures is that it is broad and flexible and allows for specific processes and tools that schools use to be included. This is particularly helpful because, given the wide range of infrastructure and practice considerations for the universal tier, there is not a single tool that will help a school capture all of the information they need. For example, the Center on Response to Intervention (*www.rti4success.org*) has developed a rubric for assessing the implementation of an MTSS framework. The multilevel instruction section of the rubric focuses on the universal tier, and five key areas are included as indicators of its quality: (1) research-based curriculum and materials, (2) articulation of teaching and learning, (3) differentiated instruction, (4) standards-based, and (5) exceeding benchmark.

TABLE 5.8. Examples of Data Collection Using RIOT Procedures

Types of data collection	Examples of data sources
• Review	• Meeting agendas and notes, previous student achievement data
• Interview	• Conversations with teachers, students
• Observe	• Classroom walk-throughs, student-led video conferences
• Test	• Universal screening data, teacher knowledge surveys

This rubric is well developed and incredibly helpful for schools to use. However, it does not address the full range of the unpacked components listed in Table 5.2 at even a broad level. Thankfully, the RIOT framework allows a school to use a tool like this rubric and incorporate the information gathered from it into the bigger picture of what is happening in the school. For example, if a school chose to use the rubric to have discussions with teachers during team time, the information gathered from those conversations could be listed under the *interview* section of the RIOT framework. Or, a school could choose to use the rubric to create a survey and send that out to staff via email. The resulting information could be listed under the *test* section of the RIOT framework.

Prioritizing Implementation Barriers for Action Planning

Once barriers have been validated, the school will need to prioritize which barriers they will focus on removing (Form 5.4). In essence, this is the step when the school finally decides where to allocate resources to resolve issues. Prioritizing the removal of barriers (e.g., "special" classes and assemblies reducing literacy instructional time) should happen during collaborative conversations with all staff. School discussions about prioritizing barriers to remove should focus on issues that staff can take action on, that are feasible given existing resources, and that have the potential to make the greatest impact on student learning.

Administrators and staff need to come to consensus regarding which barriers should be prioritized. Reaching this agreement may require some ongoing conversations to provide opportunities for staff input and to provide clarity around the implications of the decisions for staff. Once barriers are prioritized, they will become the focus of the action planning process. This, in turn, will impact how resources are allocated and what staff members are going to do until the barriers are removed. In other words, this decision should have wide-sweeping implications, so it is important that staff support the prioritized barriers if the plan is to succeed in increasing implementation of desired practices.

Pulling It All Together

The structure and process for identifying and prioritizing universal tier implementation barriers is one that can be difficult for schools. For some, it may not feel very satisfying because it requires the delay of immediate solutions. For others, it can easily devolve into "problem admiration." Problem admiration occurs when all available time is spent discussing reasons problems are occurring that are outside the control of educators rather than discussing actionable ways to solve the problem. It takes strong leadership and a clear, common understanding about why it is so important to identify implementation barriers to successfully engage in this work. Identifying and prioritizing barriers allow schools to develop action plans that are more likely to lead to improved implementation of universal tier practices.

As was previously mentioned, it is important to make identifying and prioritizing barriers manageable and collaborative, involving both staff and administrators. Three things schools can do are (1) Prioritize missing practices for barrier identification, (2) learn about common implementation barriers, and (3) gather information to identify barriers. Similar to the work of identifying universal tier practices to celebrate and those that need improvement, school leadership teams should work collaboratively with all instructional staff to do this work. Examples of potential barriers can be found in Table 5.7. Schools can use the worksheets provided (Forms 5.2, 5.3, and 5.4) to keep track of this work so that barriers can be accurately identified and reasonably prioritized. Schools that accurately identify and prioritize barriers are in a better position to improve implementation of effective universal tier practices.

THINGS TO KEEP IN MIND THROUGHOUT THE PROCESS

In this chapter, we have covered many things that schools should do to determine what needs should be addressed to improve their universal tier. Our observation is that if schools are not careful, there are several places where the process can fall apart. To help avoid a breakdown in the process, the following sections identify tips for keeping the process manageable, words of caution and common pitfalls, and the role of collaborative teams. Attending to these areas will increase the likelihood of accurately identifying implementation barriers.

Tips for Keeping the Process Manageable

If schools do not get past surface-level responses to implementation questions. the end result is that there are rarely any meaningful short- or long-term changes. This breakdown is often due to the complexity of trying to examine universal tier practices. As tempting as it is to try and account for every detail and solve implementation challenges all at once, it is important for schools to keep the process manageable. Schools can take several steps to keep the process manageable; keep the momentum; and make sure that change is deep, meaningful, and can be sustained over time.

- *Tip 1.* Give the process time to come to a completion. With the growing amount of tasks schools are expected to undertake, collaboratively engaging in gathering information to determine areas of missing implementation and barriers can be hard to let unfold over time. We have observed schools sometimes rush the process so they can get to the next task, or they never get the work done because it is too hard to prioritize issues. Meaningful and sustainable change is unlikely to occur overnight, even under the best of circumstances, because these issues are complex and the work can be difficult. Schools should understand the long-term nature of this work and prepare appropriately. To prevent teams from rushing the process, we recommend that the teams develop action plans with the understanding that this process will take time, and that slow and steady will win the race.

• *Tip 2.* Keep increased resources allocated until at least 80% of students are consistently proficient: Given the need to increase resources to improve the universal tier if less than 80% of students are on track for proficiency, the magnitude of the work and energy needed to complete it can put a strain on the system, especially since there are still students that are going to require targeted and intensive supports. In an era and environment of decreasing resources, it is important to acknowledge that to keep this work manageable, there needs to be a point where a school can confidently decide to shift resources away from universal tier improvement work. In short, schools should use the evaluation process described in Chapter 8. In this specific case, if a school is successfully maintaining at least 80% of students on track for proficiency with only universal tier, regardless of how many questions have been answered and how many practices have been changed, it is reasonable to move on to the next step in the process.

• *Tip 3.* Work on sustainability and shift additional resources to targeted and intensive interventions: If at least 80% of students are on track for proficiency with only universal tier, keeping this process manageable would entail developing and implementing a plan to sustain the new practices and then shifting resources to other work in the school. Although schools should always be dedicated to continuously improving their practice, the intense focus on universal tier can be defensibly scaled back if student achievement data indicate that the universal tier is considered "healthy."

Words of Caution/Common Pitfalls

In this chapter, we have focused on practices, processes, and tools that we have found helpful to schools in their work to improve the universal tier. We would be remiss if we did not share some of our experiences with this work that decreases the effectiveness of school efforts to improve the universal tier. There are likely other potential pitfalls, but the following paragraphs describe pitfalls we have seen frequently.

• *Pitfall 1.* Components are artificial: In the process of creating components, subcomponents, organized questions, RIOT procedures, and identifying barriers, the process can sometimes feel artificial to some school staff. Doing work like this is not typically part of the day-to-day or even week-to-week routine for schools. It is important at the outset that the vision for the work and how staff will be involved are clearly communicated and that consensus is monitored and sustained over time to help mitigate the novelty and challenge of this work.

• *Pitfall 2.* Isolated work by the leadership team: Often, the work of improving the universal tier is initiated by a BLT. This approach can absolutely be successful. However, the potential pitfall is that the work is not collaborative beyond the leadership team. It is not possible to establish and maintain consensus, and to see high degrees of implementation fidelity related to universal tier practices, if instructional staff feel "done to" and do not understand what is going on. This potential pitfall can be mitigated by establishing early, frequent, and scheduled opportunities for communication through multiple channels, especially collaborative teams.

• *Pitfall 3.* Tackling too much at one time: Schools that have intuitive administrators and staff and maintain work to improve the universal tier usually have a culture of ambition. This is a culture that can be very effective in improving the universal tier, because the work can be intense and long-lasting. However, the potential pitfall of the ambitious school is that it becomes overly ambitious and tries to do too much at once. Trying to tackle too much at once can lead to early burnout, which in turn will likely lead to a drop in consensus and eventual abandonment of the work. This downward spiral can be mitigated or prevented entirely by getting feedback on the plan, initially and over time, from other schools or from external experts who have had success keeping the work manageable.

• *Pitfall 4.* Tackling too little: The opposite phenomenon, tackling too little, is also a potential pitfall to the work. This often happens when a school has low levels of consensus to do the work, or the school does not have knowledge of how much work should be attempted at any one time. When tackling too little, staff often do not see a great deal of progress at a rate that helps them feel successful. This can also be mitigated by getting feedback on the plan, initially and over time, from other schools or from external experts who have had success keeping the work manageable.

• *Pitfall 5.* Misunderstanding barrier identification: In this situation, a school starts digging so deeply into potential barriers that it ends up tracing barriers back to factors outside of its control. Or, the school never gets to barrier identification, instead jumping straight from implementation concerns to potential solutions. In either case, there is a lack of understanding about the purpose of barrier identification and how to go about doing it. This can be mitigated by engaging staff members in professional learning on how to effectively identify barriers, or engaging high-quality coaching and facilitation to help support them through the process as they learn how to do the work.

The Role of Collaborative Teams

Our discussion about digging into universal tier practices to identify implementation barriers has emphasized the point that the work should be done collaboratively, every step of the way. Collaboration can occur in both informal and formal ways. Informal collaboration is an excellent way to get quick, authentic contributions to the work of improving the universal tier. School administrators and teachers should look for these collaboration opportunities as much is as practically possible.

At the same time, relying exclusively on these informal opportunities to collaborate is likely not sufficient for a school to make meaningful and sustainable changes to the universal tier. It is therefore important to have planned, structured opportunities for collaboration at every step on the journey of digging into universal tier practices to minimize the potential problems and to maximize the potential benefits that can occur through collaboration. Teams that are, by design, intended to be collaborative learning teams, such as PLCs (DuFour & DuFour, 2008), have a lot of built-in structures for collaboration that we do not discuss here. But it is clear that collaborative teaming structures like PLCs can be an excellent vehicle for engaging in the collaborative teaming needed to improve the universal tier. There are also several processes and tools that are used for grade-level and problem-solving teams, typically used for work related to targeted and intensive interventions, which can also be used for the work described in this chapter to improve the universal tier. Examples of those processes and tools are developing a mission statement and action plans, meeting at least weekly or biweekly, involving the principal and leadership, using a standard agenda, defining team roles, providing training on how to engage in the universal tier improvement process described in this chapter, frequently communicating about improvement efforts, and documenting the process.

CASE IN POINT

The following example depicts the process of answering the question If the universal tier is not sufficient, what are the needs that must be addressed? North County Elementary has been implementing MTSS for several years. As a result, students are screened three times per year in the areas of reading and math, and staff are very comfortable administering progress monitoring assessments. As part of the building's ongoing work to meet the needs of struggling students, the BLT reviews the screening data for each grade level after each assessment window. They consistently find that most grade levels during most assessment windows over the years have less than 80% of students on track to be proficient. This deficiency occurs, despite the fact that the school generally implements interventions with fidelity and sees a lot of positive growth for those students as measured by regular progress monitoring assessments. For example, this spring they found that the percentage of students at benchmark was between 55 and 78% on CBM-R, depending on the grade level.

Other than purchasing a new set of research-based curriculum materials within the last 3 years, the school has not spent a great deal of time making systemic changes to the universal tier. Despite having the new curriculum materials and using a PLC structure to review data and discuss potential changes to instructional strategies, overall there has been no significant improvement in student outcomes. Staff members are becoming more and more frustrated because they are working hard but not seeing the improvements in student outcomes that they expected. As a result, at the end of the school year the BLT decided to prioritize a schoolwide collaborative review of universal tier practices to better understand what kinds of supports teachers require to better meet the needs of students in the universal tier. They hope to be able to answer the question "If the universal tier is not sufficient, what are the needs that must be addressed?"

The building principal worked with other members of the BLT for 1 week right after the last contract day, as well as for 3 days before the first contract day of the next school year, to prepare to dig into universal tier practices with instructional staff during the next school year. During the week after the last contract day, the BLT discussed ideas for keeping the process manageable, identified potential pitfalls and barriers to success, and came to consensus about how learning teams will work differently during the next school year, within the school's PLC structure, to spend more time digging into universal tier practices.

To accomplish these goals, the BLT decided to use the UTC-EE framework to organize the examination of universal tier practices. Next, they identified an initial set of questions for all staff members to collaboratively answer in their teacher learning teams.

Learning Targets

- To what extent is the content of the learning targets aligned with state-required academic content standards?
- To what extent have the learning targets been organized for teaching, from the beginning to the end of the school year?

Curriculum

- How aligned is the organization of the curriculum materials with the scope and sequence of learning target skills?
- What do teachers know and not know about the content and design of the curriculum materials?

Instruction

- To what extent do school personnel work to determine the need for classwide intervention?
- How much time is allocated to universal tier standards? Is it sufficient to engage all students in meaningful learning of the learning targets?
- To what extent are research-based instructional strategies and routines regularly implemented?

Assessment and Data-Based Decision Making

- To what extent have learning goals and success criteria been developed for each learning target?

The BLT also decided to use the BIP-SIT approach to identifying implementation barriers: that is, to focus on how teachers can be supported through making changes to the universal tier. Finally, the BLT located, reviewed, and selected resources from research and best practices aligned with the UTC-EE framework, such as practices guides from What Works Clearinghouse (*http://ies.ed.gov/ncee/wwc*), research and instructional resources aligned with the Common Core from Student Achievement Partners (*http://achievethecore.*

org), and *Visible Learning* by John Hattie (2009). The BLT selected those resources most directly related to the universal tier that they felt were user-friendly to be used by teacher learning teams to learn more about research-based and best practices during the next school year.

During the all-staff meeting to kick off the school year, the BLT shared with staff the overall vision and purpose for working in learning teams with the school's PLC structure to answer the question "If the universal tier is not sufficient, what needs must be addressed?" They also let staff know that the process would not be used to evaluate teachers, the role of BLT members in representing them, and that the principal was going to make sure that teachers have the support they need to meet the learning needs of 80% of their students in the universal tier, without additional interventions. After answering staff questions, they used a "fist-to-five" process and determined that over 80% of staff agreed to pursue answering this question collaboratively.

Action 5.1. Examining Universal Tier Practices

Teacher learning teams started the year discussing the purposes of the universal tier and working toward consensus regarding their beliefs about whether or not all students can learn what is defined in the grade-level Common Core ELA Standards. This included defining what the universal tier is and organizing it in terms of learning targets, curriculum, instruction, and assessment for the purposes of making data-based decisions. Meeting twice a month, the teams spent the next 2 months reviewing the resources curated by the BLT during the previous summer to develop common understanding about research-based and best practice recommendations for the universal tier.

From the end of October through the end of March, teacher learning teams collaboratively answered the questions identified by the BLT the previous summer. Teams reviewed documents and other resources together. They brought problems of practice to their learning teams to discuss and solve together. They were able to set aside a small amount of time to observe each other in the classroom to provide each feedback and help answer the questions about universal tier practices. BLT members collected the information, perspectives, and interpretations of the teacher learning teams using Form 5.1 and brought it to the whole BLT every 2 weeks. At those BLT meetings, the team interpreted that information in an ongoing way, and ultimately answered those questions (see Figure 5.1, pp. 110–111). Based on this collaborative work, the BLT identified the following areas of universal tier practice to celebrate: the time dedicated for literacy instruction and the alignment and articulation of learning targets. The BLT also prioritized the following universal tier practices for which to explore implementation barriers: alignment of curriculum materials with the learning targets, teacher knowledge of the content and design of curriculum materials, and implementation of research-based instructional strategies and routines.

Next, the building principal shared the decisions about celebrations and areas for barrier identification with all staff. Staff members celebrated their successes together and learned about the steps they would be taking to collaboratively identify implementation barriers in their learning teams. Teachers were able to ask questions, share concerns, and get clarification on the process. The main message communicated by the building principal was that the purpose of this process was to identify why some practices were not being implemented in order to determine how to best support teachers to meet the needs of their students in the universal tier.

Action 5.2. *Identifying Barriers to Universal Tier Practices*

The process of identifying and prioritizing implementation barriers occurred in teacher learning teams during April and May. The first step taken by learning teams was to learn about common implementation barriers (Table 5.7) to help them generate potential barriers for their own implementation challenges. Next, they discussed each of the prioritized implementation concerns to establish a common understanding of those concerns. Each team then generated a list of potential barriers for each of the implementation concerns. Each team then prioritized the list of potential barriers to those for which they could achieve at least 80% consensus. Those BLT members who were also on the teacher learning teams recorded this information on the Identifying and Prioritizing Implementation Barriers Worksheet (Form 5.4) and brought it back to the whole BLT.

BLT members discussed each of the identified barriers for each implementation concern and used RIOT procedures to determine if they could verify any of the prioritized barriers. They reviewed existing documents and had conversations with both building staff and central office administrators to verify and prioritize barriers. The BLT summarized the results of their work (Figure 5.2) and shared it with all staff, as well as with central office administrators, during the first week of June. These results will be used to develop an action plan for professional learning and resource allocation for the following school year.

CONCLUSION

We started this chapter by identifying the main question schools need to answer if they have an insufficient tier for students: If the universal tier is not sufficient, what are the needs that must be addressed? To pursue answers to this question, schools need to be able to identify which research-based and best practices are not in place. Once those missing practices have been identified, schools need to identify the barriers in their system, over which they have control, that are getting in the way of implementation. We have provided a structure and process for examining universal tier practices, and we have discussed common implementation barriers to those practices. Once implementation barriers have been identified, schools should prioritize those barriers to address that are most likely to result in supporting improved implementation of desired practices. This prioritized list of barriers then serves as the focus of action planning by the school that will provide the roadmap for removing barriers and improving implementation. Once barriers have been successfully removed and implementation of universal tier research-based and best practices improves, schools are much more likely to see increases in student achievement as a result of their efforts in these areas.

Key Component	Embedded Elements (Check all that apply.)	Question and Answer (From *Examining Universal Tier Practices Worksheets*)	Status (Celebration or needs improvement)	Priority Level (High, medium, low)	Notes
Curriculum	X Alignment ___ Student engagement ___ Professional learning/coaching ___ Time ___ Collaboration	Question: How aligned is the organization of the curriculum materials with the scope and sequence of learning target skills? Answer: Low	Needs improvement	High	Textbooks and supplemental materials sequenced fairly differently than learning targets for all grades but K–1.
Curriculum	___ Alignment ___ Student engagement X Professional learning/coaching ___ Time X Collaboration	Question: What do teachers know and not know about the content and design of the curriculum materials? Answer: Moderately knowledgeable of content, low knowledge of design	Needs improvement	High	Materials have been in use for 4 years and most veteran teachers know what's in them. Most teachers do not know as much as they'd like about the design. No recent professional learning on the materials.
Instruction	___ Alignment X Student engagement ___ Professional learning/coaching ___ Time X Collaboration	Question: To what extent do school personnel work to determine the need for classwide intervention? Answer: Not at all	Needs improvement	Medium	This has never been discussed as a school. Most grades in most years' universal screening data between 65 and 75% at benchmark.
Instruction	___ Alignment X Student engagement ___ Professional learning/coaching X Time ___ Collaboration	Question: How much time is allocated to the universal tier? Is it sufficient to engage all students in meaningful learning of the learning targets? Answer: 90 minutes/day for	Celebration	Low	More time might be beneficial in kindergarten.

Practice		Question / Answer	Celebration / Needs improvement	Priority	Notes
Instruction	__ Alignment __ Student engagement __ Professional learning/coaching __ Time __ Collaboration	all grade levels, sufficient for almost all grade levels. Question: *To what extent are research-based instructional strategies and routines regularly implemented?* Answer: *Unknown*	*Needs improvement*	Medium	*No applicable embedded elements.* *Discovered that teachers are generally unclear about this and there are not any processes currently in place to better understand this.*
Assessment and Data-Based Decision Making	X Alignment __ Student engagement __ Professional learning/coaching __ Time __ Collaboration	Question: *To what extent have learning goals and success criteria been developed for each learning target?* Answer: *Somewhat*	*Needs improvement*	Medium	*Learning targets for K–6 are "I can" statements, but no success criteria have been developed.*
Learning Targets	X Alignment __ Student engagement __ Professional learning/coaching __ Time __ Collaboration	Question: *To what extent is the content of the learning targets aligned with state-required academic content standards?* Answer: *Mostly*	*Celebration*	Low	*K–3 stronger alignment than 4–6. Slight adjustments needed in 4–6.*
Learning Targets	X Alignment __ Student engagement __ Professional learning/coaching __ Time __ Collaboration	Question: *To what extent have the learning targets been organized for teaching from the beginning to the end of the school year?* Answer: *Completely*	*Celebration*	Low	*Learning targets sequenced month by month for entire school year as part of curriculum mapping for grades K–6.*

FIGURE 5.1. Example of a Summary of Universal Tier Practices Worksheet for North County Elementary School.

Implementation Concerns *High-Priority Practices Needing Improvement*	Potential Barriers *Reasons for Implementation Concerns*	Verified Barriers *Use RIOT to Verify Implementation Barriers*	Priority Level *High, Medium, Low*
Alignment of curriculum materials with the learning targets	Curriculum materials adopted before learning targets developed	Curriculum materials adopted before learning targets developed	Low
	Low levels of consensus among administrators and staff to adjust curriculum materials to better align with learning targets	Neither administrators nor staff know how to increase alignment	High
	Difference in opinion about alignment between central office and teachers.		
	Neither administrators nor staff know how to increase alignment		
	Lack of sufficient funding to complete alignment work		
Teacher knowledge of the content and design of curriculum materials	Low levels of consensus among administrators and staff regarding the importance of curriculum design	Low levels of consensus among administrators and staff regarding the importance of curriculum design	High
	Difference in opinion between central office and teachers about what teachers know	Lack of adequate professional learning and coaching support for new teachers	Medium
	Lack of adequate professional learning and coaching support for new teachers		
	Lack of existing documentation that teachers could use to learn more.		
Implementation of research-based instructional strategies and routines	Low levels of consensus among administrators and staff regarding research-based instructional strategies and routines	Low levels of consensus among administrators and staff regarding research-based instructional strategies and routines	Medium
	Neither administrators nor staff knows how to determine if strategies and routines are research-based or not	Lack of adequate professional learning and coaching support for teachers	High
	Lack of adequate professional learning and coaching support for teachers		

High-priority verified barriers will be used to help develop an action plan to remove barriers and improve implementation.

FIGURE 5.2. Example of an Identifying and Prioritizing Implementation Barriers Worksheet for North County Elementary.

DISCUSSION QUESTIONS

1. How would you describe the key components of the universal tier in your school and district that can be examined for implementation fidelity?

2. How are questions developed, organized, and used to collaboratively examine implementation of effective universal tier practices? How effective is that process?

3. By what process do administrators and staff collaboratively identify barriers to implementation of effective universal tier practices? How well are the purposes and procedures of that process understood among both teachers and administrators in your school and district?

4. How are the results of identifying implementation barriers used to prepare for action planning to improve the universal tier in your school and district?

5. How is consensus established, monitored, and maintained when prioritizing areas of universal tier practice to improve?

6. How does your school and district make the process of celebrating and improving the universal tier manageable and meaningful?

Universal Tier Barrier Identification Checklist

If the universal tier is not sufficient, what needs must be addressed?

EXAMINE UNIVERSAL TIER PRACTICES

☐ Establish common understanding of the purpose and features of the universal tier.
☐ Organize the universal tier into key components.
☐ Dig into key components.
☐ Build common understanding of research-based and best practices.
☐ Collaboratively answer a small set of focused, sequentially organized questions.

IDENTIFY AND PRIORITIZE BARRIERS

☐ Prioritize missing practices for barrier identification.
☐ Learn about common implementation barriers.
☐ Gather information to identify barriers.
☐ Prioritize implementation barriers for action planning.

NEXT STEPS

☐ Share the results of the examination of universal tier practices and identification of barriers with building staff.
☐ Communicate areas of celebration and focus areas with central office stakeholders.
☐ Prepare to use information gathered to answer the question How will the needs identified in universal instruction be addressed?

POINTS TO KEEP IN MIND THROUGHOUT THE PROCESS

☐ Review tips for keeping the process manageable.
☐ Review words of caution and common pitfalls.
☐ Establish and maintain consensus on the role of collaborative teams.

Examining Universal Tier Practices Worksheet

GENERAL INFORMATION

Building Name: _____ Date(s): _____

Team Members' Names: _____

_____

Focus of Examination

Key Component: _____ Embedded Element(s): _____

Question: _____

_____

METHOD FOR EXAMINATION OF UNIVERSAL TIER PRACTICES

Sources of evidence used to answer question (check all used):   **Notes**

_____ Review of existing information

_____ Interview/conversations

_____ Observation of practice

_____ "Test"/examination of knowledge/skills

Describe how all instructional staff were involved in collaboratively answering the question: _____

_____

_____

_____

SUMMARY OF RESULTS

	Desired State *Briefly describe below; SMART goal*	**Current Reality** *Based on data collected*	**Notes**
What is the answer to the question?: ____ ____ _____	_____	_____	

Transfer results to Summary of Universal Tier Practices Worksheet (Form 5.3) for conversations about prioritizing areas for barrier identification.

_____

Summary of Universal Tier Practices Worksheet

Key Component	Embedded Elements (Check all that apply.)	Question and Answer (From Examining Universal Tier Practices Worksheets)	Status (Celebration or needs improvement)	Priority Level (High, medium, low)	Notes
Curriculum	___ Alignment ___ Student engagement ___ Professional learning/coaching ___ Time ___ Collaboration	Question: Answer:			
Instruction	___ Alignment ___ Student engagement ___ Professional learning/coaching ___ Time ___ Collaboration	Question: Answer:			
Assessment and Data-Based Decision Making	___ Alignment ___ Student engagement ___ Professional learning/coaching ___ Time ___ Collaboration	Question: Answer:			
Learning Targets	___ Alignment ___ Student engagement ___ Professional learning/coaching ___ Time ___ Collaboration	Question: Answer:			

Identifying and Prioritizing Implementation Barriers Worksheet

Implementation Concerns *High-Priority Practices Needing Improvement*	Potential Barriers *Reasons for Implementation Concerns*	Verified Barriers *Use RIOT to Verify Implementation Barriers*	Priority Level *High, Medium, Low*

High-priority verified barriers will be used to help develop an action plan to remove barriers and improve implementation.

CHAPTER 6

Action Planning to Address Barriers to Universal Tier Instruction

In the previous chapters, we presented information on learning targets, universal assessments, evaluating effectiveness of universal instruction, and identifying barriers to universal implementation. We now combine these elements to discuss how to develop an action plan to improve universal instruction. Developing action plans requires collaboration, consensus, and buy-in regarding identifying needs and developing plans to address these needs. We strongly recommend using the grade-level team or PLC framework described in Chapter 3 for developing plans. Many would agree that it is nearly impossible for one teacher to possibly possess all the knowledge, skills, time, and resources needed to ensure high levels of learning for all students. Collaborative teams have been recommended as a way to share collective knowledge and work together toward a common mission (Buffum, Mattos, & Weber, 2009). Schmoker (1996) stated that the determining factor in whether goals are met is the effectiveness of the "educational team." The key elements in collaborative teams are a focus on the end result (i.e., goals for student achievement) and data-based decision making. The combination of goals and teamwork is essential to student performance.

Throughout this book, we have suggested using an action planning process that incorporates answering the following five questions:

1. Is our universal tier instruction effective?
2. If the universal tier is not sufficient, what needs must be addressed?
3. How will the needs identified in universal instruction be addressed?
4. How will the effectiveness and efficiency of universal instruction be monitored over time?
5. Have improvements to universal instruction been effective?

Previous chapters have discussed the first two questions. This chapter focuses on the third question: How will the needs identified in universal instruction be addressed? Strategies for answering these questions are described in detail in this chapter. Finally, a case study illustrates the process of addressing questions 1–3.

DEVELOPING A PLAN
TO IMPROVE UNIVERSAL TIER INSTRUCTION

Developing a plan to address the needs identified in universal instruction requires teams to address three questions: (1) What is the goal for student proficiency?; (2) What is the plan to address the identified gap in proficiency?; and (3) How will progress toward the goal be monitored?

Goal Setting

Goal setting is important because the goals "establish clear benchmarks of progress and milestones on the improvement journey" (DuFour & Dufour, 2008, p. 159). Goals must be formulated to be specific, measurable, attainable, realistic, and time-focused. A common acronym that helps teams remember these necessary components of a good goal is *SMART* (specific, measurable, attainable, realistic, and time-focused). The SMART goal format evolved from the management field (Doran, 1981) and is commonly applied in education. Specific goals provide focus to teams and allow all team members to work together toward the same goal in an organized fashion that maximizes the probability of improved student outcomes. Measurable goals allow the grade level or building to monitor ongoing progress and adjust the action plans if the data indicate a lack of progress. Goals should be ambitious, yet realistically attainable in the time period set by the team, and they should include criteria determining success. Finally, goals should be time-focused and include the projected date of their accomplishment. Components of effective goals are described in Table 6.1.

TABLE 6.1. Components of Effective Goals

Necessary component	Example
• A *time frame* is included that specifies when the goal will be accomplished.	In *x* number of weeks or months,
• The *conditions* under which the outcome or behavior to be measured is identified.	when examining fifth-grade spring benchmark screening data,
• A *specific outcome* or behavior is described in observable and measurable terms.	The percentage of students reaching grade-level benchmark targets will increase
• A *criterion for success* is identified.	from 40% of students reaching grade-level proficiency targets to 50%.

Districts implementing an MTSS framework typically strive to maximize the percentage of students who are meeting grade-level benchmark targets, the criterion for which is typically established as at least 80% of students to be at, or above, grade-level benchmark scores. Although many districts use 80% as the criterion, it is important to note that this criterion is not empirically derived. Rather, the criterion of 80% evolved from the public health model of resource allocation and has been adopted by the education field for the pragmatic reason that most school districts do not have the resources to provide supplemental or intensive intervention to more than 20% of the student population.

Schools should begin by examining baseline data of student performance and use these data to set realistic yet ambitious goals for the school year. Many school districts use their fall screening data as baseline data so they can track progress throughout the school year. For districts that are using the 80% criterion, it is important to consider the magnitude of the problem when setting improvement goals. For example, if a seventh-grade team finds that only 35% of students reached or exceeded the fall benchmark score, setting a goal that 80% of students will reach the spring benchmark goal would likely be too ambitious. A more realistic goal may be to set a criterion of 50% of students reaching proficiency by spring. As such, the goal would be as follows: In 30 weeks, when examining seventh-grade spring benchmark data, student proficiency will increase from 35% of students meeting the spring benchmark score to 50%.

In addition to setting goals around the percent of proficient students, another appropriate goal is to increase or maintain the percent of students who stay proficient over the course of the year. In our experience, we have seen cases where 80% of students are proficient in the fall, but when proficiency is examined in the spring, fewer than 70% of students are proficient. We recommend that districts set goals that at least 95% of students who started the year proficient end the year proficient. If fewer than 95% stay proficient, a universal instruction problem may exist. Here is an example of the wording for an appropriate goal of maintaining the percentage of students who stay proficient: "By spring of 2018, when examining spring benchmark data, 95% of students who started the year on target will remain on target."

ACTION PLANNING TO ADDRESS IDENTIFIED NEEDS

Identifying a plan for improving universal instruction may be one of the hardest and most overwhelming parts of the action planning process! However, if you follow the systematic process outlined in this book, we promise the task will be much easier. In Chapter 5, we discussed how schools can identify missing universal tier practices and then identify barriers to implementing those practices. Common implementation barriers include low levels of consensus among staff to implement the practice, a lack of adequate professional learning and coaching support for teachers, a lack of access to the necessary tools to implement the practice, too many competing priorities in the school, and a lack of initial success with students when trying to implement the practice. Often, these various factors work together to form implementation barriers.

To remove barriers, we suggest using empirical research to identify policies, programs, and instructional strategies for accelerating student achievement. When buildings find that they have large numbers of students who test below grade-level expectations, classroom teachers will need to provide differentiated instruction and identify strategies that will help students to achieve more than 1 year's growth in 1 year's time. When large numbers of students are below grade level, teams may examine whether classwide interventions and instructional routines are being used. If not, these strategies should be considered.

Classwide Interventions

When large numbers of students are below grade-level standards, classroom teachers will have many students in their class who need further skill development. When more than 40% of students are performing below expectations, the most efficient way to ensure that all students receive needed assistance is through the implementation of classwide interventions. A classwide intervention is provided to an entire grade level. All students in the class receive the intervention, regardless of indication of need. Classwide intervention is different than differentiation in that it is the *addition of resources* to the universal tier and is typically focused on skills that students would have been expected to have previously mastered. Classwide intervention may need time resources and thus may require extending the literacy class period. It may be the addition of instructional strategy resources that target specific areas that are found to be lacking in current instruction. Or it may include the addition of staff resources and may, for example, decrease group size for a particular portion of instruction in order to increase student opportunities to respond. Whatever the strategy, the goal is to provide all students with an intervention that is matched to the needs of a large portion of the class.

Another component of classwide intervention is progress monitoring. Those students who are below targets on universal screening assessments are monitored frequently during a classwide intervention to ensure that they are progressing as expected. If they are already monitored as part of another intervention they receive, the students do not need to be monitored again.

A Classwide Intervention Checklist is displayed in Form 6.1. This checklist provides grade-level teams with the considerations needed to implement classwide intervention. The checklist has four sections: Data Review, Classwide Intervention Description, Evaluating Outcomes, and Next Steps. We recommend that grade-level teams use the checklist when they first implement classwide intervention.

The first consideration when implementing classwide intervention is reviewing the classwide (grade-level) data and identifying the primary area of need. For example, a kindergarten team may note that most students started school this year below targets for letter sounds. The team may decide to focus a classwide intervention on an explicit instruction routine for letter sounds, thereby targeting a specific skill that some students are lacking, while keeping the instruction accessible to all students in the grade.

After an area of focus is identified, the team describes the intervention. This approach allows the team to ensure that all teachers will implement the intervention in a similar manner. The description should be clear to all teachers.

Because evaluating the impact of the classwide intervention is important, the team will plan for this evaluation prior to implementing the intervention. This includes identifying the students who need monitored regularly and specifying how the team will evaluate the success of the classwide intervention. In most cases, teachers report that classwide intervention increases the skills of all students in the class, not just ones who began below target. In our experience, teachers also report that students who are not at risk continue to remain engaged in classwide intervention as long as all students are included and are actively engaged in explicit instruction.

Last, the team determines the next steps. For instance, we recommend that in the first week of implementation of a classwide intervention, teachers monitor the fidelity of implementation process and discuss any needed supports to improve implementation if needed. Identifying next steps prior to implementation can support both success and sustainability of the classwide intervention.

Although schools will always use their own data to choose a classwide intervention that meets their needs, two classwide interventions that have good empirical support are Peer Assisted Learning Strategies (PALS) and Classwide Peer Tutoring (CWPT). Both of these programs use peer tutoring to supplement the primary reading curriculum (Fuchs, Fuchs, Kazdan, & Allen, 1999; Mathes & Babyak, 2001). Teachers who use PALS have students work in pairs on reading activities intended to improve accuracy, fluency, and comprehension. The student pairs take turns being the tutor and tutee and engage in activities such as reading aloud, listening to the partner read, and providing feedback during structured activities. Students receiving training on describing the main idea and predicting what will happen next in the reading passage.

CWPT is an instructional model based on reciprocal peer tutoring that can be used at any grade level. Typically, students are pretested on skills that will be targeted for instruction. Following the pretest, students are paired together and then each pair is assigned to one of two teams. Students take turns tutoring each other in basic skill areas and then test each other's learning. Students are awarded points based on their activities, and points are reported to the teacher and summarized by team. The team with the most points is announced daily, with weekly reinforcement provided to the winning team.

Instructional Routines

Instructional routines provide teachers with a standardized format for teaching a particular skill (Kosanovich, 2012). They are similar to lesson plans but are flexible in that they can be used repeatedly with varying content. For example, a vocabulary instructional routine would allow a teacher to use the same evidence-based strategy for teaching new vocabulary across content areas. Instructional routines often prioritize effective instructional strategies as part of their design. For example, many instructional routines are intended to provide students with modeling, guided practice, and independent practice all in the same routine! Instructional routines are popular with teachers for several reasons. First, they require less preparation than new lesson plans, and evidence-based strategies are right at their fingertips when needed. Also, instructional routines tend to allow for multiple opportunities to respond in a brief period of time, making them efficient educational techniques that tend to be highly engaging for students. Examples of a basic instructional routine and a vocabulary instructional routine are displayed in Figures 6.1 and 6.2.

Although classwide interventions and instructional routines are good places to start, teachers and teams often want more detail on what specific instructional strategies work best to accelerate student achievement. In his seminal book, Hattie (2009) conducted a meta-analysis on over 800 meta-analyses relating to student achievement. Hattie's goal was to find out what works best in accelerating student achievement. He argued that most everything we do in education has some type of effect on student achievement, and that the most important task is to identify those policies, procedures, and practices that have large effects on student achievement. Hattie organized the results of the meta-analysis around a statistic called an effect size (d). An effect size compares how much larger the gains of one group is compared to the gains of another group. An effect size of $d = 1.0$ means that student learning is increased by one standard deviation and is typically associated with increasing student achievement by 2–3 years in 1 year's time. Hattie (2009) classified effect sizes above 0.40 as the "zone of desired effects." The typical effect of 1 year of schooling has effect sizes between 0.15 and 0.40. As a result, he argued that if we want to close the achievement gap with some students, then we have to identify practices that will result in more than a year's worth of learning in a year's time. Ideally, if we can identify practices with high effect sizes (e.g., the zone of desired effects), we have a much higher likelihood of increasing the learning rigor for all students and closing the achievement gap between at-risk students and their peers.

Hattie categorized the variables impacting student achievement according to whether they were specific to the (1) student, (2) home, (3) school, (4) teacher, (5) curriculum, or (6) teaching. Of the top 10 variables with the highest effect on student achievement, six were related to teaching practices, two to the student, and two to the school. These results are very powerful in that they should convey to educators that there are many factors within

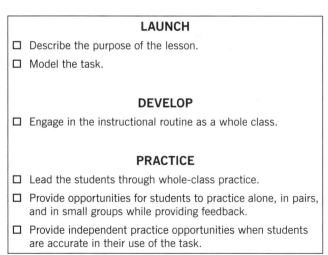

FIGURE 6.1. Example of a generic instructional routine.

LAUNCH	
Lesson Part	**Sample Script**
Describe the purpose of the lesson.	Today we will learn about the word *apprehensive*. We will discuss what it means and how it is used in writing.
Model the task. a. Say the word. b. Engage students. c. Use the word in a sentence. d. Define the word. e. Give other examples.	a. The word is *apprehensive*. b. Say the word with me: *Apprehensive*. c. Nora was apprehensive about her first day in a new school. d. Apprehensive means fearful or anxious. e. Let's think about other times people may be apprehensive. Some people are apprehensive when going to the dentist. Others are apprehensive around big dogs.

DEVELOP	
Lesson Part	**Sample Script**

Engage in the instructional routine as a whole group.
 	
a. Say the word with the students.
b. Engage the students in defining the meaning of the word.
c. Engage in whole-class practice of the word. Practice at least three times.
	a. Say the word apprehensive with me: *Apprehensive*.
	b. What word means fearful or anxious? *Apprehensive*. Yes. The word *apprehensive* means fearful or anxious.
	c. Let's answer some questions together.
	  i. Might you be apprehensive if you were lost? Yes.
	  ii. Might you be apprehensive to go to the library? No.
	  iii. Might you be apprehensive to get a shot at the doctor's office? Yes.

PRACTICE	
Lesson Part	**Sample Script**

Lead the students through whole-class practice.
 	
a. Say the word with the students.
b. Engage the students in defining the meaning of the word.
c. Engage in practice of the word. Practice at least three times.
	a. Say the word apprehensive with me: *Apprehensive*.
	b. What word means fearful or anxious? *Apprehensive*. Yes. The word *apprehensive* means fearful or anxious.
	c. Tell me if these sentences use the word apprehensive correctly.
	  i. Molly is apprehensive about flying on a plane alone for the first time. Yes.
	  ii. Sean is apprehensive about eating his favorite flavor of ice cream. No.
	  iii. Dominick is apprehensive about the science test tomorrow. Yes.

Provide opportunities for students to practice alone, in pairs, and in small groups while providing feedback.	**Sample Practice Activities** *Writing Practice* • Finish this sentence: I am apprehensive when _____. Write the sentence. • Tell the sentence to your partner. • Call on one or two students to share their sentences. *Partner Practice* • Turn to your partner. Partner number 1 will define the word *apprehensive*. Partner number 2 will use the word *apprehensive* correctly in a sentence. • Now switch. Partner number 2 will define the word *apprehensive*. Partner number 1 will use the word *apprehensive* in a sentence.
Provide independent practice opportunities when students are accurate in their performance on the task.	**Sample Independent Practice Opportunities** • Write three sentences about a time you were apprehensive. • Ask a friend or family member about something that makes him or her apprehensive. Finish this sentence: My _____ gets apprehensive when _____.

FIGURE 6.2. Example of a vocabulary instructional routine.

the control of teachers that will accelerate learning. Rather than focusing on factors that are outside of the control of educators (e.g., student's home life, socioeconomic status, student personality, family structure), we should be focus on the things that we can change during the course of the school day: teaching, curriculum, school, and teacher variables.

What Doesn't Work?

Before we review the research on strategies that were found to accelerate student growth, we think it is worthwhile to review practices that have been found to be ineffective in that area. We encourage grade-level teams to take an inventory of programs and practices at their grade level and review whether there are some that can be abandoned for more effective practices. Although there are many practices that do not produce a significant impact on student achievement, there are practices that have resulted in reverse effects or negative effect sizes. A negative effect sizes means that not only did the program, practice, or policy *not* improve student achievement, it made it worse! In his meta-analytic research, Hattie (2009) identified five practices that resulted in reverse effects on student achievement: (1) summer vacation, (2) welfare policies, (3), retention, (4) television, and (5) student mobility. We briefly review these five practices in the next sections and advise districts to review their policies and programs in these areas, where applicable.

Summer Vacation

Most school districts in our country operate on a schedule that allows a large break in the summer months. This summer break was originally established to accommodate the needs of agricultural communities. With substantial nationwide shifts in agricultural practices, many school policymakers are challenging the need for these long summer breaks when only about 3% of U.S. citizens' livelihoods are linked to agriculture (Cooper, Nye, Charlton, Lindsay, & Greathouse, 1996). Hattie (2009) found the largest loss in achievement over the summer was in the area of math ($d = -0.14$) followed by reading and language ($d = -0.05$). The implications of these findings suggest that districts may want to consider providing summer programming for at-risk students and/or providing data to teachers in the beginning of the school year about their students' levels of proficiency, based on prior-year data. Perhaps if teachers can provide a high level of differentiation and skill instruction based on data, the first month of school could be focused on recoupment of lost skills in an efficient manner.

Welfare Policies

Although meta-analyses studying the impact of welfare on student achievement have found negative effects (Gennetian et al., 2004), this is an area that is not within the control of educators. Hattie (2009) found only one meta-analysis comprised of eight studies; he concluded that "there are other more powerful effects on achievement than the welfare status of the family" (p. 64).

Retention

Retention is the practice of having students repeat a grade level. Proponents of retention assume that having a student repeat a grade will allow him or her to learn more and to fill skill gaps. Unfortunately, most students who are retained experience the same curriculum presented in the same manner; nearly all the studies examining retention have concluded that it is not an effective practice (Hattie, 2009). Not only do students who are retained do more poorly in the future, but also they are at significant risk of dropping out of school. House (1989) concluded that it would be very hard to find another educational practice that has so much empirical evidence supporting poor outcomes. We encourage school districts to reexamine retention policies and move toward abandoning this practice! Some states have even *mandated* retention policies (Iowa Early Literacy Law, 2010). In these cases, it is imperative that districts implement an MTSS framework to catch problems early and reduce the number of students retained.

Television

Studies focusing on the impact of television on student achievement have found a negative effect ($d = -0.18$; Hattie, 2009). The results of recent meta-analyses suggest negative effect sizes for more than 10 hours per week of television watching. Razel (2001) found that younger children can watch more television with no negative effects, but children age 7 should watch no more than 1 hour, and students age 17 should not watch any television. Similar to the areas of student mobility and social welfare policies, schools do not have control over the amount of television children watch at home. However, they can share this information with parents in a variety of ways (e.g., conferences, websites, newsletters) to help parents understand the impact. In addition, it is important to note that the research summarized around television does not include time spent on devices and social media.

Student Mobility

Student mobility refers to students who move across schools multiple times in their school career. In the United States, as many as 20% of students change their residences each year, and this mobility produces a negative effect on achievement (Hattie, 2009). Interestingly, other researchers have reported that an important aspect of mobility is its impact on friendships, particularly friendships that support learning (Galton & Willcocks, 1983). Others have noted that a key factor in successful transition after a move is whether the child makes a friend in the first month of school (Pratt & George, 2005). Although schools do not have control over whether students and their families move, they do have control over setting up screening systems that track student mobility and flag students who have mobility issues as at risk. In addition, schools should have "new student" procedures in place to help these youngsters make friends and feel welcomed. Other practices with low effect sizes are summarized in Table 6.2.

TABLE 6.2. Teaching, School, and Curricular Practices with Low Effect Sizes

Instructional practice	Domain	Effect size (d)
Open versus traditional schools	School	0.01
Student control over learning	Teaching	0.04
Multiage classes	School	0.04
Whole-language programs	Curriculum	0.06
Perceptual–motor programs	Curriculum	0.08
Out-of-school curricula experiences	School	0.09
Distance education	Teaching	0.09
Teacher knowledge of subject matter	Teacher	0.09
Teacher training	Teacher	0.11
Diet	Student	0.12
Gender	Student	0.12
Ability grouping	School	0.12

Note. Data from Hattie (2009).

What Works?: Instructional Strategies Related to the Curriculum for Teachers

When reviewing Hattie's (2009) findings, we highly recommend focusing on those factors that educators can realistically influence or control. Hattie found a number of practices with high effect sizes that building leadership and grade-level teams should review to determine if they are part of the instructional repertoires of teachers in the building. A summary of teacher and curricular practices with effect sizes above 0.66 are summarized in Table 6.3 and should be examined along with the hypothesis developed for why universal instruction is insufficient. These practices, which are described in more detail in the next section, can form the basis for the plan that is developed to improve universal instruction.

Formative Evaluation

Formative evaluation involves collecting assessment information while instruction is occurring and using this information to address any weaknesses in that instruction. As a major component of the MTSS framework, formative evaluation has an effect size of 0.90 (Hattie, 2009). Building leadership and grade-level teams should begin by reflecting on whether teachers in the building regularly collect formative assessment data to guide their decisions in the classroom with all students. Next, they need to examine whether formative evaluation (i.e., progress monitoring) procedures are in place for all students receiving supplementation and intensive intervention. If not, this would be an excellent area on which to focus,

TABLE 6.3. Teaching, School, and Curricular Practices with High Effect Sizes

Instructional practice	Domain	Effect size (d)	Description
Formative evaluation	Teaching	0.90	Data used to inform instruction.
Micro-teaching	Teacher	0.88	Analysis, reflective teaching, and videotaped role play with debriefing.
Acceleration	School	0.88	Accelerating students through the curricula.
Comprehensive interventions for students who are learning disabled	Teaching	0.77	Teachers who use a combined approach of direct instruction and strategy instruction model for students with leaning disabilities.
Teacher clarity	Teacher	0.75	Teachers who organize their instruction by providing clear explanations, examples and non-examples, and guided practice; and by assessing student learning.
Reciprocal teaching	Teaching	0.74	Teachers who use an instructional process to teach students cognitive strategies that lead to increased reading comprehension.
Feedback	Teaching	0.73	Teachers seeking feedback about what students know and understand, where they make errors, when they have misconceptions, and when they are not engaged.
Teacher–student relationship	Teacher	0.72	Teachers who establish positive relationships with their students by providing empathy, conveying warmth of personality, encouraging higher-order thinking, providing encouragement, and displaying genuineness.
Spaced versus mass practice	Teaching	0.71	Distributed practice and review over time.
Metacognitive strategies	Teaching	0.69	Teaching students to apply a strategy to solve a problem and to self-monitor the use of the strategy.
Vocabulary programs	Curriculum	0.67	Explicit teaching of vocabulary by providing both definitional and contextual information, involving students in deeper processing, and providing students with many exposures to the words.
Repeated reading programs	Curriculum	0.67	Having students with at least 95% accuracy reread short and meaningful passages until a satisfactory level of fluency is reached.

Note. Data from Hattie (2009).

as the general education teacher can also review progress monitoring data and use these to determine the amount of differentiated instruction needed during universal instruction.

Teacher Clarity

Teacher clarity refers to a composite of qualities in teachers who organize their instruction by providing clear explanations, examples and non-examples, and guided practice and who frequently assess student learning. In other words, degree of teacher clarity reflects how well teachers convey to students specifically what is expected and how to accomplish the desired task. Teacher clarify has an effect size of 0.75 (Hattie, 2009). Chapter 2 emphasized the importance of learning targets. In fact, teacher clarity relates to learning targets because it is a measure of how well teachers communicate the intention of each lesson and how they measure student learning to evaluate the impact of their instruction.

Feedback

Another teaching practice with a high effect size is feedback ($d = 0.73$; Hattie, 2009). When asked to define feedback, many teachers will indicate that *feedback* refers to the information and observations teachers make to students. In fact, Hattie (2009) found the opposite to be true. The most important aspect of feedback was teachers' attention and their willingness to seek feedback from their students about what the students know and understand, where they have misconceptions, and when they are not engaged. Feedback from teacher to student should be immediate and should address the exact steps the student needs to correct. For example, if a teacher provided written feedback on a student essay, saying only "Needs improvement" or simply put a letter grade on the essay, the student would not know *what* needed to be improved to meet expectations. Many teachers have begun to use rubrics to clearly define expectations for satisfactory work products. Research has also shown that positive feedback shapes behavior better than negative feedback. For every negative or corrective feedback statement given to students, there should be five positive statements (Bickford, 2012).

Positive Relationships

Many have argued that positive teacher–student relationships are critical for student learning to occur. With an effect size of 0.72 (Hattie, 2009), it is apparent that it is an essential element for engaged learning. Some of the variables found to relate to positive teacher–student relationships are high levels of empathy, conveying warmth of personality, encouraging higher-order thinking, providing encouragement, and displaying genuineness. We encourage teachers to reflect on the following questions:

- How do teachers in your district connect with students who display challenging behaviors?
- How do teachers in your district connect with students who lack motivation?

- How do teachers in your district connect with students who are very shy and withdrawn?
- How do teachers in your district connect with students from different ethnic backgrounds?

Teams can discuss these questions and work together to identify strategies for improvement!

Spaced Practice

Distributed practice and review over time (i.e., spaced practice) were found to have an effect size of 0.71 (Hattie, 2009). Spaced practice is in contrast to mass practice, wherein students practice a skill at one time or study by "cramming" the night before a test. When students are in the acquisition phase of learning, they need a number of deliberate practice opportunities followed by corrective feedback (Walker, Greenwood, Hart, & Carta, 1994). Nuthall (2005) asserted that students need at least three to four exposures to learning over several days for acquisition to occur. Repeated exposure and practice allow students to develop automaticity, and once automaticity or fluency is reached, retention of material is improved. Teachers should reflect on the amount of deliberate practice and exposure to new material over time they provide to their students and build in daily cumulative reviews to their lessons.

Metacognitive Strategies

The use of metacognitive strategies has an effect size of 0.69 (Hattie, 2009). *Metacognition* refers to the practice of thinking about one's thinking. In the school context, it also refers to a student's ability to plan his or her thinking. Examples of metacognitive strategies include (but are not limited to) the use of advance organizers, engaging in comprehension monitoring tasks, making outlines to assist with writing, checking work before handing it in to the teacher, taking notes, and verbalizing the steps to solve problems. Teachers can model metacognition by using a "think-aloud" approach, in which they describe to students how they are thinking—that is, how they are engaging in certain learning or study behaviors. The most important consideration for teachers is that the variety of metacognitive strategies used within a lesson appears to be a powerful factor. Collaborative teams are encouraged to review the metacognitive strategies currently used (or not used) at their grade level and discuss how these strategies can be used consistently across the grade level to support learning.

Vocabulary Instruction

Hattie (2009) found that students who received vocabulary instruction showed major improvements in reading comprehension and overall reading skills, with an effect size of 0.67. The most effective vocabulary instruction includes providing both definitional and contextual information, involving students in deeper processing, and providing students with more than one or two exposures to the word to be learned. Effective vocabulary instruction starts with a student-friendly definition that is simple and clear. Then time is spent practicing use of the word in rich and wide examples. In addition, Feldman and Kinsella (2005) identified six components of effective vocabulary instruction: (1) an advance organizer, (2) a consistent instructional process, (3) well-organized instruction, (4) time dedicated to important words, (5) visual representations of the words being taught, and (6) a written record. These effective elements of vocabulary instruction are in stark contrast to typical vocabulary instruction, in which students identify bolded words in a chapter, looking up the word, writing the definition, and using the word in a sentence. This technique does not involve explicit teacher-directed instruction or involve students in deep processing.

Reciprocal Teaching

Palinscar and Brown developed a type of peer tutoring in the 1980s called *reciprocal teaching*. Hattie (2009) reviewed meta-analytic research on reciprocal teaching and found an effect size of 0.74. The approach is an instructional process to teach students cognitive strategies that lead to improved learning outcomes. Students take turn being the "teacher" and work on strategies such as summarizing, questioning, clarifying, and predicting. Students check their understanding of content by generating questions and summarizing. Reciprocal teaching is similar to peer tutoring methods in that they improve student engagement connected to classroom instruction (Brown-Chidsey & Bickford, 2015). In order for this strategy to be effective, teachers must ensure that students have been trained on how to use the steps in reciprocal teaching. Teachers should conduct frequent fidelity or spot checks to ensure that the procedure is implemented correctly.

Micro-teaching

When using micro-teaching, teachers record their lessons and then view the recorded lessons and debrief with a mentor or evaluator. Micro-teaching may also involve having an instructional coach observe short lessons and give feedback to the teacher. The goal is to improve the teaching and learning experience by having teachers reflect on their teaching and make changes in instruction to improve student learning and engagement. This technique allows teachers to see what worked, which aspects have fallen short, and to identify what needs to be done to enhance their teaching practice. Hattie (2009) reported four meta-analyses on micro-teaching with an effect size of 0.88.

Repeated Reading

Repeated reading was first identified as an effective intervention to increase reading fluency in 1979 (Samuels, 1979). Since that time, many studies have continued to demonstrate the effectiveness of this intervention for increasing fluency. Students reread short passages on which they are at least 95% accurate until a satisfactory level of fluency is reached. Larger effects were found when students were timed than when students were untimed. Repeated reading produces effects both on reading comprehension as well as reading fluency. The most important caveat to repeated reading is that students must read text in which they are at least 95% accurate. If repeated reading is conducted on passages for which students are below 95% accurate, fluency will not improve because students will spend time practicing errors. Hattie (2009) found an effect size of 0.67 for repeated reading interventions.

Differentiated Instruction

Numerous articles have been written promoting the use of differentiation as a way to address the multiple levels of learning and student needs with which teachers are faced in the classroom today (Bender, 2005). *Differentiated instruction* is a term that is widely used but often is not clearly defined, resulting in confusion over what the term really means. When teachers are asked what the term means, a common response is that it means working in groups. Although instructional grouping is certainly a key consideration in differentiation, it also involves changing content, process, and product based on student needs and interests (Tomlinson, 1999). Differentiated instruction provides a variety of ways to meet student needs and allow each student to meet the learning target. Differentiation means doing whatever it takes to maximize instruction over what could otherwise be achieved through whole-class, one-size-fits-all approaches. It means identifying ways in which students learn best, rather than presenting material and documenting students' success (or lack thereof) with it (Wormeli, 2006). The term *zone of proximal development* (Vygotsky, 1978) is often used as an argument that students learn best when they are taught at an instructional level that is slightly higher than the level they are functioning at. Differentiation allows teachers to provide appropriate challenges for students to help them grow at each stage of their development. While individualization is occasionally used in differentiated classes, it's more common to find students grouped and regrouped flexibly.

Instructional grouping is a way that some teachers have attempted to address the "zone of proximal development." When choosing a grouping option, there are pros and cons related to effectiveness of instruction, and two important factors must be considered. First, the instructional level of every student needs to be considered to determine the extent to which he or she is receiving instruction that is within the zone of proximal development. Second, the amount of engaged learning needs to be considered. Students who spend large portions of time in independent or center-based work may not receive the desired level of teacher-directed instruction, thus impacting their level of engaged learning.

There are three common ways in which teachers typically approach grouping: (1) whole-class instruction, (2) grouping within a class, and (3) flexible grouping across classrooms. The traditional model of schooling involves whole-class instruction. Under this model, the teacher usually teaches to the "middle" of the instructional range in the class. As a result, some students are not challenged because the instruction is below their instructional level, typically resulting in boredom, whereas other students are too challenged because the instruction is above their instructional level, often resulting in frustration. Both of these groups of students may be at risk for lower levels of academic engagement due to the mismatch between their instructional level and the level of instruction being provided.

Teachers who do within-class grouping are able to maximize the instructional levels of their students. For example, a teacher who had established three instructional groups within the class would be able to teach each group within its instructional level, but each of the groups would need to work independently about two-thirds of the time. There is a high probability that students would spend too much unengaged and/or off-task time, especially students who need the most teacher-directed instruction to progress. One way to counteract this problem is to add in instructional help (e.g., paraprofessionals, specialists) so that both the amount of teacher-directed instruction and engaged time are maximized.

A third option is flexible achievement grouping across classrooms. Flexible instructional groups are formed based on student need, such as students' instructional programs, the levels of instruction, the amount of time each student needs, and the student–teacher ratio needed (Howe, Scierka, Gibbons, & Silberglitt, 2003). Groups change regularly based on the same variables. No student is left in a group after the group is no longer appropriate for that student. Grade-level teams collaborate to determine groups and make decisions about students entering and exiting groups based on data. This type of grouping maximizes teaching to the instructional level of every student and results in maximized engaged time. In order for this type of grouping to work, common scheduling needs to occur. For example, all first-grade teachers may agree to teach reading from 9:30 to 11:00 each morning, and math from 12:30 to 1:30 each afternoon. Setting up a schedule such as this for all grades requires some planning and coordination with regard to lunch/recess and special class schedules, but is entirely feasible within the context of a typical school schedule. In addition, we encourage principals to schedule basic skill instruction at different times *across* grade levels. There are two primary benefits to this type of grade-level scheduling. First, it is possible that teachers may opt to create flexible instructional groups that are different from initial classroom assignments. Second, it allows building-level resources to be concentrated at each grade level during the most opportune times each day.

Differentiation at the Secondary Level

The National Research Council conducted a synthesis of the research on factors critical to student learning in history, mathematics, and science and found three principles of sound instruction: (1) understanding students' initial level of knowledge and anticipating their misconceptions, (2) developing a solid foundation of factual knowledge, and (3) teaching for metacognition so they can be active learners (National Research Council, 2004). These instructional practices involve a number of approaches, including formative and summative assessments, scaffolding curriculum, and flexible grouping practices to tailor instruction, similar to content in previous sections. At the secondary level, differentiation begins with consideration of the demands of the curriculum and what methods of instruction will be used to deliver the content. A summary of reflective questions teachers can ask about curriculum, presentation of material, and the ways in which students acquire knowledge is provided in Table 6.4. Through a process of planning instruction using reflective inquiry, secondary content-area teachers can design engaging and effective lessons for their students.

TABLE 6.4. Reflective Questions for Teachers to Consider across Domains

Domain	Questions
Curriculum	• What are the standards and goals for this unit? • What are my students' interests and talents? • What important background knowledge do my students possess? • What misconceptions are my students likely to have?
Instructional delivery	• How will I provide a range of materials? • In what ways can students show me that they have learned the content?
Student acquisition of knowledge	• Where are the opportunities for students to work collaboratively? • How will I use metacognitive strategies to promote deeper learning?

THE INSTRUCTIONAL HIERARCHY

Although Hattie (2009) identified several instructional practices that have high effects on student achievement, a key issue remains on how to design instruction in relation to student needs. The *instructional hierarchy* is "a way of understanding the 'order of operations' that teachers should follow when teaching specific content" (Brown-Chidsey & Bickford, 2015, p. 153). This hierarchy is based on research that demonstrates how students move through predictable stages of learning. Think about playing a musical instrument. Most people do not instantly start playing Mozart on the piano. Instead, they learn to play notes and simple songs. They practice simple notes over and over until the process becomes automatic, and then they move to the next progression. Learning anything requires a stepwise progression for students to attain mastery. Haring and Eaton (1978) were the first to operationalize the instructional hierarchy and proposed four stages: (1) acquisition, (2) fluency, (3) generalization, and (4) adaptation.

Acquisition marks the first stage when initial learning begins. Students learn the most basic steps of the overall skill, with ample teacher modeling and feedback to students. Students typically need repetition to acquire new skills. Once students have acquired a new skill, they need to practice the skill so that it becomes automatic. Practice needs to take place with materials at the students' current skill level. If the material is too hard, students will become discouraged, disengaged, and likely give up. If the material is too easy, students will become bored and disengaged. There is a great deal of research emphasizing the importance of matching materials to the students' instructional levels during the fluency stage (e.g., Jimerson, Burns, & VanDerHeyden, 2007). Once fluency is achieved, the next step is to help students generalize what they have learned to other settings. If students are able to read out of the basal reader but cannot read from other materials or in different settings, generalization has not occurred. Although generalization seems to be a natural next stage, it is actually very difficult to achieve without explicit planning and teaching for it (Brown-Chidsey & Bickford, 2016). Teachers facilitate generalization when they set up their instruction to have students apply what they are learning in new situations. In the last stage of adaptation, students change some feature of a skill to make it work in a new situation.

Not all students reach this stage, but it is important for teachers to set adaptation ability as a goal. In summary, using effective instructional strategies *and* having an understanding of the where each student is positioned in the instructional hierarchy are critical to ensure success.

Putting It All Together

This section has summarized several high-impact instructional strategies that can be used to increase student achievement. Although it is easy to become overwhelmed by all of these strategies, there is a straightforward way to proceed: We recommend that teachers conduct an inventory of instructional practices used within the school and at various grade levels. The items on this inventory or list can then be compared to the strategies presented in this chapter and used to facilitate discussion on strategies to target and prioritize as well as strategies that can be abandoned. A form to guide teams through discussion around effective universal instruction considerations is found in Form 6.2. These strategies and practice form the basis for the plan. The next step is to determine how the effectiveness and efficiency of universal instruction will be monitored.

HOW WILL THE EFFECTIVENESS AND EFFICIENCY OF UNIVERSAL INSTRUCTION BE MONITORED?

Once a goal is clearly defined and strategies have been selected for the improvement plan, teams need to determine how to monitor progress toward their goals and how to evaluate whether the action plan is being implemented with fidelity. When monitoring progress, teams are encouraged to reflect on the data that were used to identify the problem and use the same information to monitor progress toward the system goal of improving universal instruction. Thus, if teams used data from the building screening process to validate the problem, then we suggest that teams continue to use data from the screening process to monitor progress. If 35% of students were at or above the fall screening benchmark target, and a team set a goal that 50% of students would be at or above the spring screening benchmark target, then the team would use the percentage of students at the benchmark target to monitor progress.

ACTION PLAN FORMAT

Once decisions are made regarding any needed changes to the universal tier, the team should document the plan and decide upon the specific logistics of implementation. A suggested action plan format is included in Form 6.3. In addition to the specific changes, the action plan should include anything that is being given up due to the change, the staff member in charge of ensuring the changes take place, timelines for each action, and the monitoring strategy for each action (discussed in more detail in Chapter 7).

CASE IN POINT

To illustrate the process of action planning described above, we use a case study to outline the action planning steps. Happy Valley Elementary School has been implementing an MTSS framework for the several years. As a result, they screen students three times per year in the areas of reading and math. As part of the building's continual improvement process, the BLT review the screening data for each grade level in the spring. They found that 51% of students were below the benchmark target in the spring of first grade on CBM-R. They worked with the first-grade team to develop an action plan for improvement.

Step 1: Is Universal Instruction Sufficient?

The first-grade team begins by meeting to review their spring screening data. They determine that only 49% of students are reading 70 words per minute or greater. The district uses the target of 70 words correct per minute because this target has predictive validity with the statewide accountability tests administered in third grade. The team concludes that a problem exists with universal instruction because only 49% of students have reached the spring target, compared to the expectation that 80% will reach the spring target.

Step 2: Why Is Universal Instruction Insufficient?

The team explores a variety of hypotheses in the areas of curriculum, instruction, environment, and organization. They review the screening data from kindergarten of the previous year and find a similar pattern that only 40% of current first-grade students had reached the spring target for letter–sound fluency when they were in kindergarten. The first-grade team examines its reading curriculum and finds that it is well aligned with state reading standards and has empirical research support. However, the teachers question whether there is enough instructional time allocated. The current time allocation of 90 minutes includes language arts instruction. They also determine that each of the four first-grade teachers is using a combination of whole-class instruction with three or four small skill groups within each classroom. The team hypothesizes that students are not receiving enough teacher-directed instruction during the reading block and that the amount of total instructional time for the reading block is insufficient. In addition, the team hypothesizes that the beginning reading instruction that occurs during the kindergarten year needs to be examined to determine why so many students are entering first-grade below target.

Step 3: How Will the Needs Identified within Universal Tier Instruction Be Addressed?

The team begins by setting a goal that 65% of students will reach the spring benchmark target. Next, the team develops a plan to address the needs identified in the universal instruction. First, the team members work with their building principal to increase the reading block from 90 to 120 minutes per day. Second, they agree that the first 20 minutes of each day will be spent implementing a classwide peer-tutoring program (e.g., PALS). They identify a training plan for their own professional learning on the program and the procedures needed to train their classes on the procedure. Third, they develop a flexible grouping model across the four, first-grade classrooms. They decide to use the fall screening data in conjunction with other data sources to group students according to need. It is determined that the teacher who works with the students who have the most needs will have additional resources in the classroom, including "push-in" special education services and paraprofessional support. Finally, the team recommends joint planning with the kindergarten teachers to examine the vertical alignment between kindergarten and first-grade curriculum.

Step 4: How Will the Effectiveness and Efficiency of Universal Tier Instruction Be Monitored over Time?

For each instructional strategy proposed, the team develops a clear plan that identifies the resources needed to implement the plan along with timelines for review. Team members work with the building principal to receive training and coaching on the PALS program. Regular fidelity checks are completed to ensure that the program is being implemented correctly. Grade-level team meetings are scheduled on a weekly basis. The team meets after the fall screening period to establish flexible instructional groups. Subsequent meetings are spent reviewing student assessment data to determine movement between groups and to review PALS implementation data. Team meeting agendas and notes are shared with the building principal to keep her informed of progress. The team meets shortly after the winter benchmark screening period and finds that 58% of students have reached the proficiency target for that benchmark period. They conclude that they are on track to reach their spring goal!

Step 5: Have Improvements to Universal Tier Instruction Been Effective?

The team meets after the spring benchmark screening period and find that 63% of students met the spring proficiency target. Although the goal was 65%, the team is encouraged by the percent increase from fall to spring, and decides to maintain the plan for another year. There has also been substantial work done with the vertical alignment of kindergarten and first-grade curriculum, so the hope is that this work will increase the percent of students who enter first grade meeting the fall proficiency targets.

CONCLUSION

Identifying and addressing barriers to effective universal instruction can be a challenging and overwhelming task. This chapter emphasized the use of collaborative grade-level teams to make this task easier and more efficient by asking and answering five foundational questions. A review of research-based instructional strategies and practices was included to assist teams in developing hypotheses in the areas of curriculum, instruction, environment, and organization. Although this process can be challenging to undertake, it is *essential work* that must be completed if schools want to improve outcomes for *all* students and be able to intervene effectively with a manageable number of students in need of supplemental and/or intensive instruction.

DISCUSSION QUESTIONS

1. How aligned are your building's current instructional practices and programs with empirical research?

2. What ideas do you have about how universal instruction could be improved in your content area or grade level?

3. How will you prioritize your ideas?

4. How will you work to ensure consistency and buy-in of universal tier strategies at your grade level or within your building?

5. How will you evaluate fidelity of universal instructional practices?

Classwide Intervention Checklist

DATA REVIEW

☐ What data indicate a need for classwide intervention?

☐ What do screening data indicate regarding the primary area of need (e.g., fluency, phonemic awareness, math facts, behavior)?

CLASSWIDE INTERVENTION DESCRIPTION

☐ What is the name of the classwide intervention that will be used?

☐ Describe the intervention. How will it look when teachers implement the classwide intervention?

☐ When will the classwide intervention be implemented (time of day)?

☐ How often will the classwide intervention be implemented (e.g., daily, twice a week)?

EVALUATING OUTCOMES

☐ How will we monitor progress for students who are below targets at the start of the classwide intervention?

☐ When will we examine student outcomes to determine the success of the classwide intervention?

☐ How long do we plan to implement the classwide intervention before deciding next steps?

NEXT STEPS

☐ Do all teachers know how to implement the classwide intervention?

☐ Will we check fidelity of implementation? If so, how?

☐ How will we provide teachers with support as needed?

Universal Instruction Checklist for Action Planning

Universal Instruction	Not in Place	Limited Practice	Partially Implemented	Well Established
1. All **universal curriculum materials** are research-based for the target population of learners (including subgroups).				
2. There are clear, high-quality universal curricula in academic and social behavior areas, implemented with **well-defined scope and sequence** plans across grades.				
3. Staff can articulate information and factors they consider when adopting **culturally and linguistically relevant** universal instructional practices and assessments.				
4. The **teaching and learning objectives** are well articulated from one grade to another and within grade levels so that students have similar experiences regardless of teacher.				
5. Teachers are **well trained** to implement universal curricula.				
6. Curricula and instruction are differentiated based on student needs.				
7. Ongoing work to **align** the universal curricula with state standards is evident.				
8. Universal **screening results are linked** to ongoing discussions about high-quality universal curriculum for academics <u>and</u> social behavior.				
9. The district has a plan for systematically evaluating the **fidelity** of universal curriculum implementation on a regular basis and addressing deficiencies.				
10. Systematic **evaluation of the effectiveness** of universal instruction for both all students and subgroups of students is conducted on a regular basis, based on data from multiple measures.				

(continued)

Universal Instruction	Not in Place	Limited Practice	Partially Implemented	Well Established
11. Teachers are knowledgeable about and implement principles of **effective instruction** (e.g., high rates of engagement, opportunities to respond, immediate error corrections).				
12. Teachers are knowledgeable about and implement research-based principles for effective instruction in **basic skill areas** (reading, writing, math).				
13. Teachers understand how to embed basic skills instruction within **content-area classes,** and do this regularly.				
14. The school provides **enrichment opportunities** for students exceeding benchmarks at all grade levels.				

Comments:

Universal Instruction Action Plan

Area of Need	Identified Barriers	Actions to Address Barrier	Lead for Next Steps	Timeline

CHAPTER 7

Implementing Universal Tier Improvements

Systems-level change is complicated and rarely implemented without challenges. BLTs develop action plans that, for a variety of reasons, are unable to be implemented as intended. This chapter is designed to provide support to schools when implementing improvements to the universal tier. We describe the processes and considerations for answering the question How will the effectiveness of universal tier improvements be monitored over time? The action plan drives the identification of improvements to the universal tier, which then needs to be monitored (see Figures 7.1 and 7.2 for examples of building-level and district-level action plans, respectively). It is important to include this implementation monitoring because items discussed during action planning are often more difficult to implement than the team originally anticipated. Strategies for monitoring implementation are discussed in this chapter. In addition, we discuss ways to identify barriers if issues exist with fidelity of implementation. Last, teaming opportunities that may be utilized during implementation are outlined. A checklist for conducting action plan implementation monitoring is provided in Form 7.1.

Several tools related to monitoring the implementation of the universal tier (Algozzine et al., 2014; St. Martin, Nantais, & Harms, 2015; St. Martin, Nantais, Harms, & Huth, 2015) are available. In addition to using published monitoring tools for overall MTSS implementation, we encourage schools to specifically monitor those changes being implemented. For instance, if a schedule change is being implemented, we recommend conducting observations of literacy instruction in order to monitor the specific implementation of that schedule change. In this chapter we first address monitoring implementation of school action plans to improve the universal tier. Then we provide considerations for using established implementation monitoring tools.

Action	Grade(s)	Person Responsible	Completion Date	Follow-Up Method	Notes
Lengthen reading instruction from 75 to 100 min. per day.	K–3	Principal	Start of third trimester	Observe Interview teachers	
Implement a new vocabulary teaching routine.	K–3	GLT leaders	Oct. 1st	Observe Review information	
All kindergarten classrooms will teach literacy from 9:30 to 11:00 each morning.	K	Principal	First day of school	Observe Review Information	
Sustained silent reading will be removed from universal instruction.	2–3	GLT leaders	Sept. 16th	None needed	Replace with fluency routine (teacher's choice)
Fluency routine will be implemented as part of universal instruction.	2–3	GLT leaders	Sept. 16th	Observe	
Classwide intervention in phonemic awareness will be implemented in all kindergarten classrooms.	K	MTSS building lead	Within 1 week from today	Observe Interview teachers	

FIGURE 7.1. Example of a universal instruction building-level action plan. GLT, grade-level team.

Action	Building	Person Responsible	Completion Date	Follow-Up Method	Notes
Lengthen reading instruction from 75 to 100 min. per day.	Elementary	Principal	Start of third trimester		
BLTs include action plan review on all meeting agendas.	All	Principals	Summer BLT retreat		
BLTs participate in common learning regarding MTSS implementation and sustainability.	All	Curriculum Director	August		
District leadership team reviews progress on building-level action plans.	All	Principals	Sept. 15th		
BLTs will implement data review days three times per year.	All	MTSS building leads	Oct. 15th		
Resource allocation for universal instruction priorities will be decided.	All	Superintendent	July 1st	Allocations communicated to all principals.	Data discussed during June administrator retreat.

FIGURE 7.2. Example of a universal instruction district-level action plan.

WHAT IS IMPLEMENTATION EVALUATION?

Implementation evaluation, also known as *implementation fidelity,* specifically examines what is currently being implemented and is an important and often forgotten form of evaluation. As opposed to considering the outcomes of instruction, implementation monitoring considers how changes were implemented, leading to information regarding additional system supports that may be needed to reach the desired state of universal tier improvements. Collecting fidelity of implementation information is important because, without it, teams will not know whether lack of improvement is related to a particular improvement strategy or is a result of an improvement strategy not being implemented as intended. Having information about fidelity of implementation leads to more helpful and effective discussion and formulation of next steps.

SUPPORTING ACTION PLAN IMPLEMENTATION

Implementing change requires ongoing, focused support. When implementing changes to the universal tier, we recommend providing a structure that includes the following components: vision, resources, data, and accountability. Providing vision involves ensuring that all staff members understand the need to make improvements to the universal tier. Although they may not all agree that this would be their first choice of action plans to implement, they agree to willingly implement the change and are given opportunities to discuss the reasons the BLT recommends these changes.

When all staff understands the need for the proposed action plan changes, the BLT ensures that necessary resources are allocated toward implementing the change. For instance, if the schedule is changed and teachers are allocated more time each day to devote to literacy instruction, they must also have opportunities to engage in specific conversations about how to modify other scheduled subjects that are now given less time and about which specific strategies to use during the additional literacy time. An action plan is a necessary resource with which to implement change, but it will not be put into place until all staff has the necessary resources to support successful implementation.

Most of this chapter discusses the process of collecting and analyzing implementation data. We often consider student data when making changes, but it is essential that we also collect data on our implementation to best utilize resources to support the change. These data will inform the leadership team when additional vision discussions, resource allocation, and accountability are needed.

Accountability is essential to ensuring that any action plan is implemented. Without accountability in place, other activities will take priority for some staff. This does not mean that staff members are attempting to sabotage the change. It simply means that people tend to spend more time doing those things for which there is accountability, as well as those things that are more preferred activities. For example, for many people, an accountability buddy is an essential part of a workout plan. When skipping workouts, most people are not actively thinking about how they don't want to be in shape. They simply are choosing either a more preferred activity (sleeping in) or an activity for which they are held accountable (staying late at work). The same is true for staff in schools. Needing accountability as a component of an action is not a sign that staff lacks motivation. It is simply a necessary support for implementing complex change.

When providing vision for the plan and resources to implement changes, BLTs can anticipate the action plans to be implemented. Holding staff accountable for making the changes is necessary, as is collecting data on those changes taking place. That data collection can be completed through varying types of information, described in detail in upcoming sections.

IMPLEMENTATION OF FIDELITY DATA

There are two types of fidelity data: component fidelity and session fidelity (Lane, Bocian, MacMillan, & Gresham, 2004). Monitoring the implementation of the key components of the improvement strategy is referred to as *component fidelity*. For instance, group responding may be identified as a key component of a vocabulary routine. When monitoring the fidelity of implementation of that routine, the school would want to ensure that each teacher implementing the routine elicits group responding.

The second type of fidelity, session fidelity, is used to monitor the dosage provided of the improvement strategy. Monitoring session fidelity can be as simple as monitoring the key components across several days or by checking the duration or frequency with which the improvement strategy is implemented. Session fidelity is an often-overlooked component of implementation, but is as important as component fidelity. If the improvement strategy is implemented exactly as planned but only half as often, outcomes would likely be substantially different than expected if the dosage of the improvement strategy were higher. We recommend that teams develop checklists to use when monitoring both types of implementation fidelity. These checklists can then be used with any of the implementation collection methods described later in this chapter.

CHECKLISTS TO MONITOR

When developing the implementation checklist, schools will need to distinguish between checklists to monitor specific instructional strategies and those designed to monitor other types of changes, such as the length of the literacy period. Here, we provide two generic checklists for teams to use. The first is designed to evaluate the basic implementation of the universal tier—to see if an adequate amount of time is provided to each and every student in universal tier instruction. It is often a necessary, but not sufficient, first step in monitoring implementation of the universal tier. The second checklist specifically monitors the changes the school has identified through the processes described in this book.

Session Fidelity Checklist

Form 7.2 provides an example of a checklist designed to monitor session fidelity of a literacy period by identifying if all students are receiving access to universal tier instruction. The first two items in the form provide information about how much instruction students are receiving. If a teacher or grade level experiences frequent interruptions that result in starting the literacy period late or ending early, teams will want to provide support.

The third item allows the team to identify if scheduling has resulted in some students missing teacher-directed literacy instruction. If a student's time with a speech–language pathologist overlaps with large-group reading instruction, that student does not have access to the universal tier. If a student who has an individualized education program with a reading goal around decoding skills misses the small-group instruction focused on comprehension skills because of the special education schedule, the student may be missing critical universal tier instruction. This item provides information to ensure that all students have access to the universal tier.

The final item helps teams to identify any instructional gaps. If the school has a weekly early dismissal to allow for teacher collaborative learning and the literacy period is always shortened on those days, over the course of a year the missed instructional time could accumulate to a large amount of time! On most days this item, "Shortened school day contains at least 90 minutes of literacy instruction," would be marked as N/A and removed from any calculations. It will only be used on shortened school days.

This checklist can be implemented in multiple ways. It may be used to design questions for teacher or student interviews. It could also be used during an observation of instruction or for a teacher log. Later in this chapter we discuss considerations for choosing how to collect implementation information.

After completion, this checklist is totaled to identify the percentage of universal tier implementation that is taking place. It will not inform the team about the instruction occurring during universal tier instruction but is often a necessary first step in determining that all students have access to an adequate dosage of universal tier instruction.

Example of a Completed Session Fidelity Checklist

Figure 7.3 depicts an example of a completed session fidelity checklist. In the example, the items were implemented 4 out of 5 days. The third item, including all students in teacher-directed instruction, was not implemented at all throughout the week, suggesting a more persistent lack of implementation. Taken together, this information suggests potential areas of focus for the BLT to address the gaps in availability of universal tier instruction to all students.

Action Plan Fidelity Checklists

When making changes to the universal tier, schools will also want to know if those key components in the action plan were implemented as intended. Form 7.3 provides a check-

Teacher: Ms. Jackson   Grade: 2nd

Week: 10/15–10/19

Monitoring Type (T. Int., T. Log, Obs., Review): *Observation*

	Mon.	Tues.	Wed.	Thurs.	Fri.	Total
1. Literacy period begins on time.	Yes	Yes	Yes	No	Yes	4/5
2. Literacy period lasts the expected duration.	No	Yes	Yes	Yes	Yes	4/5
3. All students participate in the teacher-directed instructional opportunities.	No	No	No	No	No	0/5
4. Shortened school day contains at least 90 minutes of literacy instruction.	N/A	N/A	N/A	N/A	N/A	N/A
Total	1/3	2/3	2/3	1/3	2/3	

Notes: The Title 1 teachers came and removed four children during the whole-class instruction portion of the literacy period. Additionally, the speech–language pathologist removed two children during their small-group instruction during the literacy period.

FIGURE 7.3. Example of a completed Implementation Checklist for Literacy Period.

list schools can use to monitor the implementation of these action plan changes. This form allows schools to analyze both the adherence to expected implementation (component fidelity) and that adherence over time (session fidelity).

METHODS OF EVALUATING UNIVERSAL TIER IMPROVEMENTS

When evaluating implementation, many schools think about evaluating specific instructional strategies. Although this is important, each action plan item should be evaluated in some way. Depending on the action's complexity, the method for monitoring will change. For instance, scheduling and communicating a data review meeting may need no additional implementation check other than if it occurred. However, implementation of a classwide intervention into all kindergarten classrooms will be more challenging to monitor.

Evaluating the implementation of universal tier improvements can be completed in multiple ways (Gresham, 1989). The most common methods include interviewing teachers and students, observing universal tier instruction, teacher logs, and reviewing existing information.

Interviewing Teachers

Teacher interviews can be used to determine the changes that have been made in universal tier implementation. Interviews are semistructured in nature to ensure that consistent information is garnered, to be used later by the leadership team. When interviewing teachers, it is highly recommended that open-ended questions be used. The action plan should serve as a guide for developing the questions. For example, if the action plan indicated that shortened school days due to professional learning meetings or weather-related delays would not impact the length of the literacy period, an interview question for teachers may be, "What time was your literacy period during last week's snow delay?" Table 7.1 provides examples and non-examples of potential teacher interview questions based on sample actions identified in an action plan.

Interviewing Students

Student interviews are valuable for multiple reasons. First, they can provide evidence of how students interpreted the experience the teacher was attempting to create. Second, student interviews allow for comparing information with other forms of data collected. For instance, when implementing schoolwide expectations, a handful of students are often asked, "What are the expectations at our school?" The answers to this question allow teams to examine if the goal of instruction has been achieved.

Observing Instruction

Observing instruction is the most valid way of ensuring that action plan changes have been implemented. Observations allow teams to see both the change as well as the environment

TABLE 7.1. Examples and Non-Examples of Teacher Interview Questions

Action	Example of teacher interview questions	Non-example of teacher interview questions
Lengthen reading instruction from 75 to 100 minutes per day.	• What time were you able to start your reading period yesterday? • What time did you transition to a different subject?	• How long is your reading period each day?
Implement a new vocabulary teaching routine.	• Tell me about your lesson plans for teaching vocabulary words this week.	• Did you use the vocabulary routine when you taught vocabulary last week?
Reinforce students' adherence to school expectations by using the schoolwide system.	• What did you give Tiger tickets for in your second-period class today? • How many Tiger tickets did you distribute during your homeroom today?	• Do you use Tiger tickets when students follow school expectations?

in which the change occurred. Before observations can be completed, the BLT creates an observation protocol using the action plan. Some examples of observation items to verify (or not) the implementation of specific actions are included in Table 7.2.

Teacher Logs

Individual teachers can use checklists, when organized in a clear manner, to log their implementation of universal tier instruction. To complete the log, the teacher would have the checklist close by during instruction and would check off the components either during or immediately after the instructional period. The timing of the completion is important. Logs should not be completed in retrospect, as we may not remember the answers to each of the questions explicitly. For example, if asked in retrospect when an instructional topic ended, a teacher may not have looked up at the clock to see when she transitioned to the next subject, and any data collected would likely just reflect the times on the class schedule. However, if the teacher documents the time the lesson is completed in the log immediately, she will note the exact time the instruction ended on that day. Teacher logs are rather simple to implement and can provide useful data, given that they are used during instruction, as opposed to as a reflection tool later in the day.

Reviewing Existing Information

Existing information is sometimes the quickest way to examine implementation of changes. With many evidence-based universal tier programs, student materials provide an account of implementation. Existing student materials can reveal which components were implemented, the pace at which they were implemented (e.g., at least five lessons a week), and which students had access to the instruction. The BLT will identify the components that all teachers are expected to implement. For instance, if the basal series has "optional" activities that we decided all classrooms would implement this year, those activities would be included as a key component for review.

TABLE 7.2. Observation Protocol Example Items

Action	Question to answer	Example
Implement a new vocabulary teaching routine.	• Is each key component of the routine being taught?	• Observe during literacy instructional time with a checklist of each of the key components of the routine and check off those that are present.
All kindergarten classrooms will teach literacy from 9:30 to 11:00 each morning.	• Is literacy taught at the same time of day in each section of K? • Is the literacy block 90 minutes long?	• Complete walkthroughs throughout this period of the day to check that literacy is the subject of instruction. • Observe classrooms briefly from 9:30 to 9:45, then again from 10:45 to 11:00, to monitor duration of literacy instruction.

When the school does not have an evidence-based, published program, reviewing existing information is still recommended. In this situation, the team will identify the common elements in the instruction of the subject and the existing products that demonstrate those elements. For example, if daily student paragraph writing is expected in every core content area in the middle school, teachers could bring samples of writing from a specific day to a grade-level team meeting.

With or without evidence-based universal tier programs, the key elements of the action plan will be examined to identify potential existing information. The key to selecting existing information is to choose that which will provide information about important actions that are deemed critical to the successful implementation of the universal tier. Maximizing that selection process and minimizing the collection of every existing piece of information are crucial to avoid fatigue.

Finally, existing information can often be combined with other methods of collecting implementation information. For instance, if a teacher's initials are on each PBIS ticket she distributes, the team may ask during an interview why the number of PBIS tickets she has given out has increased significantly recently. Or, we may have a teacher's plan for using a vocabulary routine during a specific unit with us during a lesson observation.

SELECTING IMPLEMENTATION METHODS

Although none of these methods may indicate if all changes to implementation of the universal tier were made, a combination of one or more may provide satisfactory information for the leadership team to decide whether improvements were implemented adequately. The BLT will use components of the action plan to determine the method to use and how to collect the information. The team must also consider what resources are available with which to collect implementation information. Although interviewing teachers is likely the simplest method to use, it is also the least reliable of methods. Observing instruction is often the most valid method to use, but it is also the most resource-intensive. Table 7.3 provides considerations and examples to aid in selecting and combining implementation evaluation methods.

SETTING AN IMPLEMENTATION EXPECTATION

After a method for monitoring implementation is selected and checklists of key components to monitor are developed, the team needs to set an implementation expectation. That is, the team needs to determine what amount of implementation demonstrates that the practice is indeed being implemented. A common implementation expectation is 80% (Arkoosh et al., 2007). This criterion presumes that if a practice is implemented most of the time, it is likely to be enough to have the intended impact, if it is a successful practice. Although we typically want to set expectations at 100%, it is not always realistic to expect 100% implementation. There are sometimes events beyond our control that impact implementation.

TABLE 7.3. Considerations for Selecting an Implementation Evaluation Method

Action	Question to answer	Method
Implement a new vocabulary teaching routine.	• Is each key component of the routine being taught?	• Observe.
	• Is the routine being used by all teachers each week?	• Review vocabulary lesson plans.
All kindergarten classrooms will teach literacy from 9:30 to 11:00 each morning.	• Is literacy taught at the same time of day in each section of K?	• Observe.
	• Is the literacy block 90 minutes long?	• Observe.
	• Does the schedule conflict with the ability to implement this practice?	• Review building master schedule.
Reinforce students' adherence to school expectations by using the schoolwide system.	• How many Tiger tickets are teachers distributing?	• Review tickets redeemed by teacher.
	• Do students know why they receive Tiger tickets?	• Interview students.
	• Are teachers distributing Tiger tickets for correct behaviors?	• Interview teachers.

Hopefully, our improvement strategies are robust enough to be effective with less than 100% implementation fidelity.

ANALYZING IMPLEMENTATION INFORMATION

One way in which many schools choose to hold implementation conversations is through the regular BLT and district leadership team meeting structures. Each team meeting should include a time to review progress on action plan items. Those staff members responsible for implementing each change report on progress toward implementation. In order to make this a sustainable and feasible process to implement, we recommend the following actions to support this work. First, team agendas should include the review of action plan progress. When the teams meet each month, progress on action plan items are discussed. Any items that teachers and other staff are struggling to implement can be problem-solved during this time. It is possible that additional support to get progress moving on an action item may be needed, and the team members can problem-solve those needs together. Second, we recommend that teams celebrate completed action items together. Making universal tier improvements is not the most exciting work in a school, so celebrating progress and successes along the way is essential to maintaining momentum and motivation to engage in this work.

Implementation information is analyzed in order to identify any grade levels and classrooms that may need additional support to implement changes to the universal tier. Implementation checklists make the analysis of implementation information rather simple.

By determining if there are concerns with implementation at any level, including individual classrooms, each grade level, and across the building, teams can prioritize resources to support greater implementation of universal tier improvement efforts. The BLT is responsible for organizing and summarizing implementation information. Then the team examines the data and identifies any gaps between expected actions to be implemented and what the collected information suggests is actually being implemented. When gaps are identified, the team then determines if the implementation is not occurring at a classroom, grade, or building-wide level. Depending on the level of the concern, implementation may be supported in different ways.

SUPPORTING IMPROVED IMPLEMENTATION

More often than not, at least one component of the action plan may need additional support to be implemented as intended. When this is the case, it is essential to identify the pervasiveness of the lack of fidelity in order to determine the appropriate support. If the fidelity is low in only one or two classrooms, individual support will likely be the most efficient and effective method. This level of support is often provided via a team leader or an instructional coach. However, if the lack of fidelity is found across an entire grade level or more, it is likely a concern that should be addressed by a grade-level team or an entire staff. In this case, additional learning and discussion should determine why the practices are not being implemented as intended and the barriers addressed as a system, as opposed to one by one.

INSTRUCTIONAL COACH SUPPORTS

When supporting an individual teacher to implement a change, an instructional coach may be selected to provide that support. At the grade level, the grade-level team may focus on the action for a period of time. At the building level, professional learning time, grade-level team time, and the instructional coach support may all focus on the actions identified for improved implementation. Each of these methods of supporting implementation will be used based upon the level of implementation that is of concern. For example, if data suggest that implementation of a change is occurring in most grade levels but a specific grade level is struggling, support should extend only to that grade level. Carefully planning the allocation of supports allows the school to efficiently use limited professional learning resources and to target supports for teachers in a similar manner that resources are targeted in an MTSS framework for students.

Essential Components of Support for Improved Implementation

It is essential that these supports meet several criteria in order for them to be effective both in the short and long term. First, the support offered must not be communicated as evaluative or punitive in nature. Just as an intervention with an individual student is intended to be short term and nonpunitive, additional resources for a team member are intended to provide support to help her successfully attain building goals.

Support must also be focused and intentional. If an individual teacher needs to work with an instructional coach because the duration of his reading period is too brief, the focus of the work needs to be on that concern. If he tries to change the focus to writing instruction, or if the coach modifies the focus to a new strategy she learned, the goal of the coaching is likely to be missed. These modifications in coaching goals are more common than you may expect and greatly dilute the potential benefits and power of instructional coaching. Table 7.4 shows examples of common uses of instructional coaches, contrasted with more powerful uses of coaching resources.

EXAMINING MTSS IMPLEMENTATION

In addition to monitoring implementation of the building-specific action plan, many schools choose to also monitor implementation of their overall MTSS framework. This implementation evaluation is more general in nature than the monitoring of specific action plan items. When schools are monitoring their overall implementation of the universal tier, we recommend utilizing one of several validated tools (Algozzine et al., 2014; St. Martin, Nantais, & Harms, 2015; St. Martin, Nantais, Harms, & Huth, 2015). These tools can serve schools in multiple ways. First, they allow BLTs to examine the implementation of the universal tier compared to recognized standards. These tools also support BLTs to have conversations regarding implementation that they may not have without such a tool. Comparisons of growth in universal tier implementation are also supported through the use of implementation monitoring tools. Most importantly, these tools can be used to set priorities for universal tier improvements and the work of coaches in the building. A checklist is provided in Form 7.4 to assist teams in evaluating their MTSS system implementation.

TABLE 7.4. Common versus Recommended Uses of Instruction Coaches

Common use	Supporting implementation use
The teacher contacts the coach when support is needed.	The coach has a schedule of working with specific teachers and grade levels.
The coach works on practices that are requested by the teacher.	The coach focuses on the school improvement efforts that have been prioritized by the BLT.
The coach spends most of his or her time meeting and talking with teachers and grade-level teams.	The coach spends time observing and modeling classroom instruction. Conversations may support these efforts, but do not replace observation and modeling.
The primary data used during one-to-one and grade-level instruction are teacher anecdotes about implementing a strategy.	Student data and implementation data are used during each reflection conversation.

When BLTs use these tools, it is important that they understand that setting priorities and providing a comparison to implementation of recognized MTSS standards are the reasons the measures are being utilized. We have seen teams become defensive in this context because some of the practices that are being evaluated with the tools were never practices that the BLT had focused on implementing. In other words, the team members felt they were being evaluated on something they were never expected to implement. However, when the team goes into the implementation evaluation process knowing that they are learning about these standards for implementation of MTSS and are using the tool as a way to set priorities for their building action plan, the process can be powerful!

COMPONENTS OF MTSS IMPLEMENTATION MONITORING

When monitoring implementation of MTSS universal tier supports, schools consider multiple supports for engaging in a change process. MTSS universal tier implementation monitoring often considers the following variables, discussed in more detail in the following sections: leadership team, infrastructure, implementation, and evaluation.

Leadership Team

The leadership team is a crucial component to implementation of any system change, especially those changes that require a modification in practice for all instructional staff. Because of that central leadership role, universal tier implementation tools often examine the functioning of the BLT. Having a team that meets regularly, has appropriate representation, and operates with efficient and effective processes will best support change within the building. When leadership teams have little vision for the purpose, lack consistent meeting structure, or lack an ability to make decisions, team members appear resistant to change. This barrier should be addressed directly when identified.

Infrastructure

Having an infrastructure that supports universal tier improvement is essential to changes. MTSS requires that a school function as a system, as opposed to separate classrooms that all operate as their own individual educational kingdoms. When infrastructure for an effective universal tier is not implemented in a planful and systemic manner, frustration and confusion can occur within staff, and implementation will suffer. For example, if a new teaching routine is expected to be used as part of an action plan to improve the universal tier, but teachers receive minimal training on the routine and no follow-up conversation occurs, teachers will likely be confused and/or frustrated when attempting to implement the routine.

Implementation

Implementation of evidence-based practices is also monitored via implementation monitoring tools. Implementing curricular materials with fidelity, providing adequate knowledge of pedagogy and content to teachers, and providing professional learning related to implementation of universal tier improvements are all essential components of MTSS universal tier improvements, and BLTs will want to monitor these infrastructure components regularly.

Evaluation

Evaluation, discussed in more detail in the next chapter, is another essential component of an MTSS framework. When monitoring implementation, both evaluation practices and the infrastructure to support them are considered. These include having agendas to support grade-level teams in conducting regular evaluation, system-level evaluation considerations, and leadership use of evaluation in planning and decision making.

CHALLENGES TO MONITORING IMPLEMENTATION EFFORTS

Ensuring successful implementation is not a task without challenges. If staff members are not used to having discussions and expectations around new practices, they may feel that these implementation efforts are evaluative in nature. That is, of course, not the intention. Based on our work in implementation efforts, we have some recommendations for supporting teachers during these changes.

Explain the Rationale

Before adding implementation evaluation to your practices and action plans, discuss why this component is important to your school improvement efforts, and give teachers a chance to engage in some discussion and planning. This effort may include using a staff meeting to explain that, in order to ensure that everything is done to increase student achievement at the trajectory intended, it is important to monitor both student learning and implementation of the changes in the action plan. Including an analogy in the explanation is often helpful when discussing implementation evaluation. Popular ones include brushing daily and the dentist office visit, or a blueprint and a house remodel. This dual-focused monitoring will help to identify areas in which support is needed as well as ensure that if the leadership team has identified a practice that is too difficult to implement, teachers will have a mechanism to engage in that discussion. Emphasize that the information is not being used for staff evaluation purposes and will be paired with student outcome data to determine next steps in school improvement.

Pair Implementation with Outcome

When presenting implementation information to staff, always pair implementation and outcome data. This dual emphasis takes the focus away from solely discussing what a teacher may or may not have done. Instead, it focuses on practices that were implemented and their impact on student learning. We have found that teachers engage easily in this conversation without feeling threatened or guarded. When presenting implementation information alone, teachers (everyone, really) are more likely to focus on the barriers they face in implementation, rather than confront the conversation as a problem-solving one. Keeping the focus on the fact that these changes in practice are solely for the purpose of improving student learning is more likely to result in productive conversations and openness to change.

Be Flexible

The leadership team will decide how implementation information is gathered for each practice. However, there may be times when it is difficult to gather the information in the manner you would most like. This may be because of a staff member's schedule, or because a building teacher-leader is uncomfortable collecting information in the manner first identified. In these cases, we recommend being flexible about how the information is collected. Be willing to modify the plan if the person collecting the information identifies another manner that the data could be collected. What is important here is that the information gathered represents an accurate picture of implementation, not that it was collected using a certain method, such as observation. A teacher on your BLT may initially feel more comfortable having a conversation with a teacher (teacher interview) about a lesson plan (review existing information) then he may be in observing the lesson. Both methods could use the same checklist of critical components that could be checked off either during the observation or during the discussion. Over time, as teachers learn that these implementation checks are not a threat to them, they should be willing and able to complete them in any way designed. In the beginning, though, we encourage you to be flexible with those BLT members who are more comfortable with collecting the information in one way versus another.

TEAMING OPPORTUNITIES

During implementation, both grade- and building-level teams have responsibilities for monitoring action plan implementation and outcomes. Although each team will monitor different components of implementation, communication and collaboration regarding implementation are critical throughout universal tier improvement efforts.

Grade-Level Teams

Grade-level teams are responsible for ensuring that any grade-level improvement activities are implemented. Team members meet at least once per month to consider data relating to universal tier improvements. For example, if a specific writing routine for teaching text summarization was an action for the grade level to implement, team members will bring student work samples and data about student performance after using the routine. The team will then use these data to analyze student performance and discuss implementation questions.

Grade-level teams also support implementation by serving a problem-solving function when barriers to implementation begin to arise. If a team member is struggling with implementing the summarization routine, the grade-level team can provide ideas, feedback, and modeling to support the team member. These just-in-time learning opportunities are critical for sustainable change implementation.

Building-Level Teams

Responsibilities of BLTs during implementation are twofold. First, they ensure that implementation is monitored and that those data are examined. Second, they monitor the overall plan for the identification and problem solving of any barriers.

BLTs arrange for the monitoring of actions on the building-level plan. They then analyze the information to determine if implementation is on track and to allocate resources if implementation is not on track. They monitor the overall plan to proactively remove barriers that arise. For example, a building's action plan indicated that the fourth-grade literacy block should last at least 110 minutes a day. The team interviews the fourth-grade teachers as part of implementation monitoring and discovers that during the early dismissal day that occurs once per week, the grade-level team decided to teach for only 50 minutes. The BLT will need to work with the fourth-grade team to identify the barrier to implementing the full instructional period and provide supports to administer the necessary change.

The BLT also monitors implementation by considering overall universal tier MTSS implementation. This work includes regularly and systematically applying a framework for MTSS implementation, specifically focused on universal tier implementation. This practice allows the team to celebrate areas of improvement as well as to plan for future areas of need.

CASE IN POINT

Empowered Elementary School staff has identified several improvements both to their behavior and to their reading universal tier instruction:

1. Schedule monthly BLT meetings.
2. Implement K literacy instruction for at least 90 minutes per day.
3. Implement a main idea comprehension routine in third grade.
4. Review building expectations in each setting once per month.
5. Ensure that teachers are rewarding appropriate student behavior with tickets.

The BLT knows that they will not be able to adequately gauge the reasons for either their improvements or lack of improvements unless they have implementation information. They also believe it is important to provide staff with additional support to implement when needed, so they decide to collect fidelity information on their changes.

First, the team identifies the key components of their universal tier improvement efforts. These are outlined in Form 7.5. Notice that some improvements can be monitored quickly and easily, whereas others have more key components to be implemented with fidelity.

After key components are identified, the team decides the best methods for monitoring fidelity for each improvement. Figure 7.4 shows their decisions. The BLT discusses the monitoring plans with each grade-level team, and data are collected as intended. The team discusses the information and prioritizes three implementation areas that need further support. They then discuss potential supports for each of the implementation concerns, identifying a combination of some individual and some group supports. The first prioritized area is the increase in the time spent in literacy instruction in kindergarten. The kindergarten literacy instruction is being implemented only between 70 and 80 minutes a day, depending on the classroom. This means in 1 week, students are receiving between 50 and 100 fewer minutes of reading instruction than intended. The building principal met with the grade-level team and asked about the reasons behind not meeting the literacy expectation. Two

Improvement Strategies	Method for Monitoring
1. Schedule monthly BLT meetings.	
At least nine meetings throughout the school year are scheduled by September 1st.	Review existing meeting schedule information.
2. Implement K literacy instruction for at least 90 minutes per day.	
Each K teacher implements at least 90 minutes of literacy instruction per day.	Classroom observation of the beginning and ending time of literacy instruction. Teacher interviews during grade-level team meetings.
3. Implement a main-idea comprehension routine in third grade.	
Materials are ready.	Classroom observation using a checklist with all components of the routine. Teacher log using a checklist with all components of the routine.
Routine instruction lasts 15 minutes.	
Reason for the routine is discussed.	
Each step in the routine is followed.	
Students have time to practice.	
When needed, error corrections are immediate.	
Pacing of the routine is adequate to keep students engaged.	
4. Review building expectations in each setting once per month.	
Each teacher reviews expectations in each setting each month.	Review teacher lesson plans. Conduct teacher interviews during grade-level team meetings.
5. Ensure that teachers are reinforcing student behavior.	
Each teacher, in all grade levels, distributes at least 10 tickets per day.	Review ticket activity of each teacher.
Teachers inform students why they are receiving the ticket, including naming the expectation the students exhibited.	Conduct student interviews regarding reasons they earned tickets.

FIGURE 7.4. Exquisite Elementary School's implementation fidelity monitoring methods.

primary reasons emerged. Some teachers were counting some free playtime as literacy time because they encouraged communication and language practice during that time. Once they understood that these 90 minutes are those that are guaranteed for each student, they realized that they cannot ensure that all students will practice their language and communication skills during free play and switched their schedules to include additional literacy time within the school day. Other teachers indicated that they thought that 90 minutes was developmentally inappropriate for kindergarten students. The principal assured the teachers that this was not only developmentally appropriate, but evidence-based and provided access to professional articles that supported this time parameter. She also then met with the instructional coach and the teachers to discuss some developmentally appropriate, evidence-based activities that would teach the kindergarten standards as well as keep the young students active and engaged.

Second, although most third-grade teachers were implementing the comprehension routine with fidelity, one was struggling to follow each step in the routine and allow enough practice for students. The BLT decided that the instructional coach would meet individually with the teacher and review the routine, answering any questions he has. Then the teacher and coach would decide if the coach would model, and then observe, the teacher using the routine or simply observe the teacher using the routine. Then the coach would provide feedback about the implementation of the routine. This observation and feedback would continue until weekly observations revealed sufficient implementation for 3 weeks in a row.

Last, one kindergarten, two first-, two third-, and all fourth-grade-level teachers were not reviewing building expectations with students regularly. Because this is a more global implementation need, a staff meeting will be devoted to teachers' sharing and generating ideas for regularly reviewing building expectations with students. Teachers with low implementation will be encouraged to obtain support from the instructional coach if needed, but will not be required to consult with the coach as long as future teacher logs indicate that they are reviewing building expectations monthly with fidelity. After identifying these supports, the team continues to meet regularly to discuss any additional needs, and, more importantly, to review the outcomes of these improvement efforts in the coming months.

CONCLUSION

When implementing complex changes, schools cannot rely on the plan to be followed without regular monitoring and problem solving. Intentional monitoring and data-based conversations need to occur in an ongoing manner to support teachers and building leaders. These efforts include gathering objective data about the implementation of the universal tier changes the team decided to enact. These may be collected through interviews, observations, or teacher logs. Additionally, thoughtful planning and a willingness to admit when that planning fails are critical to continuous improvement. Providing support and data-based resource allocation during the implementation of change is critical to sustained improvement.

DISCUSSION QUESTIONS

1. In what ways have expectations for implementation been monitored in the past (either for individual intervention plans or for other instructional changes)?

2. Why is it important to monitor the implementation of changes?

3. What are ways in which all leadership team members can access the most recent action plans?

4. Who is responsible for ensuring that actions on action plans are implemented as designed?

5. When are action plans updated and monitored for implementation?

6. How will you explain the importance of monitoring implementation to other teachers in your building?

7. How do you ensure that staff has the skills to implement effective instructional strategies? Do you have instructional coaches in your building? If so, how are they used?

Action Plan Checklist

How will the effectiveness of universal tier improvements be monitored over time?

DATA COLLECTION AND REVIEW

☐ What changes need to be monitored?
☐ How will we monitor them?
    ☐ Interviewing teachers
    ☐ Interviewing students
    ☐ Observing universal tier instruction
    ☐ Teacher logs
    ☐ Reviewing existing information
☐ What will we evaluate?
    ☐ Will we consider component fidelity?
    ☐ Will we consider session fidelity?
☐ Were changes implemented as intended?
    ☐ If not, which changes were not implemented to an acceptable level?

NEXT STEPS

☐ Are there practices that are not implemented by more than one or two staff that need whole-staff support?
☐ Are there practices that need support for only one or two staff?
☐ How will we provide support as needed?

Implementation Checklist for a Literacy Period

Teacher: _____   Grade: _____

Week: _____

Monitoring Type (T. Int., T. Log, Obs., Review): _____

	Mon.	Tues.	Wed.	Thurs.	Fri.	**Total**
1. Literacy period begins on time.						
2. Literacy period lasts the expected duration.						
3. All students participate in the teacher-directed instructional opportunities.						
4. Shortened school day contains at least 90 minutes of literacy instruction.						
Total						

Notes: _____

_____

_____

_____

_____

_____

_____

_____

_____

_____

_____

_____

_____

_____

_____

_____

Implementation Checklist for Action Plan Changes

Teacher: _____ Grade: _____

Week: _____

Monitoring Type: _____

	Mon.	Tues.	Wed.	Thurs.	Fri.	**Total**
All materials prepared and used						
Duration						
Key component						
Key component						
Key component						
Key component						
Key component						
Key component						
Key component						
Total						

MTSS Implementation Checklist

How will the effectiveness of universal tier improvements be monitored over time?

DATA COLLECTION AND REVIEW

- ☐ Choose tool to monitor overall MTSS implementation.
- ☐ Communicate reason for implementation check to all building staff.
- ☐ Complete the implementation review as a BLT.
- ☐ Discuss the MTSS implementation information.
    - ☐ Identify celebrations.
    - ☐ Identify areas for prioritized focus.
    - ☐ Identify focus areas for instructional coaches.

NEXT STEPS

- ☐ Share the results of the MTSS implementation evaluation with building staff.
- ☐ Communicate celebrations and focus areas with central office stakeholders.
- ☐ Plan for support for areas of improvement.
    - ☐ Add any needed items to the building action plan.

Checklist for Key Components of Universal Tier Improvement

1. Schedule monthly BLT meetings.

☐ At least nine meetings throughout the school year are scheduled by September 1st.

2. Implement K literacy instruction for at least 90 minutes per day.

☐ Each K teacher implements at least 90 minutes of literacy instruction per day.

3. Implement a main-idea comprehension routine in third grade.

☐ Materials are ready.
☐ Routine instruction lasts for 15 minutes.
☐ Reason for the routine is discussed.
☐ Each step in the routine is followed.
☐ Students have time to practice.
☐ When needed, error corrections are immediate.
☐ Pacing of the routine is adequate to keep students engaged.

4. Review building expectations in each setting once per month.

☐ Each teacher reviews expectations in each setting each month.

5. Ensure that teachers are reinforcing student behavior.

☐ Each teacher, in all grade levels, distributes at least 10 tickets per day.
☐ Teachers inform students why they are receiving the ticket, including naming the expectation the student exhibited.

CHAPTER 8

Evaluating Core Improvement Efforts

Throughout the book, we have described actions the BLT can take to focus on universal tier improvement. From identifying learning targets through implementing actions to remove barriers to achieving the desired state of universal tier instruction, readers of this book have been very busy! In this chapter, we describe how to examine the impact of the changes made to improve the universal tier. Just as we examine the impact of interventions for individual students, it is essential to consider the impact of improvements made on a systemwide level. We discuss the questions to ask and the data to examine to explore the effectiveness of changes.

REVIEWING THE DESIRED STATE

MTSS is about resources, and more specifically, the efficient use of resources to impact student achievement. Figure 8.1 shows two pyramids. One is the traditional MTSS pyramid with which most readers are familiar. This pyramid has often been used (by ourselves included) to graphically display student levels of proficiency. The result of this interpretation has created some misunderstanding in our schools. Whereas many schools now strive to demonstrate that 80% of their students are proficient, it has also sensitized some educators to the idea that it is acceptable if 20% of students are not proficient. The original idea of MTSS and data-based decision making is to ensure that building-based resources are used effectively and efficiently to support all students to work toward proficiency. Although there will likely be students who do not reach proficiency, resources are always provided, and teams consistently meet to support those students in their attempts. In Figure 8.1, the first pyramid is intended to depict the resources needed for various groups of students in order to be successful. When used in this way, the universal tier should support the majority of

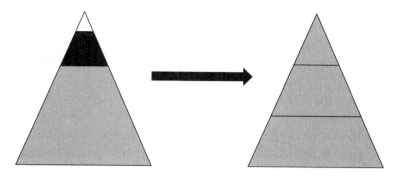

FIGURE 8.1. MTSS pyramid depiction of resources versus student achievement.

students to be successful, while additional resources may be needed for a small number of students to become proficient. That is the vision of an MTSS. If the pyramid were actually meant to represent individual students and their success, it would look more like the second pyramid in Figure 8.1. In the spring, our goal is that all students to meet expectations. The goal of universal tier improvement efforts is to work toward a use of resources that allows for about 80% of students to be successful with universal instruction. It takes a strong foundation of instruction to achieve this goal and BLTs to thoughtfully guide this work. Summative evaluation allows for reflection on the impact of universal tier improvement efforts to achieve this goal.

SUMMATIVE EVALUATION

Summative evaluation is the process of evaluating the impact of actions after they are completed. It is an important part of a change process that is often overlooked because teams move on to solve new problems. Unfortunately, unless time is devoted to examining the impact of work, teams will never know if their actions were successful. As a result, they may miss an important opportunity to either improve efforts or to celebrate successful improvements. Summative evaluation allows the team to take a step back, review the big picture of universal tier improvement work, and determine next steps in these efforts. As the team is reflecting on the current school year, it is also planning for the next school year. Summative evaluation allows for the identification of areas on which to focus and goals to seek for the coming school year. As we discuss the process of summative evaluation, teams may find it useful to periodically refer to Form 8.1. This checklist depicts the summative evaluation process in which a team will take the following actions to improve the universal tier.

EXPECTATION FOR POSITIVE CHANGE SYSTEMWIDE

We are often asked how quickly schools can expect to see change in achievement rates with universal tier improvements. The brief answer is slowly and fast. Because systemwide change requires everyone in the system to teach and team differently, results are expected to take longer than when an intervention is implemented by only one or two staff, such as with a student intervention. Academic interventions with groups of students often result in change within a month's time, and behavioral interventions often are successful even more quickly. It is expected that effective systemic changes will realize notable and significant improvements within a range of 12 weeks (one benchmark period) and 1 school year. For instance, a classwide intervention would be expected to show significant results by the next universal screening period. However, the change in a building schedule may result in changes being noticed by the end of the school year in which the changes took place. In some cases, changes should be noticed almost immediately, especially in the behavioral domain. If common expectations are developed, taught, and monitored for hallway behavior, office referrals related to hallway misbehavior would be expected to decrease dramatically almost immediately.

In reality, schools can expect changes to take place most quickly in those grade levels and content areas in which more resources have been invested. For instance, if fourth grade was prioritized for classwide intervention in writing routines, it would be anticipated that large changes in fourth-grade writing (and potentially in reading comprehension as well) would occur during the same instructional year. However, it would not be expected that third- or fifth-grade writing scores would demonstrate the same level of improvements.

In addition to seeing changes within the first year of working on universal tier improvement, a school should not anticipate that after a year's worth of focus, all changes to the universal tier would be complete. Schools should *always* monitor the current sufficiency of their universal tier practices. Additionally, implementation of a full MTSS framework takes years to develop. However, by impacting the universal tier, additional changes to the system are likely to achieve even greater impact than they would have without a sufficient universal tier.

It is our assertion that when a building's data suggest that the universal tier program is not sufficient for students in the building today, it is not appropriate to prioritize only changes that will take multiple years to yield student data improvement. Changes that need to be prioritized in this situation are those that will have impact for students in the building this year! If I (S. B.) am in a restaurant and see someone choking, I may think to myself that this would be a good time to schedule a refresher course in the Heimlich maneuver. That may be a fine idea, but I also need to apply what I remember today, to help the person who is choking. In schools, we cannot allow ourselves to say that we are going to begin improvements for next year's students. We must implement short-term changes to the universal tier while we prepare for more long-term implementation considerations.

OTHER CONSIDERATIONS FOR EXPECTED IMPROVEMENTS

A BLT needs to be realistic and should expect to achieve only those gains that are consistent with the intensity of the changes put in place. When more intensive and systemic changes are implemented with fidelity, greater change can be expected. On the other hand, when changes have not been implemented with fidelity, are being pilot-tested as opposed to being implemented building-wide, or are relatively small, then the BLT should not expect large gains in student success.

When considering among an array of possible universal tier improvement efforts, choosing activities that are more intensive and can be implemented broadly are recommended (see Chapter 6). Although potentially more difficult to implement, more intensive activities are more likely to continue to garner consensus to implement additional, necessary changes when instructional staff see improvement with these efforts.

STUDENT ACHIEVEMENT DATA

As part of a summative evaluation process, student-level data are used to determine if improvements to the universal tier have been effective. Student-level data will include both the districtwide assessments administered at each grade level and the universal screening data. Questions answered during this summative evaluation include the following:

1. What percentage of students who met benchmarks in the fall continued to meet benchmarks in the spring?
2. Were at least 80% of students at each grade level successful on districtwide high-stakes assessments without additional intervention?
3. Were any changes seen in subgroup gaps?

Each of these questions is examined in more detail in the following sections.

Students Meeting Targets

Schools will examine the percent of students at each grade level who met benchmarks on the universal screening assessment in the fall and who continued to meet benchmarks in the spring. This question was also considered as a basic question in Chapter 4, when teams were conducting universal tier screening. Answering this question allows teams to determine if universal instruction, examined at each grade level, is robust enough to ensure that students who began the school year meeting expectations grew at a pace that was sufficient for them to continue to meet expectations at the end of the year. In order to consider universal tier instruction to be robust, 95–100% of students at a given grade level who begin the year meeting benchmarks should continue to meet them at the end of the year. Think about it, in what school would we anticipate that students would slip from meeting expectations to no longer meeting expectations?

Districtwide Accountability Assessment

Another metric utilized to evaluate the success of universal improvements is the success of students on the districtwide accountability assessment. Summative assessments provide the data to ascertain if the overall goal—that all students are proficient—has been achieved. If resources are maximized and the universal tier is robust, the number of students proficient on the districtwide accountability assessment would increase. When possible, these analyses should also be completed on those students who did not receive interventions. This allows a BLT to see if the universal tier alone is supporting students to become proficient, or if the building is relying heavily on intervention resources to do so. When students who receive intervention are included in this analysis, a school receives a distorted image of the impact of the universal tier because intervention success will also be included in the equation. Of course, successful interventions are a piece of the MTSS process to celebrate! However, successful interventions will not, in and of themselves, compensate for a universal tier that is not meeting the needs of students sufficiently. Because of that, examining the success of students, at each grade level, on the universal tier alone is an important consideration.

Subgroup Gaps

Lastly, BLTs will examine the change in subgroup gaps over the year as part of the evaluation of universal tier improvements. To do this, the team will compare the change in gaps for subgroups from the fall to the spring. When a team sees a dramatic decrease in achievement gaps after universal tier improvement efforts, it may mean that instruction is more sensitive to the needs of various groups of students in the school. Equity considerations need to be examined on a regular basis, but the less the gap in the success of subgroups, the more equitable universal tier instruction can be assumed to be.

THE FIDELITY DATA CONNECTION

Fidelity data are also crucial to any summative evaluation of universal tier improvement efforts. As discussed in Chapter 7, fidelity data allow BLTs to determine if universal tier improvements have been implemented as intended. These data, when used in combination with summative achievement data, can support the building in identifying areas where additional intervention may be needed. For instance, imagine a building that has two grade levels that did not fully implement all improvements identified for the universal tier. Considering fidelity data alone would not help the BLT determine where to provide additional resources. However, this team also considered achievement data and found that in one grade level, over 80% of students were proficient on accountability assessments, whereas fewer than 80% of students were proficient on accountability assessments in the other grade level. This team was then able to prioritize resources for universal tier fidelity improvement. Fidelity data are designed to be considered in conjunction with outcomes.

THE 80/20 DILEMMA

The traditional conversation about the MTSS pyramid has created what we call the *80/20 dilemma*. As educators, we have become sensitized to the fact that it is acceptable for 20% of our students to be less than proficient. When we view the MTSS pyramid as representing *students,* as opposed to resources, we edify this misunderstanding. The truth is, we want all students to be proficient, even when we know that is unlikely. Nevertheless, having this ambitious goal does two things for schools. First, it supports a culture of never settling with our current results; we are always learning and working to improve outcomes for our most challenging learners. Second, it prevents us from expecting less from struggling learners. In too many schools, the response to students who struggle is to lower expectations. MTSS is about flipping that paradigm around. When students struggle, we provide more educational resources, more intense instruction, and more frequent monitoring of progress. We make these efforts toward the goal of closing the achievement gap. In cases where students remain less than proficient, we remain steadfast in our attempts to provide effective intervention and supports. Then, even when the year ends and a student is less than proficient, we are confident that we gave it our all and, more importantly, that the student learned as much as possible in the time we were together.

Although the *80/20 dilemma* refers to students and their learning, it is also an important concept as we examine the success of our universal tier improvement efforts. When a school examines data, we recommend focusing on several aspects of the journey, as opposed to simply the percentage of students who are proficient. And, when considering the percent of proficient students, we encourage schools to focus on the *growth over time in proficiency in the school,* as opposed to examining one pyramid. This shift in focus should help avoid the trap of the 80/20 dilemma. Throughout this chapter, we provide multiple considerations when examining improvement efforts, and there are many opportunities to celebrate those efforts.

DETERMINING NEXT STEPS

As they are reviewing the data and answering the questions, the teams should also focus on next steps. It is inevitable that more questions will arise, and these should be documented and, as much as possible, answered while in the meeting. If additional information or time is needed, the questions may remain unanswered until the next team meeting, and a team member (preferably the one who raised the questions) can be assigned to research and share the needed information. The team will also want to plan explicitly for the future. After engaging in these school improvement efforts, celebrating successes is essential. Hopefully there have been many celebrations throughout the year. Now is another time to reflect on the progress made and how far the team has come. Identify specific areas of celebration in the data, both from the perspective of implementation as well as student outcomes.

The teams will also want to identify areas of future focus and note those in the action plan. As current efforts are evaluated, there will likely be some work that will need to continue. Ensure that those plans are documented to keep the momentum of improvement.

Lastly, it is essential to communicate the results of the efforts to improve the universal tier to all staff and any other appropriate stakeholders. Form 8.2 contains a checklist to support identification of communication needs. First, the team should determine the communication needs. These include, but are not limited to, changes in student data, new practices that will continue, celebrations, and next areas of focus. Additionally, the team should identify the stakeholder groups with which it needs to communicate. Often times these groups include all building staff, central office staff, the school board, the parent organization, and the broader community. Once the message and the stakeholders have been identified, the BLT should make a communication plan. Communication plans are important because they ensure that key messages are both consistently communicated and reach all the right groups. A template for a communication plan can be found in Form 8.3.

TEAMING OPPORTUNITIES

Teams will analyze outcome evaluation data at various levels and with different perspectives. This work mostly happens in the spring or summer, after spring data are available, and the goal of the teaming is to consider the effectiveness of changes, to celebrate successes, and to plan for priorities in the upcoming year. Form 8.4 provides an organized means of reviewing assessment data to determine the impact of changes to the universal tier. This form can be used to aid in the discussions and can be modified for use with both building- and grade-level teams.

Building Leadership Team

The BLT will consider each of the questions outlined in this chapter. First, the team will consider how successful the universal tier was at supporting students who began the year meeting benchmark expectations. When grade levels are identified that have lower percentages of students with adequate learning trajectories, the BLT will support those grade levels in undertaking universal tier improvement efforts.

The BLT also examines implementation fidelity data and districtwide accountability assessment data to determine if overall improvements have supported student learning. In turn, these analyses will support the BLT as it identifies areas of focus for the next school year.

Lastly, the BLT will examine subgroup data to ensure that equity exists in the system. When equity concerns arise, the team will continue to implement universal tier improvements until subgroup gaps are no longer apparent.

In addition to examining data and setting priorities for the upcoming year, the BLT also has the opportunity to use summative evaluation information to identify areas of learning and celebration. It is sometimes easy to get mired in the details of the things still needed in the system. The BLT can also serve as a champion of the school's successes. Pointing out areas of strength and growth are critical for continued motivation and building staff members' sense of efficacy. During a conversation about universal tier improvement recently, I (S. B.) asked the members of a BLT to individually list and describe the five big ideas of reading. After they easily completed the task, I asked them if their staff could do this. The principal was confident that teachers in the building could do this, and another team member quickly agreed and added, "because of our work over the past few years." The entire team started smiling and discussed how just 2 years ago, they would not have been confident that everyone would be able to do this. It was a reason to celebrate and an opportunity to build confidence that they are moving in the right direction.

Grade-Level Teams

Grade-level teams review the types of data discussed in this chapter, along with their implementation fidelity data, to determine areas of focus for their learning in preparation for the upcoming year. This summative analysis allows for the celebration of successes throughout the year as well as ongoing prioritization of areas needing continued focus. When identifying areas of success, the team should focus both on the outcomes as well as those areas where greater consistency has been reached in implementation of the universal tier. When considering priorities, the grade-level team members should discuss priorities they have identified with the BLT to ascertain the areas about which both teams agree as well as to uncover priorities that one team noticed but the other may have overlooked.

CASE IN POINT

Exceptional Elementary School

Exceptional Elementary School identified needs in the area of reading for their fourth-grade students in the fall, based on the screening data shown in Figure 8.2. They decided to address their concerns in multiple ways. First, they implemented a classwide intervention for the fourth grade in which all students received an additional 20 minutes of reading prac-

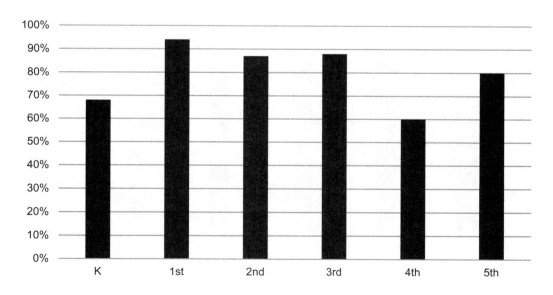

FIGURE 8.2. Exceptional Elementary School's fall universal screening data.

tice in their content classes each day, through the implementation of some evidence-based fluency-building routines, including partner reading. This intervention was accomplished by having students engage in an evidence-based routine to promote reading fluency for 5 minutes during each subject throughout the day. The content used was the content used for that subject. For example, in science class, they may use the science textbook or a research summary. In math, they may use a summary of a real-world problem that was solved by the type of math they were currently learning.

In addition to the classwide intervention in reading, Exceptional Elementary fourth-grade teachers also intensified the universal tier instruction through the implementation of a routine to teach multisyllabic word reading by teaching etymology. This routine was implemented for the whole class and replaced a 20-minute period of time in which students were working individually on various reading practice tasks.

The fourth-grade level teacher team and the BLT worked together to examine data throughout the year to evaluate their efforts. They used universal screening data during the winter window to ensure that they were on the right track—and they saw signs of progress (see Figure 8.3). At the end of the year, they considered three questions. First, they asked if students who began the year on track remained on track. Table 8.1 depicts the progress of students who started the year on track. The fourth-grade students who started the year on track all made enough progress to end the year on track. Additionally, the teachers were surprised to see that even though many of them did not receive interventions, a majority of students who began the year at risk also made enough progress to end the year on track. The team hypothesized that these at-risk students had benefited greatly from the extra practice during classwide intervention, as well as from the more intense universal tier instruction.

The team also hoped to see that at least 80% of fourth graders were proficient on the statewide assessment. Unfortunately, they fell short of this goal, with 73% of fourth graders meeting proficiency on the statewide accountability assessment. However, when compared

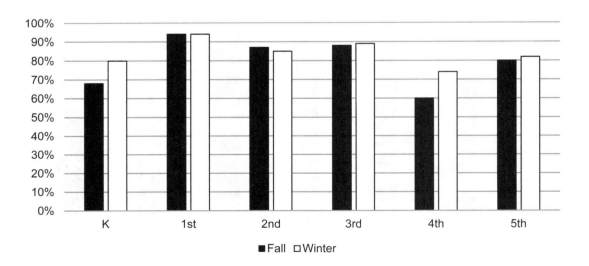

FIGURE 8.3. Exceptional Elementary School's winter universal screening data.

TABLE 8.1. Exceptional Elementary School's Fourth Grade Fall to Spring Data

Level of risk	Fall (No. of students)	Spring (No. of students)	Level of risk	Movement from fall to spring (No. of students)
Low risk	197	272	Low risk	197
			Some risk	0
			High risk	0
Some risk	85	26	Low risk	72
			Some risk	12
			High risk	1
High risk	46	30	Low risk	3
			Some risk	14
			High risk	29

with fall screening data that predicted only 60% of students meeting proficiency, the data suggested that many students had benefited from the universal tier improvements. The team saw this gain as a celebration, despite not meeting their goal.

Last, the team hoped that the large gap they noticed in the fall had lessened through their universal tier improvement efforts. Figure 8.4 compares subgroups from the fall to the spring. Although they did not implement practices aimed at specific subgroups, the team hypothesized that intensifying the universal tier for all students would benefit students who came to school with various backgrounds—and they were correct! The gap was greatly reduced throughout the year.

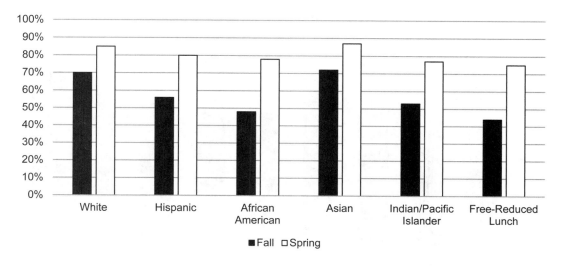

FIGURE 8.4. Exceptional Elementary School's fourth-grade subgroup data.

Given the changes in outcomes from the fall to the spring, the teams decided that their efforts in improving the universal tier in the fourth grade were greatly successful. As they reflected on the spring and the following year, they decided on two areas for additional focus. First, the BLT decided that they would need to share the data and the story with the fifth-grade teachers, as this group of students would continue to need robust universal tier instruction. Second, the grade-level team decided to add the strategy they used for classwide intervention into universal tier instruction for the future. They decided that extra practice in a variety of subjects would be beneficial for all students and likely help to reduce their subgroup gaps. The grade-level team determined that they would continue these evidence-based routines as part of their universal tier.

Miraculous Middle School

The principal at Miraculous Middle School approached the BLT about her concerns with the increasing number of office referrals and escalating behavioral concerns in the building (see Figure 8.5). Over the course of the previous year, more than 1,300 office referrals had been issued. In addition, 107 students had received more than two office referrals over the course of the year. She also brought information about positive behavioral interventions and supports (PBIS), an evidence-based framework for addressing behavioral challenges in schools. The team read about PBIS, visited a nearby middle school implementing the framework, and watched several online videos describing practices and outcomes associated with PBIS. After thoughtful discussion and debate, the team decided that the data could not be ignored and that PBIS would be the best choice to address the school's behavioral concerns. The team chose some initial readings and videos and introduced the idea to the rest of the building staff through both staff meetings and discussions in content teams and grade-level teams. After about a month of discussion and data review as a building staff, the BLT

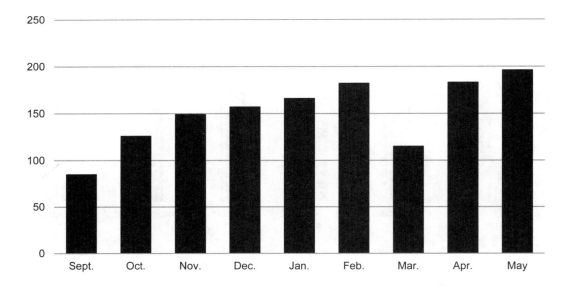

FIGURE 8.5. Miraculous Middle School's office referral data.

conducted a survey of all staff to measure consensus to implement PBIS. Over 90% of staff agreed that PBIS would be an appropriate choice to address their behavioral concerns.

The BLT spent the next several months planning for implementation of PBIS. They identified schoolwide expectations, decided how to teach the expectations, and determined specifically what consequences and rewards would be used for both following and choosing not to follow the expectations. Throughout the planning process, they met with building staff to get input on the decisions and to update staff on the progress. Anticipation was growing; staff members were ready to try this new way of addressing behavioral concerns when they returned to school in the fall.

During implementation of PBIS, the BLT examined ongoing data frequently and suggested areas of increasing behavioral concerns that needed additional teaching. They conducted checks of implementation fidelity and identified areas of needed support and coaching.

After the first year of implementation, the team stepped back and reflected on the progress the school had made. Office referral data suggested there was a significant decrease in both the number of total referrals and the number of students receiving than two referrals over the course of the year. Figures 8.6 and 8.7 depict the office referral data change over the course of the school year. The principal indicated during the discussion that she also noticed throughout the year that she was able to spend more time in classrooms because she was spending less time responding to behavioral concerns.

The BLT was also examining the school's achievement data and noticed something peculiar. Even though there was no focus on providing additional resources to improving students' reading and math scores, both had increased in the past year (see Figure 8.8). The BLT investigated further and realized that many schools implementing a PBIS framework experience something similar. Discussing the data, the team realized that this unexpected improvement may have occurred because students were in class more since they were in the office less often. They were excited to show the data to the rest of the building staff and students to celebrate!

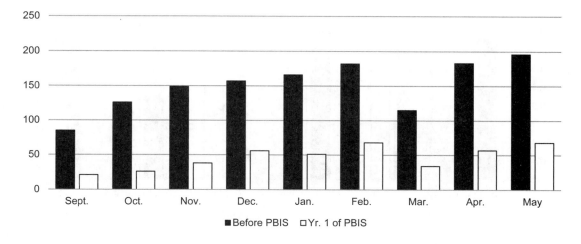

FIGURE 8.6. Miraculous Middle School's office referral change data—after implementation of PBIS.

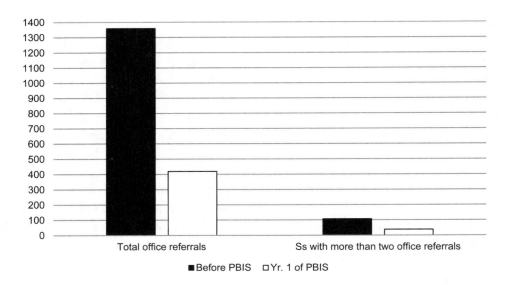

FIGURE 8.7. Miraculous Middle School's total data change—after implementation of PBIS.

CONCLUSION

Evaluating the impact of universal tier improvements is an ongoing endeavor and includes the summative evaluation described in this chapter as well as the ongoing, formative evaluation described in Chapter 7. Taking time at the end of each school year to review successes and identify areas for continued focus is essential to a school improvement effort. This thoughtful reflection will support continued planning and improvement of universal tier efforts. Supporting the success of the universal tier will always be the work of every

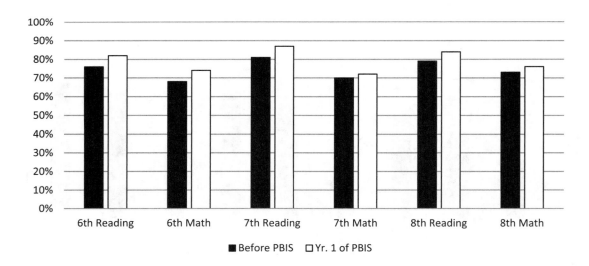

FIGURE 8.8. Miraculous Middle School's reading and math achievement data.

school. Summative evaluation will allow teams to determine if additional resources need to be added to this effort or if the current intensity of focus is sufficient.

DISCUSSION QUESTIONS

1. Why is summative evaluation important?

2. What are ways in which we currently use summative evaluation information?

3. How much impact do we expect to see from our universal tier improvement efforts?

4. What does the 80/20 dilemma mean to us? Do we need to talk to staff about this dilemma?

5. Who would be interested in knowing the impact of our universal tier improvements? Who are our stakeholders?

6. Do we have experience with communication plans? In what other circumstances do we use them to support our work?

Checklist of the Summative Evaluation Process

What is the impact of changes to the universal tier?

DATA REVIEW

- ☐ What percentage of students who met benchmarks in the fall continued to meet benchmarks in the spring?
- ☐ Were at least 80% of students at each grade level successful on districtwide assessments?
- ☐ Were any changes seen in subgroup gaps?

NEXT STEPS

- ☐ Identify additional questions.
- ☐ Identify celebrations.
- ☐ Identify changes and practices that need to continue as part of the universal tier.
- ☐ Identify areas of future focus.
- ☐ Identify communication needs.

Checklist of Communication Planning Efforts

What are our communication needs?

MESSAGES

Data Review
☐ What data should be shared?
☐ How will the data best be depicted (e.g., what kind of charts, graphs)?
☐ What explanations, if any, are needed with the data?

Successful Practices
☐ Which implemented changes had the most impact?
☐ Which changes will be continued in the future?
☐ Are there other celebrations to report?

Next Steps
☐ What do data suggest about content areas that need future focus?
☐ What do data suggest about grade levels that need future focus?

STAKEHOLDERS

Which stakeholders need to be part of the communication?

☐ Building staff
☐ Central office staff
☐ School board
☐ Parent organization
☐ Community
☐ Other(s): _____

Communication Plan

Message: *(Summarize message here.)* _____

Who needs to know?	How will we inform them?	Who will be responsible for informing them?	When will we inform them?

Message: *(Summarize message here.)* _____

Who needs to know?	How will we inform them?	Who will be responsible for informing them?	When will we inform them?

Leadership Team Agenda:
Summative Evaluation Data Review

What is the impact of changes to the universal tier?

DATA REVIEW

☐ What percentage of students who met benchmarks in the fall continued to meet benchmarks in the spring?

☐ Were at least 80% of students at each grade level successful on districtwide assessments?

☐ Were any changes seen in subgroup gaps?

☐ What do data suggest should be our future universal tier improvement efforts?

    ☐ Content focus?

    ☐ Grade-level focus?

NEXT STEPS

☐ What other questions do we have about the data?

    ☐ Who will prepare those data for our next meeting?

☐ What changes are we celebrating?

    ☐ What changes had the most impact?

☐ What changes and practices do we need to continue as part of our universal tier?

☐ What are our areas of future focus?

    ☐ Do we have a written multiyear building action plan?

☐ How will we communicate our results and next steps?

    ☐ Have we documented the communication plan?

CHAPTER 9

Continuing the Journey

This book is focused on providing a framework to help educators implement effective universal instruction, evaluate the effectiveness of universal instruction, and identify barriers preventing the educational success of all learners. The resource allocation model of MTSS functionally places the primary jurisdiction over MTSS in general education. Therefore, it is most effectively accomplished through a multi-tiered model of increasing intensity of service and frequency of assessment (Tilly, 2008), all of which are operated by general education. Tier 1, or universal instruction, involves quality universal instruction in general education and benchmark assessments to screen students and monitor student progress in learning. Students who do not made adequate progress in general education, despite a sound universal curriculum, receive additional support in Tier 2, which involves providing small-group interventions to approximately 15–20% of the student population. Tier 2 interventions have a standardized component to assure efficiency and are delivered in small groups of four to six students. Tier 3 consists of intensive, more individualized supports for students who are not successful with supplemental instruction alone. These interventions are matched specifically to a student's identified skill deficit. This book focused specifically on improving universal instruction through data-based decision making to prevent large numbers of students from needing Tier 2 or 3 supports.

Although there is general consensus in the field in favor of a multi-tiered model of instruction, as we stated multiple times throughout this book, most practitioners first think about providing supplemental and intensive interventions when implementing MTSS. Schools typically jump immediately to designing and implementing Tier 2 and Tier 3 supports, regardless of the data showing lack of success of the universal instruction with their current population. In some respects, it is much easier to design and implement interventions for at-risk students than it is to analyze universal instruction to determine why it isn't working. This work is hard and requires time for collaboration, extensive professional learning, and instructional coaching to fill in the gaps. It requires solid school leadership at a time when turnover among school administrators is at an all-time high. It requires setting aside our beliefs about what we think works and examining the research base to discover what works *best*. It requires embracing a fundamental belief that all children can learn, despite a number of obstacles that are outside the control of educators. It requires an understanding that if we keep doing what we have been doing, we will keep getting what we have been getting: great variability in outcomes and further disadvantaging of the most disadvantaged. And finally, it requires a sense of urgency and a conviction that we can and must do better for large numbers of students.

How do we rise to this challenge? Many believe that we rise to this challenge by disrupting the educational system substantially and quickly by rolling out large-scale changes across whole districts and whole states. These initiatives make extraordinary demands on teachers' time. Directives change, guidance is absent, and key provisions sometimes do not work at all. In this book, we argued that we rise to this challenge by being thoughtful, planful, and using our data to guide our decisions. We do not jump on every new educational bandwagon that comes along. We are careful and deliberate in our planning and not focused on implementing more in 1 year than the system can handle. We also recognize the importance of connecting the work we do on universal instruction to other programming within the building or district.

CONNECTIONS TO OTHER PROGRAMMING

Proficiency on standards is the educational goal, and the universal tier is intended to be the main vehicle to reach that goal. Supplemental programming in schools is intended to provide students with additional resources in order to make progress and/or meet proficiency. Because supplemental programming is just that, *supplemental*, this programming can be more effective when added to a strong universal tier foundation and related to the content of universal instruction. When supplemental and intensive interventions are aligned with and supportive of grade-level standards, outcomes are maximized.

Additional Resources

As was discussed in Chapter 1, the universal tier is a student's first intervention. Improving the universal tier has the potential to impact all other programming within a school. When more students are successful without additional intervention, more resources are available to provide intensive instruction to the few students who need it. With fewer students who struggle, intervention group sizes are smaller, the frequency and duration of interventions increase, and interventions can be individualized and further intensified when needed.

Access to Instruction

Schools with strong universal instruction are also able to provide greater scaffolding and supports in the general education setting. The strong universal tier is differentiated to meet the needs of learners, allowing intervention resources to truly teach to skill deficits, as opposed to providing all instruction in a given content area. For instance, if a first-grade student has significant a learning disability and deficits in the area of reading, special education services will be provided. In a school with a strong universal tier, the student will likely be able to benefit from at least some portion of the universal instruction. For instance, if the learner struggles with phonemic awareness and decoding skills, he or she should, at the very least, remain in the classroom for vocabulary and comprehension skill work. Removing this student from all classroom instruction will likely result in skill gaps in additional areas while his or her decoding skills are being remediated.

Special Education

Special education services are intended as supplemental services provided to support those students who qualify to help them access and make progress in the Standards. In a school with a strong universal tier, special education services are truly supplemental, and special educators have time to work with general education teachers to accommodate and modify as needed to support students, as well as to work with individual students to close skill gaps. These educators are experts at providing individualized instruction that is targeted toward specific deficits, and at modifying instruction to accommodate learning needs. Special educators can have the greatest impact when they are allowed to focus on individualizing instruction, as opposed to teaching all of the Standards to the students they serve. At the same time, special education students are general education students first. Therefore, universal instruction needs to be designed and implemented in ways that support all students, including those students with deficits and/or disabilities. General education teachers need to be supported in their efforts to differentiate instruction to meet the needs of all learners.

Title Services

Title services are provided to support at-risk students and are meant to supplement, not supplant, universal instruction. Again, when strong universal tier instruction is available, fewer students need these specialized services and have smaller achievement gaps than when the universal tier is not meeting the needs of a large portion of students.

Gifted and Talented Services

Gifted and talented services are different because they are intended to support students who may have already mastered the Standards. However, again, high-achieving students can often make greater progress in a school implementing a strong universal tier through an MTSS process, because differentiation is available to support them in continuing to learn and achieve in ways that fulfill their capacities. We argue that students who are at or above the 90th percentile in achievement have as much need for intensive differentiation as students who are at or below the 10th percentile.

This chapter summarizes and connects information from the previous chapters with a focus on sustaining effective universal instruction practices over time. We discuss seven imperative components of any change process, connecting these components to universal instruction, and we provide a tool for self-reflection. We conclude the chapter by focusing on 10 lessons, learned from our practice, about improving and sustaining effective universal instructional practices.

SUSTAINING EFFECTIVE UNIVERSAL INSTRUCTIONAL PRACTICES

Many districts that are focusing on universal instructional practices are doing so through implementation of an MTSS framework. As mentioned earlier, MTSS has quickly emerged as a methodology for improving outcomes for all students. A recent national survey of K–12 administrators indicated that 61% of respondents have fully implemented or are in the process of implementing an MTSS framework districtwide, up from 24% in 2007 (Spectrum K–12 Solutions, 2010). Although it is encouraging that so many school districts around the country are implementing the MTSS framework, the focus needs to shift from implementation to sustainability. This shift in focus is also true for changes to universal instructional practices. The problem facing schools is not how to initiate change; rather, it is how to implement changes in process and performance that will endure. We know that issues will arise, within individual districts, as implementation occurs on a national level. We can predict themes that will occur if key components are not addressed or not implemented with fidelity. The field of education is full of examples of school districts implementing an innovation with great enthusiasm at the beginning, but later abandoning it. School leaders and teams need to institutionalize changes to universal instruction in ways that preserve the positive changes and resist efforts to revert back to the old ways of doing things. Gibbons and Coulter (2016) suggest that in order to effectively manage and sustain the change process, districts need to attend to seven imperative components: (1) leadership; (2) vision and culture; (3) infrastructure; (4) resources; (5) implementation plans; (6) professional learning to support knowledge, skills, and self-efficacy; and (7) incentives. The change process will be negatively impacted if any of these components is not addressed (Knoster & George, 2002). The next sections discuss each of these components and how each impacts the change process and the successful implementation of effective universal instruction. Form 9.1 provides a self-assessment tool of the seven components.

The Importance of Leadership

The Wallace foundation has produced study results indicating that leadership is second only to teaching in its impact on student achievement. In fact, principals are responsible for 25% of school effects on student learning (Louis et al., 2010). They found that when principals focus their efforts on improving instruction and work to create shared leadership within the building, and teachers trust them, the result is higher scores on standardized tests of achievement. Key leadership responsibilities include communicating a vision of high standards, creating an engaging and safe environment, encouraging leadership by others, focusing on improving instruction using evidence-based data, and improving outcomes through collaboration. Meeting these responsibilities will require that instructional leaders are results-oriented and data-informed. They must be responsive to feedback and be effective communicators. Above all, they must work to build consensus and articulate a vision for the building that aligns with district priorities.

Vision and Culture

Effective leaders realize that putting vision into action is only possible through setting ambitious goals and then mobilizing their teams to meet these goals. Conveying a clear vision, the intended benefits, and a plan of the supports that will be provided is thought to contribute toward readiness and acceptance when implementing a change. When we talk about vision as it relates to universal instruction, we mean that district leaders need to be cognizant of how effective instruction relates to the district's strategic plan and goals. Leaders need to establish a culture wherein all staff understands that *teaching* and *effective instruction* have the largest impact on student achievement, not factors that are often assumed, such as class size, school finances, and student socioeconomic status. School culture is defined as the "traditions, beliefs, policies, and norms within a school that can be shaped, enhanced, and maintained through the school's principal and teacher-leaders" (Ward, 2004, p. 1). Sustaining changes to universal instruction requires a shift in each school's culture to include accountability for results and a genuine expectation that *all* students can make meaningful progress.

Explicitly communicating how efforts to improve universal instruction fit within other district initiatives (e.g., braiding initiatives) and an MTSS framework is essential. This book focused on ways to evaluate and improve universal instruction. In this case, leaders need to connect how universal instruction fits within an MTSS framework and the district's vision for increasing achievement for all students. The same can be said for implementing PLCs, benchmark assessments for all students, progress monitoring for some students, PBIS, anti-bullying programs, standards-driven instruction, and pay-for-performance systems. A leader with good vision will explicitly show how each of these initiatives fits within an MTSS framework and is related to the others. Without this clear vision, staff members are likely to be confused and uninspired.

Infrastructure

Building an infrastructure to support and sustain the MTSS framework is essential for successful implementation. When focusing on universal instruction, leaders and collaborative teams need to identify resources that are already in place to support effective instruction, determine needs, design or adopt ways to document decisions and assess fidelity, and create policies and procedures that define implementation. Throughout this book, we have suggested that districts develop infrastructure through collecting regular screening and progress monitoring data, establishing collaborative teams, establishing routines for teachers and teams to use in their instruction and decision making, and providing technical assistance through professional learning with coaching. Districts that lack infrastructures will not sustain implementation of effective universal instructional practices. If BLTs do not exist, there will be no structure to monitor and manage implementation and provide support to staff. If grade-level teams do not exist, problem-solving teams will be inundated with referrals for special education evaluation. Moreover, buildings without problem-solving teams will likely have a large number of referrals to special education child-study teams. If routines are not present or changed, then schools will perceive that what is being required is transient and, like other innovations, will soon pass so that the school can get back to status quo. Finally, technical assistance is imperative to ensure the availability of people to continually support teachers in their efforts to improve instructional effectiveness. Without coaching and support, the chances that teachers will apply newly learned skills in the classroom are slim.

Resources

Without resources allocated to support improvements to universal instruction, staff will experience a great deal of frustration. At the district level, resources need to match the needs and goals of the action plan. Districts and buildings will need to examine their needs and provide high-quality professional learning in targeted areas identified by collaborative teams. As discussed above, professional learning works best when it is embedded in the job and followed up with coaching and support (Dufour & Dufour, 2010). Subsequently, districts may need to allocate resources to hire instructional coaches to help sustain implementation. We suggest that the roles of the instructional coaches remain fluid and change in response to building needs over time. Resources also will be needed to purchase or develop a measurement system that will assist with screening, diagnostic, and progress monitoring decisions. Finally, resources may need to be allocated to work on alignment with the Standard and to purchase universal curriculum programs, if needed.

Implementation Plans

As detailed in Chapter 6, action plans or implementation plans need to be developed that describe the goal, strategies, and progress monitoring procedures to improve universal instruction. Once the vision has been established and MTSS has been integrated within the district's strategic plan, an action plan should be developed that describes the district and building plans to improve universal instruction. Without an implementation plan, buildings will likely experience many false starts, and staff will be unable to see either the short-term or long-term plan for where their school building and grade level are headed. Clearly developed implementation plans provide a context for explaining why activities are occurring and where they fit within the larger picture of school district operations. During any type of change process, lack of clarity in direction often creates stress for individuals whose practice is changing (Sarason, 1996). The action plan should be viewed as a flexible plan that guides implementation, rather than as a rigid plan that cannot be modified.

Professional Learning to Support Knowledge, Skills, and Self-Efficacy

One of the most significant changes in focusing on improving universal instruction is the change pertaining to the professional practice of teachers and other support staff within the building. Successful implementation of effective universal instructional practices requires that educators need to be knowledgeable about collecting and interpreting student data, effective instructional strategies and differentiation of instruction, and matching instructional supports to student needs. In addition, educators must *believe* that the instructional strategies they are implementing will be effective with their students (Sanetti & Kratochwill, 2009). Self-efficacy fuels implementation and increases sustainability. Professional learning must precede implementation in order to ensure that staff members have the skills necessary to be successful in their attempts to improve universal instruction and that their efforts will be rewarded with improved student performance. Knowing the existing skills of the staff and what skills will be needed to inform professional learning is essential.

Perhaps the most critical skills educators lack are skills to analyze student data and use those data to differentiate instruction within universal instructional time. If these skills are weak, teachers will experience significant anxiety that may be expressed in the form of resistance (Sailor, 2009). A recent survey conducted of master's-level elementary, secondary, and special education teachers found that teachers reported the least amount of preparedness in academic assessment strategies and instructional programs (Begeny & Martens, 2006). Although special education teachers reported receiving more training in academic assessment than their regular education counterparts, their training was still limited and typically not focused on using data in a problem-solving process. Therefore, professional learning around data literacy is a critical gap to address to ensure sustained implementation (Sailor, 2009). Previous research has confirmed that teachers who received training were more likely to (1) implement the program (McCormick, Steckler, & McLeroy, 1995), (2) implement the program with fidelity (Sanetti & Kratochwill, 2009), and (3) report more favorable student outcomes (Simmons, 2012). In their seminal study, Joyce and Showers (1998) found that follow-up coaching and support are needed for teachers to utilize and maintain newly learned skills. Strong professional learning needs to be the cornerstone of any systematic plan to improve universal instruction.

Although no single model of professional learning that has emerged to represent a validated standard of professional learning practice (Kratochwill, Volpiansky, Clements, & Ball, 2007), national standards do exist to help guide the design and delivery of professional learning. Learning Forward (*www.learningforward.org*), a professional learning organization, collaborated with 40 other professional associations to develop the *Standards for Professional Learning* (Killion & Crow, 2011). The most recent version of these standards outlines the characteristics of professional learning that lead to effective teaching practices, supportive leadership, and improved student results. Educators are to take an active role in using data to determine professional learning needs and embed professional learning experiences in the contexts in which the knowledge and skills are to be applied.

Research has identified that job-embedded professional learning structures such as teacher networks, PLCs, and/or study groups were more effective in changing teacher practice than traditional workshop or conference formats and were strongest when groups of teachers were from the same school, department, and/or grade level (Porter, Garet, Desimone, Yoon, & Bierman, 2000). In addition, building opportunities within professional learning experiences for active engagement of adults, content focus, and coherence resulted in greater changes in practice, and the effect was even stronger when professional learning activities were directly aligned with teacher goals and state standards. Brown-Chidsey and Steege (2011) recommended scheduling several training sessions for educators rather than "one-shot workshops" or multi-day conferences. Educators need ongoing support and training to maintain a high degree of implementation fidelity. Learning outcomes should be clearly stated for each training session, and some type of measure of implementation fidelity should be used to determine whether teachers are applying newly learned skills in their instruction and decision making. Finally, just as we differentiate instruction for students, professional learning should be differentiated according to teacher needs.

Incentives

Providing incentives to promote implementation of effective universal instructional practices is an important component to consider. Although it may seem that a paycheck should be incentive enough, some educators are resistant to change efforts in the absence of additional incentives. Without incentives, districts and buildings will experience slower change (Hess, 2013). At first glance, many people think incentives need to involve financial resources. However, there are many nonfinancial incentives that can be provided, including giving permission to abandon existing ineffective practices, using data to celebrate incremental success, and providing public praise and recognition to grade-level teams that increase student proficiency toward district targets.

Although many districts use nonfinancial incentives, financial incentives can obviously be used to facilitate the implementation process. Some districts and states have performance pay incentives whereby staff receive additional financial compensation for reaching student achievement goals. For example, teachers or teams set goals that they want to achieve in the area of increased student achievement. If those goals are reached, teachers receive "bonus pay." Other districts provide stipends to teachers to facilitate grade-level team meetings or PLCs. Grade-level team facilitators are reimbursed for the extra time they spend in training, gathering and generating data reports, and working with their colleagues on improving instructional practices at the grade level. Another financial incentive is to offer "mini-grants" at the district level to work on a specific area of implementation. For example, some districts offer mini-grants for which teachers, buildings, or grade levels can apply to help them align curriculum and instruction with the Standards, develop standardized treatment protocol interventions, and/or develop common formative assessments.

LESSONS LEARNED REGARDING UNIVERSAL INSTRUCTION

Our own implementation experiences, along with a review of common implementation barriers across the country, have taught us many lessons and their implications for practice regarding systematic improvement to universal instruction. The top 10 lessons we learned are described in the following material.

- **Lesson 1: Understand that improving universal instruction necessitates system-level change.** Requiring collaborative grade-level teams to analyze, reflect upon, and make changes to universal instruction, based on data, requires change at the system level. We are all familiar with the statement "Change is difficult." System-level change can be incredibly complex and often requires attending to several "moving parts." Although it is imperative that districts have a sense of urgency about the need to improve student outcomes through effective universal instructional practices, implementation will likely fail if the process moves too fast without enough support. Districts should expect questions and occasional conflict. Any time a system is undergoing change, conflict should be expected. It is important for staff to focus on data and student outcomes and to work collaboratively to evaluate and improve universal instruction.

- **Lesson 2: Conduct an inventory of assessment and instructional practices to ensure that reliable and valid assessment and high-impact instructional strategies are being used.** We have found that an effective annual activity for teams is to conduct an inventory of assessments, instructional practices, and programs used across the grade levels. All too often, we have observed that buildings and districts add to their menu of options but never make strategic decisions to take things *off* the menu. An inventory can form the basis for discussion around alignment between the school's current practices and best-practice research. Teams should be given permission to abandon practices that are not well supported by research. In addition, by conducting an assessment inventory around the four purposes of assessment, buildings can determine where gaps and redundancies exist.

- **Lesson 3: Set ambitious goals.** Just as we know that setting ambitious goals for students leads to improved academic learning, the same is true for teams. Collaborative teams should be encouraged to take risks and set ambitious goals for their grade level. Failure to meet goals should be viewed in a positive manner, as an opportunity to evaluate change efforts through implementation. When goals are not met, teams need to re-cycle through the action planning process and formulate new hypotheses to test. As mentioned throughout this book, goals should be formally documented, and a system should be set up to monitor team goals throughout the year.

- **Lesson 4: Begin with a clearly defined plan with consensus from the grade level.** Written action plans increase the likelihood that goals will be attained. When written plans are in place, communication is enhanced and fidelity of the plan can be assessed. Our experience is that, without a clear plan, many "false starts" occur that may lead to increased resistance among staff. The BLT should develop a standard action or implementation plan that can be used across grade levels. A mechanism should be established whereby teams share their plans with the BLT. In turn, the BLT can look for themes across grade levels and help align well-matched building resources with the identified needs.

- **Lesson 5: Universal instruction needs to be viewed as part of a multi-tiered service delivery model.** Improving universal instruction in the context of an MTSS framework is predicated on the notion that a continuum of service delivery options is available in each building. In buildings where special education services are the only way of providing help to students, large numbers of special education referrals can be expected. Developing a multi-tiered model requires efficient use of resources and a great deal of instructional "teaming." As reiterated numerous times in this book, we recommend that districts examine benchmark data and work on improving universal instruction if large numbers of students are not proficient. Teams should then design standard treatment protocol interventions for groups of students as a starting point. Building leadership will need to develop a master schedule that supports supplemental interventions. If students do not make progress with standardized interventions at Tier 2, then individual interventions should be customized by a team using a problem-solving process for decision making.

- **Lesson 6: Leadership is critical.** Building principals need to develop shared leadership within their building to support system-level change. In our experience, it is often difficult for principals to attend every grade-level team meeting on a consistent basis. It is imperative that communication systems be established so that principals are apprised monthly of team meeting discussions, needs, and plans. Principals need to use this information to determine which meetings should be prioritized for their involvement and attendance. They need to hold grade-level teams accountable for reviewing grade-level data, setting improvement goals, and evaluating their instructional practices. Building principals also need to develop shared leadership within their building through targeting teacher leaders who are supportive of efforts to improve universal instruction. When leadership is shared, sustainability is enhanced as turnover in building administration occurs.

- **Lesson 7: Provide job-embedded training and instructional coaching to support learning and applying effective instructional practices.** High-quality professional learning on improving instructional practices using research-based strategies and on meeting the goals established in action plans should be provided to teachers. Ongoing training on data-based decision making and research-based interventions should be provided to grade-level teams. To sustain implementation, districts are advised to build in a coaching component to assist staff in skill development. Coaches should be available to model instructional strategies and provide feedback and support to teachers as they implement new instructional strategies. In addition, coaches can assist building teams in data analysis, interpretation, and data-based differentiation.

- **Lesson 8: Encourage grade-level teams to use multiple sources of data to make decisions.** Teams should be taught to never make an important educational decision about a student based on a single data point. We have seen many instances where teams make decisions about students based on single benchmark screening score. Teams need to be cautioned that error is always present in any score, and that they need to look for converging data across multiple sources that support a hypothesis.

- **Lesson 9: Team routines and protocols are essential.** Collaboration is essential in improving student outcomes through system-level change. In our experience, teams are more successful when there is a facilitator, roles are assigned, and there are clearly defined questions that teams are answering at each meeting. Throughout this book, we have included forms to guide team discussion and decision-making processes.

- **Lesson 10: Always discuss and include ways to measure fidelity of implementation.** The foundation of all change efforts rests with fidelity of implementation. The benefits of using research-based instructional strategies and programs are easy to identify by examining student outcomes; however, these benefits are not possible if instruction is not implemented correctly (Brown-Chidsey & Bickford, 2016). When all teachers in a grade level or subject are expected to teach a particular curriculum or program, and/or use specific instructional practices, and not all teachers use these programs or practices, a lack of fidelity or of treatment integrity exists. As a result, some students will be denied access to the intended learning, and a guaranteed curriculum becomes less certain for all students.

Interestingly, one of the main reasons that the CCSS were developed was to have unified standards in place to identify what students are expected to learn at each grade level. However, in order for the full impact of CCSS to be recognized, a focus on providing training and support for teachers is needed to translate *standards* into effective instructional *practices*. Determining fidelity of universal instruction will require observations of teams and classroom teachers providing daily instruction. Protocols for evaluating fidelity of teams are included in Chapter 6; the BLT can facilitate classroom observations of instruction. Many universal instructional programs contain observation checklists that can be used to evaluate fidelity of universal instructional practices. In addition, lesson plans created by classroom teachers can be used to compare the actual lesson with what was planned. By collecting fidelity information on the teaching of the universal curriculum and the process of administering and analyzing assessments, districts and buildings will have the foundation on which to evaluate their implementation efforts.

CONTINUING UNIVERSAL TIER IMPROVEMENT

Too often, universal tier improvement is seen as a short-term process. Part of this misunderstanding may be attributable to NCLB. A school could improve enough in a short period of time to become a school that was no longer in need of assistance, and their work was seen as complete. In reality, improving the universal tier should be thought of as an ongoing, continuous endeavor. As long as a school has new students, new teachers, and new materials, the universal tier will always need to evolve. This work is similar to keeping up with a yard. Short-term goals, such as adding new bushes or some new flowers, may be set and accomplished. These accomplishments should be celebrated; however, once big projects in the yard are complete, and the yard is no longer the focus of resources, regular maintenance is still needed. There is never a time the yard is ignored completely for other household projects that need financial and time resources.

Universal Tier Screening

Using universal screening data to examine the health of the universal tier, as described in Chapter 4, will continue to be essential, even after action plans have been developed and universal tier improvements are evaluated. This work is ongoing, as we have said repeatedly, and should be planned as a regular part of the building's MTSS plan. This commitment will ensure that the work remains sustainable and continues, even after the person who led the work the first time wins the lottery and retires!

Continuous Improvement

This book has laid out an argument that continuous improvement plans for schools must include a focus on the improvement of the universal tier if below 80% of students are proficient at each grade level. If the universal tier is highly effective, the plan may have few resources devoted to improvement of this level of service. However, if the universal tier is not sufficient, the continuous improvement plan will require significant percentages of resources (both time and financial) allocated toward improving the universal tier. We hope that this book has provided resources to help schools evaluate and improve universal instruction. Changing universal instructional practices requires systemic change on many levels. We hope that school leaders acknowledge the need to understand the change process and the complexities involved with making any type of systemwide change. Once changes have been made to universal instruction, those changes need to be evaluated. We need to move from implementing effective universal instructional practices to *sustaining* these practices over time. The hope is that educators and policymakers institutionalize positive changes to universal instruction and instill resilience in administrators and staff to resist efforts to revert back to the old ways of doing things—ultimately improving outcomes for all students!

CONCLUSION

We end with a fictitious story of unknown origin. The story is as follows:

> In a small town, a group of fishermen gathered down at the river. Not long after they got there, a child came floating down the rapids calling for help. One of the group on the shore quickly dived in and pulled the child out. Minutes later another child came, then another, and then many more children were coming down the river. Soon everyone was diving in and dragging children to the shore, then jumping back in to save as many as they could. In the midst of all this frenzy, one of the group was seen walking away. Her

colleagues were irate. How could she leave when there were so many children to save? After long hours, to everyone's relief, the flow of children stopped, and the group could finally catch their breath. At that moment, their colleague came back. They turned on her and angrily shouted, "HOW COULD YOU WALK OFF WHEN WE NEEDED EVERYONE HERE TO SAVE THE CHILDREN?" She replied, "It occurred to me that someone ought to go upstream and find out why so many kids were falling into the river. What I found is that the old wooden bridge was missing several planks, and when some children tried to jump over the gap, they couldn't make it and fell through into the river. So I got someone to fix the bridge.

We hope this book has inspired you to examine "the bridge" and that you will strive to use the guidance in this book to design and implement powerful universal instruction that will maximize outcomes for all students.

DISCUSSION QUESTIONS

1. Describe building leadership activities that support evaluating and improving universal instruction. How does leadership convey a clear vision and establish a positive culture for change?

2. How is the infrastructure developed to support a focus on universal instruction?

3. How are resources allocated to and aligned with the needs and goals of implementation plans?

4. What is the process for establishing buildingwide and grade-level action plans?

5. What types of professional learning and coaching are offered to educators to improve their skills in analyzing data and using those data to differentiate instruction within universal instructional time?

6. What incentives are offered to promote implementation of effective universal instructional practices? (*Note:* Think about nonfinancial incentives.)

Self-Assessment Form

- For each area, please rate each statement on a scale of 1–5:
  1 = huge strength; 2 = pretty good; 3 = much room for improvement; 4 = area of concern; 5 = major area of concern.
- *Priority Level:* H (High), M (Medium), L (Low)
- *Existence of Data:* When applicable, answer Y (yes) or N (No) on whether data exist on the degree and quality to which this practice is happening by grade level, building, or district.
- *Ideas and Notes:* Ideas about action items upon return to the district.

Sustainability Area	Rating (1–5)	Priority Level (H, M, L)	Existence of Data (Y/N)	Ideas and Notes (How can you improve this area?
Leadership				
1. There is a culture of shared leadership in my building/district.				
2. Leaders spend the majority of their time focused on instruction and improvement of outcomes for students.				
3. Teachers and colleagues trust administration.				
4. The talents and energies of teachers, pupils, and families are used toward achieving common educational goals.				
5. Administrators are fluent in the use of data as a leadership tool.				
6. Teachers in my building or district perceive that administrators are fluent in the use of data.				

(continued)

Developed by Kimberly Gibbons and Alan Coulter.

Sustainability Area	Rating (1–5)	Priority Level (H, M, L)	Existence of Data (Y/N)	Ideas and Notes (How can you improve this area?)
7. Leaders recognize their own strengths and weaknesses and pursue self-development.				
8. Leaders deal effectively with pressure; remain optimistic and persistent, even under adversity; and recover quickly from setbacks.				
9. Leaders are open to change and new information and rapidly adapt to new information, changing conditions, or unexpected obstacles.				
10. Leaders keep up-to-date on technological developments; make effective use of technology to achieve results; and ensure access to, and security of, technology systems.				
Vision				
1. Staff understands "the why" around MTSS/RTI.				
2. Initiatives in my district or building are braided together.				
3. There is a focus on goals and high expectations for student achievement in our building/district.				
Infrastructure: Data				
1. There is a focus on use of data to promote instructional activities.				
2. Staff knows what kind of data will answer key questions, along with how to use an array of data to stimulate conversations and action.				
3. The school/district has a clearly articulated local assessment plan that includes screening procedures for all students at least three times per year.				

(continued)

Self-Assessment Form *(page 3 of 8)*

Sustainability Area	Rating (1–5)	Priority Level (H, M, L)	Existence of Data (Y/N)	Ideas and Notes (How can you improve this area?)
4. Schoolwide assessment data are used to identify students who may be at risk in academic and/or social–behavioral areas.				
5. The school/district has a clearly articulated local assessment plan that includes diagnostic assessment, as needed, for some students to better understand instructional needs.				
6. The school/district has a clearly articulated local assessment plan that includes a plan for progress monitoring at-risk students.				
7. The measures identified in the local assessment plan are all reliable and valid for the purposes for which they are used.				
8. Schedules for progress monitoring are set based on the intensity of students' needs, and assessment occurs at least monthly for all identified students.				
9. Data are stored in a database that is easily accessed by all teachers and administrators in a timely manner.				
Infrastructure: Teams				
1. There is common understanding of the purpose and unique roles of each team within the building or district, and of the ways in which these teams interrelate.				
2. Grade-level, building-level, and district-level teams all consistently follow a problem-solving process to make data-based educational decisions that promote improvement in academic and social–behavioral outcomes for students.				

201

(continued)

Self-Assessment Form *(page 4 of 8)*

Sustainability Area	Rating (1–5)	Priority Level (H, M, L)	Existence of Data (Y/N)	Ideas and Notes (How can you improve this area?)
3. Team meetings at all levels are regularly scheduled, of sufficient duration, and frequently enough (e.g., monthly grade-level team meetings, weekly problem-solving team meetings) to complete necessary tasks. All members of teams regularly attend the meetings.				
4. All teams set measurable annual goals.				
5. Data on team functioning are collected regularly (number of students served, fidelity to problem-solving process).				
6. Structures for communication among teachers are created by arranging common collaborative time.				
7. Each team has defined roles and responsibilities.				
8. Building administrators participate in teams through direct attendance and/or reviewing meeting minutes.				
Infrastructure: Problem-Solving Process				
1. Team members effectively and efficiently identify and prioritize problems for every student or group of students served through intervention services.				
2. Teams generate multiple hypotheses across domains (ICEL[a]) when considering the cause of the identified problem. These are hypotheses are relevant, alterable, and observable.				
3. An individual, specific, and measurable goal is set for each student.				
4. Interventions selected by the problem-solving team are supported by research.				

[a]ICEL, instruction, curriculum, environment, learner.

(continued)

Self-Assessment Form *(page 5 of 8)*

Sustainability Area	Rating (1–5)	Priority Level (H, M, L)	Existence of Data (Y/N)	Ideas and Notes (How can you improve this area?)
5. Interventions selected by the problem-solving team address the student need identified in the discrepancy and hypothesis statements.				
6. Intervention plans are implemented in a timely manner.				
7. A procedure for collecting regular progress monitoring data toward the student goal is a part of each intervention plan.				
8. Intervention fidelity is always assessed through direct observation, and any issues are quickly resolved.				
9. Intervention sessions are of sufficient intensity, duration, and frequency to ensure growth.				
10. Student responsiveness is evaluated based on progress monitoring data, and the team uses decision-making rules.				
11. Intervention plans are evaluated in a timely manner, and the resulting decisions are documented.				
12. The team cycles through the problem-solving process again and again when students' performances are not sufficiently responsive to the current intervention.				
Infrastructure: Multilevel Instruction (Tier 1)				
1. Curriculum and instructional strategies are research-based.				
2. Teaching and learning standards are articulated within and across grade levels.				
3. Teachers understand how to differentiate instruction.				

(continued)

203

Self-Assessment Form *(page 6 of 8)*

Sustainability Area	Rating (1–5)	Priority Level (H, M, L)	Existence of Data (Y/N)	Ideas and Notes (How can you improve this area?)
4. Universal curriculum is standards-based.				
5. Frameworks exist and are used for supporting students who exceed grade-level expectations.				
Infrastructure: Multilevel Instruction (Tier 2)				
1. Tier 2 interventions are evidence-based.				
2. Tier 2 interventions are well aligned with universal instruction.				
3. Tier 2 interventions are standardized, led by well-trained interventionists, and group size and dosage are optimal.				
4. Tier 2 interventions are supplementary to universal instruction.				
Infrastructure: Multilevel Instruction (Tier 3)				
1. Tier 3 interventions are more intensive than Tier 2 interventions and are adapted to address individual student needs in a number of ways.				
2. Tier 3 interventions are individualized, led by well-trained interventionists, and group size and dosage are optimal.				
3. Decisions regarding student participation in both universal and intensive intervention are made on a case-by-case basis, according to student need; and intensive interventions address the general education curriculum in an appropriate manner for students.				

(continued)

Self-Assessment Form *(page 7 of 8)*

Sustainability Area	Rating (1–5)	Priority Level (H, M, L)	Existence of Data (Y/N)	Ideas and Notes (How can you improve this area?)
Knowledge, Skills, and Self-Efficacy				
1. Sufficient time and resources are allocated to professional learning and related activities in support of the RTI framework components.				
2. Professional learning is job-embedded and is followed up with coaching and support.				
3. Staff is knowledgeable about specific instructional strategies for accelerating student achievement (see next items).				
4. Self-review of grades				
5. Formative evaluation				
6. Feedback				
7. Practice				
8. Metacognitive strategies				
9. Relationships				
10. Teacher clarity				
11. Vocabulary programs				
12. Repeated reading				
13. Reciprocal teaching				

(continued)

Self-Assessment Form *(page 8 of 8)*

Sustainability Area	Rating (1–5)	Priority Level (H, M, L)	Existence of Data (Y/N)	Ideas and Notes (How can you improve this area?)
Resources				
1. An inventory of what exists in my building or district.				
2. Needs are clearly identified in each building and district.				
3. Funding scenarios have been explored to address needs.				
4. There is energy directed toward actively revamping the status quo (planned abandonment).				
Incentives				
1. Incentives are provided (either monetary or nonmonetary) for implementation of an MTSS framework.				
Fidelity, Evaluation, and Implementation Plans				
1. Procedures are in place to monitor the fidelity of implementation of the universal, secondary, and intensive interventions, and procedures are in place to monitor the processes of administering and analyzing assessments.				
2. A multiyear implementation plan exists for the district and building that includes both short-term and long-term objectives.				
3. The implementation plan identifies resources with which to implement the plan along with key implementation dates.				
4. The implementation plan has been shared with all staff.				
5. Data are reviewed for all students and subgroups of students to evaluate effectiveness of the RTI framework.				
6. Implementation data (e.g., walkthroughs) are reviewed to monitor fidelity and efficiency across all components of the RTI framework.				

References

Achieve, Inc., Council of Chief State School Officers, & Student Achievement Partners. (2014). Toolkit for evaluating the alignment of instructional and assessment materials to the Common Core State Standards. Retrieved from *www.achieve.org/files/Materials-Alignment-Toolkit_Version2. pdf.*

Algozzine, B., Barrett, S., Eber, L., George, H., Homer, R., Lewis, T., et al. (2014). *School-wide PBIS Tiered Fidelity Inventory.* Eugene, OR: OSEP Technical Assistance Center on Positive Behavioral Interventions and Supports. Retrieved from *www.pbis.org.*

American College Testing Program. (2008). *ACT's college readiness system: Meeting the challenge of a changing world.* Iowa City, IA: Author.

Anderson, L. W., & Krathwohl, D. R. (Eds.). (2001). *A taxonomy for learning, teaching, and assessing: A revision of Bloom's taxonomy of educational objectives.* Boston: Allyn & Bacon.

Arkoosh, M. K., Derby, K. M., Wacker, D. P., Berg, W., McLaughlin, T. F., & Barretto, A. (2007). A descriptive evaluation of long-term treatment integrity. *Behavior Modification, 31,* 880–895.

Begeny, J. C., & Martens, B. K. (2006). Assessing pre-service teachers' training in empirically-validated behavioral instruction practices. *School Psychology Quarterly, 21*(3), 262.

Bender, W. N. (2005). *Differentiating math instruction: Strategies that work for K–8 classrooms.* Thousand Oaks, CA: Corwin Press.

Bergan, J. (1977). *Behavioral consultation.* Columbus, OH: Merrill.

Bergan, J., & Kratochwill, T. R. (1990). *Behavioral consultation and therapy.* New York: Plenum Press.

Bickford, R. (2012). *Promoting student's social and academic success through teacher praise.* Unpublished doctoral dissertation, University of Southern Maine, Portland, ME.

Black, P. J., & Harrison, C. (2006). *Science inside the black box: Assessment for learning in the science classroom.* Brentford, UK: Granada Learning.

Brown-Chidsey, R., & Bickford, R. (2015). *Practical handbook of multi-tiered systems of support: Building academic and behavioral success in schools.* New York: Guilford Press.

Brown-Chidsey, R., & Steege, M. W. (2011). *Response to intervention: Principles and strategies for effective practice.* New York: Guilford Press.

Buffum, A., Mattos, M., & Weber, C. (2009). *Pyramid response to intervention: RTI, professional learning communities, and how to respond when kids don't learn.* Bloomington, IN: Solution Tree.

Burns, M. K., & Gibbons, K. (2012). *Implementing response-to-intervention in elementary and secondary schools: Procedures to assure scientific-based practices* (2nd ed.). New York: Routledge.

Carter, L. (2009). *Total instructional alignment: From standards to student success.* Bloomington, IN: Solution Tree.

Carter, S. C. (1999). *No excuses: Seven principals of low-income schools who set the standard for high achievement.* Washington, DC: Heritage Foundation.

Conley, D. T., Drummond, K. V., de Gonzalez, A., Seburn, M., Stout, O., & Rooseboom, J. (2011). *Lining up: The relationship between the Common Core State Standards and five sets of comparison standards.* Eugene, OR: Educational Policy Improvement Center.

Cooney, T. J. (1987). *The underachieving curriculum: Assessing U.S. school mathematics from an international perspective.* Urbana: University of Illinois.

Cooper, H. M., Nye, B., Charlton, K., Lindsay, J., & Greathouse, S. (1996). The effects of summer vacation on achievement test scores: A narrative and meta-analysis review. *Review of Educational Research, 66*(3), 227–268.

Deno, S. L., Mirkin, P. K., & Chiang, B. (1982). Identifying valid measures of reading. *Exceptional Children, 49*(1), 36–45.

DiPerna, J. C., Volpe, R. J., & Elliott, S. N. (2002). A model of academic enablers and elementary reading/language arts achievement. *School Psychology Review, 31*(3), 298–312.

Doran, G. T. (1981). There's a S.M.A.R.T. way to write management's goals and objectives. *Management Review, 70*(11), 35–36.

DuFour, R. (2004). Schools as learning communities. *Educational Leadership, 61*(8), 6–11.

DuFour, R., & DuFour, R. (2008). *Revisiting professional learning communities at work: New insights for improving schools.* Bloomington, IN: Solution Tree.

DuFour, R., & DuFour, R. (2010). The role of professional learning communities in advancing 21st century skills. In J. Bellanca & R. Brandt (Eds.), *21st century skills: Rethinking how students learn* (pp. 77–95). Bloomington, IN: Solution Tree.

Every Student Succeeds Act. (2015). S. 1177-114th Congress. Retrieved from *www.govtrack.us/congress/bills/114/s1177.*

Feldman, K., & Kinsella, K. (2005). *Narrowing the language gap: The case for explicit vocabulary instruction.* New York: Scholastic.

Fixsen, D. L., Naoom, S. F., Blase, K. A., Friedman, R. M., & Wallace, F. (2005). *Implementation research: A synthesis of the literature.* Tampa: University of South Florida.

Fletcher, J. M., & Vaughn, S. (2009). Response to intervention: Preventing and remediating academic difficulties. *Child Development Perspectives, 3*(1), 30–37.

Fuchs, L. S., & Deno, S. L. (1991). Paradigmatic distinctions between instructionally relevant measurement models. *Exceptional children, 57*(6), 488–500.

Fuchs, L. S., Fuchs, D., Kazdan, S., & Allen, S. (1999). Effects of peer-assisted learning strategies in reading with and without training in elaborated help giving. *Elementary School Journal, 99*(3), 201–219.

Fuchs, L. S., Fuchs, D., & Maxwell, L. (1988). The validity of informal reading comprehension measures. *Remedial and Special Education, 9*(2), 20–28.

Galton, M. J., & Willcocks, J. (1983). *Moving from the primary classroom.* London: Routledge & Kegan Paul.

Gamoran, A., Porter, A. C., Smithson, J., & White, P. A. (1997). Upgrading high school mathematics instruction: Improving learning opportunities for low-achieving, low-income youth. *Educational Evaluation and Policy Analysis, 19*(4), 325–338.

Gennetian, L. A., Duncan, G., Knox, V., Vargas, W., Clark-Hoffman, E., & London, A. S. (2004). How welfare policies affect adolescents' school outcomes: A synthesis of evidence from experimental studies. *Journal of Research on Adolescence, 14*(4), 399–423.

Gibbons, K., & Coulter, W. A. (2016). Making response to intervention stick: Sustaining implementation past your retirement. In S. R. Jimerson, M. K. Burns, & A. M. VanDerHeyden (Eds.), *Handbook of response to intervention* (pp. 641–660). New York: Springer.

Gresham, F. M. (1989). Assessment of treatment integrity in school consultation and prereferral intervention. *School Psychology Review, 18*, 37–50.

Haring, N. G., & Eaton, M. D. (1978). Systematic instructional procedures: An instructional hierarchy. In N. G. Haring, T. C. Lovitt, M. D. Eaton, & C. L. Hansen (Eds.), *The fourth R: Research in the classroom* (pp. 23–40). Columbus, OH: Merrill.

Hart, P. (2005). Rising to the challenge: Are high school graduates prepared for college and work? Retrieved from *www.achieve.org/risingtothechallenge*.

Hattie, J. (2009). *Visible learning: A synthesis of over 800 meta-analyses relating to student achievement.* New York: Routledge.

Helman, L., & Rosheim, K. (2016). The role of professional learning communities in successful response to intervention implementation. In S. R. Jimerson, M. K. Burns, & A. M. VanDerHeyden (Eds.), *Handbook of response to intervention* (pp. 89–101). New York: Springer.

Heritage, M. (Ed.). (2010). *Formative assessment: Making it happen in the classroom.* Thousand Oaks, CA: Corwin Press.

Hess, F. M. (2013). *Cage-busting leadership.* Cambridge, MA: Harvard Education Press.

House, E. R. (1989). Policy implications of retention research. In L. A. Shepard & M. L. Smith (Eds.), *Flunking grades: Research and policies on retention* (pp. 202–213). London: Falmer Press.

Howe, K. B., Scierka, B. J., Gibbons, K. A., & Silberglitt, B. (2003). A school-wide organization system for raising reading achievement using general outcome measures and evidence-based instruction: One education district's experience. *Assessment for Effective Intervention, 28*(3–4), 59–72.

Ihnot, C. (2002). Read Naturally: Group and tutoring edition level 8. Retrieved from *https://ies.ed.gov/ncee/wwc/Docs/InterventionReports/wwc_readnaturally_070913.pdf*.

Iowa Early Literacy Law. (2010). IA § 279.68

Jerald, C. D. (2008). Benchmarking for success: Ensuring U.S. students receive a world-class education. Washington, DC: National Governors Association.

Jimerson, S. R., Burns, M. K., & VanDerHeyden, A. M. (Eds.). (2007). *Handbook of response to intervention.* New York: Springer.

Joyce, B. R. (1988). Training research and preservice teacher education: A reconsideration. *Journal of Teacher Education, 39*(5), 32–36.

Joyce, B. R., & Showers, B. (2002). *Student achievement through staff development* (3rd ed.). Alexandria, VA: ASCD.

Kastberg, D., Chan, J. Y., & Murray, G. (2016). Performance of U.S. 15-year-old students in science, reading, and mathematics literacy in an international Context: First Look at PISA 2015 (NCES 2017-048). Washington, DC: National Center for Education Statistics.

Killion, J., & Crow, T. L. (2011). Standards for professional learning. *Learning Forward.*

Knoster, T., & George, H. P. (2002). Realizing durable and systemic behavior change in schools: Guiding questions. *NASP Communique, 30*(6), 34–37.

Kosanovich, M. (2012). *Using instructional routines to differentiate instruction: A guide for teachers.* Portsmouth, NH: RMC Research Corporation, Center on Instruction.

Kratochwill, T. R., Volpiansky, P., Clements, M., & Ball, C. (2007). Professional development in implementing and sustaining multitier prevention models: Implications for response to intervention. *School Psychology Review, 36*(4), 618.

Lane, K. L., Bocian, K. M., MacMillan, D. L., & Gresham, F. M. (2004). Treatment integrity: An essential-but-often-forgotten-component of school based interventions. *Preventing School Failure, 48*, 36–43.

Louis, K. S., Leithwood, K., Wahlstrom, K. L., Anderson, S. E., Michlin, M., & Mascall, B. (2010). Learning from leadership: Investigating the links to improved student learning. *Center for Ap-*

plied Research and Educational Improvement/University of Minnesota and Ontario Institute for Studies in Education/University of Toronto, 42, 50.

Mathes, P. G., & Babyak, A. E. (2001). The effects of peer-assisted literacy strategies for first-grade readers with and without additional mini-skills lessons. *Learning Disabilities Research and Practice, 16*(1), 28–44.

McCormick, L. K., Steckler, A. B., & McLeroy, K. R. (1995). Diffusion of innovations in schools: A study of adoption and implementation of school-based tobacco prevention curricula. *American Journal of Health Promotion, 9*(3), 210–219.

McKnight, C. C., Crosswhite, F. J., Dossey, J. A., Kifer, E., Swafford, J. O., Travers, K. J., & National Center for Education Statistics. (2017). 2017 NAEP mathematics and reading assessments. Retrieved from *www.nationsreportcard.gov/reading_math_2017_highlights.*

National Commission on Excellence in Education. (1983). *A nation at risk.* Washington, DC: Author.

National Reading Panel & National Institute of Child Health and Human Development. (2000). *Report of the National Reading Panel: Teaching children to read—an evidence-based assessment of the scientific research literature on reading and its implications for reading instruction—reports of the subgroups.* Washington, DC: U.S. Government Printing Office.

National Research Council. (2004). *How students learn: History, mathematics, and science in the classroom.* Washington, DC: National Academies Press.

Pluymert, K. (2014). Problem-solving foundations for school psychological services. In P. L. Harrison & A. Thomas (Eds.), *Best practices in school psychology: VI. Data-based and collaborative decision making* (pp. 25–40). Bethesda, MD: National Association of School Psychologists.

Polikoff, M. S. (2012). Instructional alignment under No Child Left Behind. *American Journal of Education, 118*(3), 341–368.

Polikoff, M. S. (2015). How well aligned are textbooks to the common core standards in mathematics? *American Educational Research Journal, 52*(6), 1185–1211.

Porter, A. C. (2002). Measuring the content of instruction: Uses in research and practice. *Educational Researcher, 31*(7), 3–14.

Porter, A. C., Garet, M. S., Desimone, L., Yoon, K. S., & Birman, B. F. (2000). *Does professional development change teaching practice?: Results from a three-year study.* Washington, DC: American Institutes for Research in the Behavioral Sciences.

Porter, A., McMaken, J., Hwang, J., & Yang, R. (2011). Common Core Standards: The new U.S. intended curriculum. *Educational Researcher, 40,* 103–116.

Porter, A. C., & Smithson, J. L. (2001). Defining, developing, and using curriculum indicators. CPRE Research Report Series.

Pratt, S. A., & George, R. (2005). Transferring friendship: Girls' and boys' friendships in the transition from primary to secondary school. *Children and Society, 19*(1), 16–26.

Razel, M. (2001). The complex model of television viewing and educational achievement. *Journal of Educational Research, 94*(6), 371–379.

Reschly, D. J., & Tilly, W. D., III. (1999). Reform trends and system design alternatives. In D. J. Reschly, W. D. Tilly, III, & J. P. Grimes (Eds.), *Special education in transition: Functional assessment and noncategorical programming* (pp. 19–48). Longmont, CO: Sopris West.

Sailor, W. (2009). *Making RTI work: How smart schools are reforming education through school-wide response-to-intervention.* San Francisco: Wiley.

Salvia, J., Ysseldyke, J., & Bolt, S. (2013). *Assessment: In special and inclusive education* (12th ed.). Boston: Houghton-Mifflin.

Samuels, S. J. (1979). The method of repeated readings. *The Reading Teacher, 32*(4), 403–408.

Sanetti, L. M. H., & Kratochwill, T. R. (2009). Toward developing a science of treatment integrity: Introduction to the special series. *School Psychology Review, 38,* 445–459.

Sarason, S. (1996). *Revisiting—The culture of school and the problem of change.* New York: Teacher's College Press.

Schmoker, M. J. (1996). *Results: The key to continuous school improvement.* Alexandria, VA: ASCD.

Shinn, M. R., Good, R. H., III, Knutson, N., Tilly, W. D., III, & Collins, V. L. (1992). Curriculum-based measurement of oral reading fluency: A confirmatory analysis of its relation to reading. *School Psychology Review, 21,* 459–479.

Shores, C., & Chester, K. (2009). *Using RTI for school improvement.* Thousand Oaks, CA: Corwin Press.

Silberglitt, B., Appleton, J., Burns, M., & Jimerson, S. (2006). Examining the effects of grade retention on student reading performance: A longitudinal study. *Journal of School Psychology, 44,* 255–270.

Simmons, W. (2012). Data as a lever for improving instruction and student achievement. *Teachers College Record, 114*(11), n11.

Spectrum K–12 School Solutions. (2010). Response to intervention adoption study. Retrieved from *http://rti.pearsoned.com/docs/RTIsite/2010RTIAdoptionSurveyReport.pdf.*

Squires, D. A. (2004). *Aligning and balancing the standards-based curriculum.* Thousand Oaks, CA: Corwin Press

St. Martin, K., Nantais, M., & Harms, A. (2015). *Reading Tiered Fidelity Inventory (secondary-level edition).* Lansing: Michigan Department of Education, Michigan's Integrated Behavior and Learning Support Initiative.

St. Martin, K., Nantais, M., Harms, A., & Huth, E. (2015). *Reading Tiered Fidelity Inventory (elementary-level edition).* Lansing: Michigan Department of Education, Michigan's Integrated Behavior and Learning Support Initiative.

Teams Intervening Early to Reach All Students (TIERS), Human Development Center, Louisiana State University Health Sciences Center. (2018). Data Action Team Integrity Checklist. Retrieved from *www.hdc.lsuhsc.edu/tiers/resources.aspx.*

Tilly, W. D., III. (2002). Best practices in school psychology as a problem-solving enterprise. In A. Thomas & J. Grimes (Eds.), *Best practices in school psychology IV* (pp. 21–36). Bethesda, MD: National Association of School Psychologists.

Tilly, W. D., III. (2008). The evolution of school psychology to science-based practice: Problem solving and the three-tiered model. In A. Thomas & J. Grimes (Eds.), *Best practices in school psychology V* (pp. 17–36). Bethesda, MD: National Association of School Psychologists.

Tomlinson, C. A. (1999). *The differentiated classroom: Responding to the needs of all learners.* Alexendria, VA: ASCD.

Vaughn, S., Wanzek, J., & Fletcher, J. M. (2007). Multiple tiers of intervention: A framework for prevention and identification of students with reading/learning disabilities. In B. M. Taylor & J. Ysseldyke (Eds.), *Educational interventions for struggling readers* (pp. 173–196). New York: Teachers College Press.

Vygotsky, L. S. (1978). *Mind in society: The development of higher psychological processes.* Cambridge, MA: Harvard University Press.

Ward, R. (2004). Defining the schools' culture. In R. Ward & M. Burke (Eds.), *Improving achievement in low-performing schools: Key results for school leaders.* Thousand Oaks: Corwin Press.

Webb, N. L. (2005). Web Alignment Tool (WAT) training manual, draft version 1.1. Retrieved from *http://wat.wceruw.org/index.aspx.*

Wiggins, G. P., & McTighe, J. (2005). *Understanding by design.* Alexandria, VA: ASCD.

Williams, D. (2006). Formative assessment: Getting the focus right. *Educational Assessment, 11,* 283–289.

Wormeli, R. (2006). *Fair isn't always equal: Assessing and grading in the differentiated classroom.* Portland, ME: Stenhouse.

Index

Note. *f* or *t* following a page number indicates a figure or table.